Dessie

Tangled Up in Blue

Seán Potts is a sports journalist with the Independent Newspaper Group. The 38-year-old Dublin native is married with two children and lives in the city. He is the author of the best-selling biography *Páidí* (TownHouse, 2001).

Dessie

Tangled Up in Blue

Dessie Farrell

with
Seán Potts

TOWN
HOUSE
DUBLIN

First published in 2005 by

TownHouse, Dublin
THCH Ltd
Trinity House
Charleston Road
Ranelagh
Dublin 6
Ireland

www.townhouse.ie

© Dessie Farrell & Seán Potts, 2005

1 2 3 4 5 6 7 8 9 10

All rights reserved. No part of this publication may be reproduced,
stored in a retrieval system, or transmitted in any form or by any
means, electronic, mechanical, photocopying, recording or otherwise,
without the prior permission of the publisher.
A CIP catalogue record for this book is available from the British
Library.

Quote on p 239 courtesy of Apple Computer Inc

ISBN: 1-86059-198-1

Cover design by Anú Design
Cover photograph courtesy of Sportsfile
Text design and Typeset by Sin É Design
Printed by Creative Print and Design (Wales), Ebbw Vale

To Frankie, Emma, Fiachra & Ellen

Contents

Acknowledgements

Thanks to Frankie and Emma Farrell, Seán, Anne and Aisling Farrell, Cora Flynn, Fiachra and Ellen Potts, Seán and Bernie Potts. Particular thanks to Kevin Nolan, the third man on the job. Thanks also to Donal O'Neill, Aaron Shearer, Cathal Ó Torna, Colm Ó Torna, Vera and Jimmy Cooper, Kitty and Tony Flynn, Mick Galvin, Dr Pat O'Neill, Ray McManus and Sportsfile, Dónal Óg Cusack, Jason Sherlock, Kenny Cunningham, Kieran McGeeney, Paul Curran, Jim Gavin, Alan Kelly, Will Heffernan, Mick Kennedy, Independent Newspapers, David Courtney, Frank Roche, Aidan Fitzmaurice and Shane Scanlon. Sincere thanks to Treasa Coady, Marie Heaney and Joanna Brogan at TownHouse, and to Deirdre O'Neill.

SECTION 1

Chapter 1

Night of the Long Knives – 1 October 2001

I have that feeling again.

Eleven years ago, I locked my bike to the railings beside Parnell Park, gestured to Gerry McCaul, and walked into the dressing room to grab a yard of free bench. I was shitting myself, averting my gaze from the eyes of any player who glanced in my direction.

Arriving at the traffic lights opposite the church in Donnycarney tonight and my hands are shaking on the steering wheel, my mind turning over constantly. I have spent over a decade playing for Dublin, captained the team for the past four years and yet, here I am, feeling like that neurotic debutant who entered McCaul's dressing room all those years ago.

I go into Parnell Park not as the Dublin captain; I have no right to be there in that role. Tonight I enter as a nominated Na Fianna hurling delegate after our regular representative, Con Ryan, graciously allowed my name to go forward so I could address the meeting. I have crossed the line, out of the sanctuary of playing into the daunting world of GAA politics.

Tommy Carr is expected to be sacked as manager tonight. He is due another year in the job, but that year was subject to review. The Dublin county board's management committee voted 4–3 for his removal last week and now it's up to the club delegates to make their choice. I wonder just how many of these people are qualified to know what's required to manage the Dublin team. What kind of system do we have? One of the top jobs in Irish sport, damn close to the top. And who'll decide? Officials? 'Blazers'? 'Decentskins', as Eamon Dunphy might call them. I try not to panic. There are a lot of good people here, I tell myself, lads who played, who care about Dublin, who can see what matters. Don't panic.

Our lack of success has divided the county on Carr's future. In fact, I'd venture that the only thing united in Dublin at the moment is the football team. Only two months ago, the county board Chairman, John Bailey, had gushed about Carr's role after our dramatic draw with Kerry in Thurles. 'Dublin is fully behind Tom Carr and his selectors. We fully support him, regardless of what happens in the replay,' Bailey said. He spoke to the players at training before the second trip to Thurles and was choking with emotion about loyalty and support for the management. Even after we lost the replay, Bailey didn't change his tune. Naively, we took what Bailey said at face value.

But two months is a long time in GAA politics. The first I learned of a heave against Tommy Carr, that he might not in fact be reappointed, came when I was tipped off by a senior member of my club who told me that he had been asked by the county board for his opinion on the 'direction' of the Dublin football team. I had to act immediately. Carr's future was worth fighting for. Yeah, he had made mistakes; the players made a lot more. Yet for all our grief, I never remember any Dublin team being as together as we are at this juncture.

When a manager's time is up you can usually tell – players cribbing, stories being leaked everywhere. This isn't the case with Carr. I started to ring around various clubs and used the Dublin players to liaise with them, trying to drum up support for Tommy.

Unfortunately, I was playing catch-up. Canvassing for votes to remove Carr had already begun. Ciarán Whelan told me that he'd heard his own club, Raheny, had struck a deal. They had lost two points for failing to complete a league fixture and were offered a refixture if they voted against Carr.

Other players confirmed that John Bailey had contacted their club with regard to supporting a possible change in the Dublin football management.

I don't know how this game works. Do you barter for votes or do you simply state your case and hope that club delegates will support your stance? I'm out of my depth.

When I arrive at the board offices, Vinny Murphy and Davy Byrne are standing outside, supporting their manager. They aren't happy. Some heads bow as certain delegates catch sight of the Dublin footballers talking outside. What the hell would a former All Star know about this situation? Mercifully, not all delegates are so inclined. A stream of arrivals salutes Murphy respectfully.

A lot of heads turn as I finally enter the room and the mumbling increases. I sense a wave of hostility crashing over me. Why? Are they thinking 'he shouldn't be here'? At first, I recognise absolutely no one at the meeting. These men will shape our future as Dublin footballers. These men will shape my future. Who are they? Then Dinny Gray, my Na Fianna colleague and my former Dublin minor manager, gestures towards me. Dinny's a welcome sight. Former Dublin player Dr Noel McCaffrey enters, representing Clontarf for the night. McCaffrey was Tommy's team doctor and felt so strongly about the situation that he wanted to be present at the meeting. Just as I had done, he also went to his club and asked if he could be appointed as a delegate for the night.

I take my seat beside Dinny who explains how things will work. The perfunctory business is dispensed with and the issue of the Dublin manager arrives on the agenda.

Bailey addresses the floor, speaks effusively about the great service given by Carr and his selectors, but adds that the management committee feels the time has come for change.

The division is stark. One speaker for Carr, the next against. I have absolutely no idea when I should speak. I'm trembling in my seat, shifting nervously. Eventually, there's a gesture and I haul myself up.

'After the sinister sequence of events this week, I would like to assure you that Tommy Carr enjoys the total support of the panel. This support is based on the considered view that they are doing an excellent job. This is not about John Bailey or Tommy Carr or Dessie Farrell. It's about Dublin football and the prospects of winning an All-Ireland title. A change now will be seriously detrimental to Dublin football. I have never played with a more spirited, passionate team, and Tommy Carr has gone a long way to creating the spirit which exists. He is an honest, intelligent, articulate man who deserves support.

'I beg the delegates here tonight to make the right decision. Go with Tommy Carr and help us bring the Sam Maguire Cup back to Dublin.'

Trouble is, it *is* about John Bailey. McCaffrey had earlier rebuked the chairman for his handling of the whole affair. McCaffrey alleged that the chairman had brought Carr's ability as a manager into question after a defeat by Roscommon in the national league earlier in the year. A whispering campaign had started that Carr was to be sacked, though nothing ever came of it.

Bailey denies this allegation and his supporters are furious. Even the clubs are divided, one delegate in favour of Carr, the other against.

As I expected, my presence at the meeting sufficiently irks one delegate who, looking over at me, suggests that nurses should stick to nursing. Ironically, I left nursing a couple of years ago. Despite the emotional support for Bailey in the wake of McCaffrey's attack, no one calls on this delegate to withdraw his comment about the Dublin captain. It would be a great Association if it wasn't for those meddlesome players now, wouldn't it?

The talking finishes and the voting slips are handed out for the secret ballot. The scene is chaotic, GAA democracy at its best: lads are milling all over the room, conversing side-mouthed to one another, going in an out of the jacks, glancing furtively at the Dublin captain who hasn't left the comfort of Dinny's company. I overhear one delegate behind explaining why he's voting against Carr. 'I never liked army men,' he says. His companion agrees.

Votes are collected and the tension eases momentarily; lads laughing, slagging one another.

There are ninety-three delegates present. The executives head off to count the votes. When they return to the top table, hush descends over the expectant gathering. The vote is split, forty-six for, forty-six against, with one abstention.

An abstention. I'm thinking: a fucking abstention! Why in the name of Jayzus would anyone come to a meeting like this and abstain? Did his club advise him to abstain? Is there really an abstention?

There's uproar in the room over the split vote. When calm is restored, the meeting is adjourned for ten minutes while the eight-man management committee leaves to make a final decision. I'm hoping, praying, that Bailey will do the right thing and side with the players. It's wishful thinking.

When the committee re-emerges, Bailey steps forth. As chairman, he will be giving his casting vote against Carr.

It's over.

'I am supporting the management committee's decision of last week,' proclaims Bailey. 'I am making it for what I regard to be the good of Dublin football.'

Every syllable of Bailey's speech pierces my heart – denying he's betraying Carr, having a go at the media for the pressure on his family, nothing personal.

'I made my decision honestly and openly and with no agendas... I am fucking raging. The delegates' eyes are burning a hole in my back. My first feeling is to find the fellow who uttered the nurse jibe. If ever a fellow deserves a good smack in the mouth, he does.

I walk up to Bailey as I'm leaving the room. He starts talking, but I can't listen to his shite anymore. It's all 'blah blah blah, in the best interests of Dublin GAA, hard decisions, blah blah blah'. I run out to the car and wheel-spin the fucking thing out of the car park. There are tears in my eyes as I turn down the Malahide Road.

I ring Tommy to tell him, but RTÉ Radio's Brian Carthy has already informed him.

I feel helpless, frustrated.

A bad situation just got a whole lot worse.

6 October 2001

The fallout from Tommy Carr's removal was severe if short-lived.

St Joseph's O'Connell Boys' club went public shortly after asserting that, under GAA rules, the procedure followed by the management committee that night was technically out of order.

The basis for the club's claim were bye-laws (Rule 56, 1.2 and 1.7) which state that every club – apart from the county chairman's – is entitled to have a maximum of two delegates officially attend the meeting and vote. According to the St Joseph's delegate, Barry Flynn, there were members of the management committee present and their own clubs also had two delegates. Flynn maintained he'd observed this at the meeting, but was unsure whether or not they had signed the official attendance book. He subsequently asked to see the attendance book and he said it recorded the fact that there were clubs with more delegates formally signed in than they were entitled to.

Management committee member, Seán O'Mahony, who originally voted for Carr to remain, then had to vote in unison with his committee to have him removed. However, there was a query as to whether O'Mahony should have voted at all, as it was suggested afterwards that his club already had its quota of delegates present.

Dessie Farrell

As the decision had been made, the county board issued no response. The line that they had 'moved on' was filtered through to the media, but the procedural question was never answered. This is how this great organisation works.

A week later, I sat with Carr and the management team at a press conference in Jurys Hotel as they bit the dust. Carr spoke eloquently and revealed that, at a meeting in September, Chairman John Bailey had asked him to remove one of his selectors, Dom Twomey, to 'freshen things up'. Carr had refused, claiming that it was too easy to look for scapegoats in this manner.

The matter was over. Carr was gone and the scramble to replace him was underway.

Who knows? If Carr had stayed would things have changed dramatically? After all, his successor, Tommy Lyons, brought back Ray Cosgrove with profound effect the following season. Carr would not have made this move, as he felt he had already given Cosgrove every chance to make the step up. In fact, he actually took him off in a Leinster final against Meath after earlier introducing him as a substitute. But the players did feel they were continuing to improve. We had a bond, a belief that we could really do something.

On the surface, it made perfect sense to me to try and hang on to our manager. Experience has taught me the value of good team spirit, how it could compensate for technical weaknesses in a team. Carr had engendered that spirit and it promised much. But there were other reasons.

Deep down, I took the stand because of my own failure to deliver for Carr. I owed this guy, big time. When I fell, he was there to pick me up and there was simply too much I wanted to rectify: losing to Kildare in the first round when I was sent off, losing to Meath when I had to limp off, losing to Kildare after being six points up at half-time, losing to Meath again when we owned the blasted ball and then, then … the nightmare, missing an open goal from two yards against Kerry in Thurles. Small things alter a team's fate; a simple score can determine your destiny. Leslie Deegan's winning point for Dublin against Offaly in the 1974 Leinster championship is considered by the 1970s players to have changed the course of history. Without it, they wouldn't have beaten Offaly – their first real breakthrough – and gone on to win the All-Ireland that year; there mightn't have been any Heffo's Heroes. I don't underestimate the significance of my miss.

Now my chance to deliver for Carr was gone. The sense of order and achievement that came with our All-Ireland victory in 1995 was a fading memory. The optimism that came with my captaincy had crumbled. My challenge was never bigger.

Trouble was, I had nowhere else to go. I would have to convince a new manager of where I was at, start all over again. I was married with two children, trying to develop a new career, trying to keep our club on the boil. I had never taken stock of where my life was heading, I had never taken stock of failure, of the trouble I'd caused for myself. I clung to the dream that a turnaround in Dublin's fortunes would lift me personally; obscure the problems, public and private, that were mounting.

Chapter 2

Flashback – March 1998

Mickey Whelan sounded me out for the captaincy when he took over as manager of the team at the end of 1995. I told him that I wouldn't be comfortable with the role, particularly because there were so many senior figures in the squad – Barr, Moran, Curran and Heery. Mickey went with Keith Barr; he picked the right man. Now, Mickey's gone, his final game tarnished by the unedifying spectacle of the Dublin fans booing him off the field, after losing a league game to Offaly in Parnell Park, and Heery responding by giving the crowd the two fingers.

I always wanted to be Dublin captain. My childhood ambition was blue, but it was also arm-banded. You've made it when you're captain. Only good footballers become captains. Captains are guaranteed respect, guaranteed their place, guaranteed proper recognition. I'd wait my turn though. 'Little boy blue', as I was once dubbed in the *Evening Herald*, won't blow his own horn.

I can't understand why some counties, like Kerry, allow the reigning county champions to name the county captain every year. It seems so arbitrary, a mere reward rather than a serious appointment. I think such an arrangement devalues the role and diminishes the authority of the manager. I mean, it's an important position, even in Gaelic football. It's not like rugby or cricket, where the captain is responsible for calling strategies, but you're still a leader.

At training on Saturday morning in the Phoenix Park Army Grounds, our new manager, Tommy Carr, calls me aside during the pre-session kick-around.

'Dessie, how would you feel about the captaincy?'

'Yeah?' I reply.

Done deal.

I'm chuffed. Driving home that spring morning the only thing tempering my pride is the challenge of my new position. What exactly would it mean to be the Dublin captain? I'd have to change my attitude. Under Paddy Cullen, Pat O'Neill and Mickey Whelan, I minded my own patch, got my own game in order. Now, I would have to liaise with Tommy, John O'Leary, Dom Twomey and Richie Crean. I would have to speak to players, listen to players. Now there would be more pressure on my own game and I would have to lead by example. More than anything, I would have to be honest; call things as I saw them.

It isn't easy. The first difficulty is being stuck in the middle; being aware, in particular, that some of the senior members of the squad are coming under the pressure of a new broom. It's easy to deal with the inexperienced lads, but we have men who have given a decade's service to Dublin. I'm twenty-six years old. Stuck in the middle.

I try to think my way into the job, be as serious as I can. I think of things to say, things to do. I won't be taken for granted and I'll never lose sight of my responsibility – lead by example. LEAD BY EXAMPLE.

A couple of weeks later, Na Fianna defeat Clontarf in the first round of the Dublin senior football championship on a Thursday night. We've bitten the bullet in the club this season as far as I'm concerned. I was one of the people behind bringing in some outside players to strengthen our hand and I'm more than happy to take the shit over it. Winning games will soon silence the doubters. Now, we've got over our first hurdle – no mean feat for Na Fianna in 1998 – and our satisfaction is reflected by the drinking session in the clubhouse afterwards that stretches into the early hours.

I'm in work on the Friday morning, working as a psychiatric nurse in the assessment unit of St Brendan's Hospital. I crawl into the hospital in a heap. The knowledge that, at some stage, I'll bunk off to meet up with the Na Fianna lads is the only thing that gets me through the day. By lunchtime, I learn of an impromptu gathering close by. The day-after session is pretty much the norm for most football teams, a reward for our temporary abstinence. It's hard to knock it. Everyone else enjoys their weekend social life, meets their friends for a pint when it suits, goes to weddings, out for dinner, plans holidays. Footballers can't, or at least aren't supposed to. So when the opportunity arises, we take it … and stretch it.

Before midday, I join the lads in Downey's Pub in Cabra, where I polish off three or four quick pints. Unfortunately, the few quick ones have topped up the considerable quota from the night before. Realising the time, I put the last glass to my throat, bid farewell and hop into the car to head back to work. As I'm driving down the Rathdown Road in my Fiat Punto, I clip the wing of an oncoming car and then swerve, smashing into a parked car on the left. When the gardaí arrive, they observe pretty quickly that I have been drinking.

Before I could even gather my senses, I am arrested, placed in the back of a squad car and taken to the Bridewell Garda Station. Once there, I'm chucked into a cell while they prepare to take a urine sample. Heads turn as I enter the station.

'I'm not a gouger,' I sheepishly tell the sergeant. 'Look,' he says, 'we have to follow the rules.'

It's a grim scene. A horrific panic engulfs me. Dublin captain, lead by example, sitting in a cell with another guy. He doesn't recognise me. 'What are you in for?' he asks. 'Mind your own business,' I say out straight. I'm still praying this will all go away, that no one will find out. A couple of gardaí stick their heads around for a look. 'Is that Dessie Farrell?'

What in the name of Jayzus was I thinking? I've never stopped to consider the implications of drink-driving. Blinded by arrogance, I behaved totally irresponsibly. Too caught up with my exemplary attitude to football, to Na Fianna, to Dublin. Now what? I was supposed to be in work when it happened. What will the hospital think? What will Noreen think? What will my parents think? What will Tommy Carr think?

By the time I give the sample and the gardaí have formally charged me, rampant paranoia has set in. I'm in a mess, I'm a criminal. My self-esteem, so high when I was elevated to county skipper only a short while ago, is crushed.

Later that evening, I'm released. My brother-in-law, Fergal, picked me up at the Bridewell and took me to the Hut in Phibsborough for a stiff drink to calm my nerves before going home to face the music. I really regret what I did, but all the regret in the world is hardly going to improve my situation.

Back in Downey's, meanwhile, word has filtered back that I'd been in an accident. 'He's after ploughing into eleven cars parked on the North Circular Road, made shite of the lot of 'em.' That's before the story even grows legs.

The following evening, Dublin are playing Mayo in a challenge game in Parnell Park, the kind of night I love. Tonight, though, it's like an out-of-body experience. I arrive at the game not knowing my arse from my elbow. I meet John O'Leary in the car park and pluck up the courage to tell him that I'd something I wanted to discuss with the management team later. 'No problem,' he says, rushing to the dressing room with a bag of balls. I line out, actually get my hands on a lot of ball, which I proceed to kick everywhere except over the bar. After an inordinate amount of wides, I'm eventually substituted, much to my relief. My mind is addled. I'm sure people in the crowd know what's going on. I shower, change, panic and shoot out the gate without talking to anyone.

Later that night the phone rings. 'Dessie, Tommy here. Have you something to tell me?' I think that Mayo manager John Maughan told him, which meant that, at that point, everyone knew. I felt awful. If it was possible to compound the unholy mess I found myself in, then not broaching the subject with Tommy earlier did just that. I haven't led by example. I presume I've lost the captaincy, maybe even my place?

'Dessie,' Tommy counters, 'my only disappointment is that you didn't pick up the phone to me immediately. You are my general, I will support you any way I can. We all have skeletons in our cupboards, and we all have to deal with them.'

I realise Carr actually cares about me, the individual, not just about Dublin or the captaincy, not even about the pressure on him. He cares about me. The relief is enormous.

'There's no way I'm taking the captaincy off you. In fact I'm envious of the way the players look up to you,' Tommy adds. 'Now, put it behind you, the stress of this will ease in time.'

It does, until the week before we are due to play Kildare in the replay of our first outing in the 1998 Leinster championship on 21 June. We drew with them last week, should have lost really. It was a proud day for me, leading the team out in the championship as captain, but two missed goal chances are still weighing on my mind. I skimmed one great shot over the crossbar and should have buried a second that was cleared off the line.

I'm in work on the Wednesday afternoon when the phone rings.

'Hello. Is this Dessie Farrell?'

'Yeah.'

'This is a reporter from the *Sunday World*. We are working on a report that you were arrested some time back for drink-driving. Have you any comment to make?'

I panic. I deny the story. I hang up.

I'm phoned again. I refuse to comment, but I ask where they got the story. They refuse to comment.

I ring Tommy. He advises me to remain calm, that we would deal with it. Calls are made to try and have the story pulled. Seán McGoldrick is rung, Pat Spillane is rung, but they are sports journalists – this, they claim, is a news story. The more calls are made, the more the paper realises how big their story is.

The night before the replay, one of the gardaí who had arrested me calls to my home. 'I'm sorry for you, Dessie. I'm sorry this is in the public domain, it's nothing to do with me.'

I believe him – I don't know who sold the story to the *Sunday World*.

At first light on the Sunday, I'm up. After breakfast, I ring my father Seán.

'Have you seen the paper?' I ask.

'I have,' Seán replies, almost apologetically.

'How bad is it? It's bad isn't it?'

Seán demurs, 'Ah…'

'Where is the story?'

'It's on page one.'

'Where on page one?'

'It's the lead story.'

'The lead! What does is say?'

'DUBS SKIPPER BUSTED'

'Ah bollix!'

Now I'm a gangland drug-pusher. Now I'm back to square one. No time to reconstruct my self-esteem now. In a few hours I've to lead my team out in Croke Park, the man the Dublin team must look up to and follow. An ongoing groin problem means that I have to go to the gym for a swim on the mornings of matches, so I head up the Navan Road to Total Fitness to loosen myself out. On the way in, I meet Tommy Carr and his daughter.

'Have you seen it?' I ask.

'I have,' he says. 'Fuck them. They've had their go and that's it. Forget about them, put it out of your head and focus on the game.'

Later we meet in Parnell Park to prepare for Croke Park. The players are shifting nervously when they see me. They try to laugh the whole episode off and it eases the tension. Jim Gavin calls me aside while we're stretching.

'Dessie, no one gives a shit about that stuff. Everyone here looks up to you. Give those bastards their answer on the field.'

Anger, shame, guilt, determination, fear... Take your pick. On the short bus journey with the team down through Fairview, determined not to allow it affect me, I'm hurtling through the full gamut of emotions. Every second player reiterates the words of encouragement, 'Give them their answer on the field Farrell.'

We take to the field and deliver a woeful performance, worse than our performance for the drawn game. A new set of guidelines has been issued for referees. You're ticked for a first offence, booked for a second, and sent off for a 'third strike'. Five minutes from the end of the game, Niall Buckley, Kildare's key player, is trying to burst out of his defence when I draw my arm across him. He grabs it, pulls me in, and down he goes. Mick Curley, not exactly my favourite referee, informs me that it's my third tick and sends me off for the first time since I became a Dublin senior player. Glenn Ryan puts Kildare four points up in injury time and Declan Darcy's late goal is a mere consolation. White jerseys and black tracksuits emerge from the four corners of the ground, forming a joyous human pyramid on the final whistle.

More hunched than normal, I pick myself up off the bench, eyes fixed on the turf. So there it is, there's my answer. Lose to Kildare for the first time since 1972, drop out of the championship after one round, play shite, get sent off and exposed in the national media as a criminal. That's the fucking tin hat on the whole situation.

Croke Park, Sunday, 21 June 1998. Longest day of the year, longest day of my life.

Chapter 3

Something Inside – 1998–2001

The Tommy Carr era was probably my most enjoyable period with Dublin, paradoxical as that must seem given the lack of success we endured. This period shaped how I think about football. The bond between me and the manager, forged during the traumatic months in 1998, grew stronger, and I think it rubbed off on most of the rest of the panel.

There were exceptions. Following our exit in 1998, Keith Barr, my predecessor as captain, didn't appear back on the panel in 1999 and the relationship between manager and player, both of whom stubbornly refused to acquiesce, deteriorated. I tried to get the two of them to meet half way, to get Barr back into the squad. It never happened, and one of Dublin's greatest players drifted into retirement. As captain I didn't shirk my role, so I was annoyed when word filtered back to me that I had done nothing to try and prevent Barr being let go. This wasn't true. I bent over backwards with Carr to try and sort out the impasse that seemed to be compounded in Barr's absence.

In different circumstances, Eamon Heery also hung up his blue jersey that year. Heery was one of the finest players of his generation, a hard bastard who was imbued with great skill and determination and who, unfortunately, missed out on an All-Ireland medal in 1995. Barr and Heery epitomised an era of Dublin football. Their commitment to the county and to their performances belied the reputation they endured outside the city. The game may have changed in time, but we have never really replaced the attitude that men like Heery and Barr possessed in abundance. I think players like that are particularly missed at training because they never held back, even in the most innocuous practice matches. This attitude stood to everyone in the full heat of battle.

Mind you, my favourite memory of Eamon Heery happened shortly before his county retirement when Na Fianna played St Vincent's in Marino. Heery decided to man-mark me for the hour and the full treatment he was dishing out was having the desired effect. I got pissed off, so when a ball was played deep into midfield, I tucked in behind him, shouted at our midfielder Seán Forde to punch the ball onwards and, as I did, gave Heery a hefty push in the back. Having taken Heery out of the game, I was left with what seemed like acres of space and managed to slip the ball to a team-mate for a handy goal. After releasing the pass, I could hear the hooves behind me and, before I could turn, he planted his elbow into my head. As soon as the ball was back in play, we engaged in a pretty tasty digging match and what I remember distinctly about the fight was that neither of us said a word, as if we didn't want our rumble rumbled, so to speak. After the game, I never got to say anything to him so, when I was going to collect my kit and saw him standing at the bottom of the stairs, I steeled myself for round two. But as I tensed, he threw out his hand with a big grin on his face. 'That's the way to play football Farrell,' he said.

With a new season underway, I faced the future with renewed optimism and with good cause. I was eventually acquitted on the charge of drink-driving. The original hearing was postponed after my solicitor had been advised by Dermot Deasy, a garda and a former Dublin team-mate whose support was invaluable throughout the whole ordeal. He discovered a flaw in the procedure adopted by the prosecution. The solicitor was a stand-in as my original choice was unable to make it. It proved crucial. When my first choice of brief, Ernie Hanahoe, took charge the next day, he argued and won the case on a technicality, as the car I was driving had apparently ceased to be 'a mechanically propelled vehicle which could be propelled forward'. Honestly. I didn't ask. My father and I met our good friend, Pat Coffey, from Na Fianna outside the court. He couldn't believe the news. However, there was no gloating, just the strong handshakes of people who cared and supported me.

I used my good fortune to launch myself into the pursuit of success, on and off the field. Only then, I believed, would I put the whole embarrassing mess behind me. I was oblivious to the risk inherent in my strategy.

The four years of Carr's tenure was one of great ambition for me. Not only was I determined to be a successful captain with Dublin, but we enjoyed a period of unrivalled success with our club Na Fianna, winning three Dublin championships on the trot, a Leinster title in 1999 and sadly, losing the All-Ireland the following St Patrick's Day. On a personal level, I had jacked in my position as a psychiatric nurse, taken up a job as a medical rep and even changed companies as my new career started to show some promise. I had also assumed a leading role in the rapidly developing Gaelic Players' Association. Before long, that role would expand even further into a full-time career. At home, my wife Noreen gave birth to our second child, a baby girl, Emma. Along with our son Frankie, it meant that, with all the responsibilities I had taken on outside of the house, there was a great deal to be getting on with at home. My commitments were mounting by the day and life was becoming more hectic in every regard.

Sadly, my aspirations for Dublin were thwarted at every hand's turn. We lost every critical game during that period and, with each setback, the burden of failure grew heavier. It was also a time when injury started to blight my contribution, which was extremely frustrating. After 1998's disaster, we had wilted in the national league final the following spring, undoing any benefit of defeating Kildare and Armagh en route to Páirc Uí Chaoimh. Then, after scraping past Laois to reach the 1999 Leinster final, we were well scuttled by Meath. I limped off in the first half with an Achilles tendon and calf-muscle problem and watched from the bench as Meath's Ollie Murphy destroyed us. Carr received a barrage of flak afterwards for his tardiness in moving debutant Peadar Andrews off the rampant Murphy. Typical of the man, he was stoical. He accepted defeat, accepted the criticism. I struggled to match him, particularly as Meath went on to lift the Sam Maguire, a sight which galled me.

Our failure in Carr's third championship in 2000 was probably our most catastrophic. Despite our emerging free-taking problems in the absence of the injured Declan Darcy, we had reached the Leinster decider and fought out a gripping 0-14 each draw with Kildare, Collie Moran grabbing an equaliser in the last minute. Our hand had been boosted by the return of Vinny Murphy from his exile in Kerry, a move which I played a small part in orchestrating the previous season when I suggested to Tommy that it might be a runner. He laughed at first, but when he considered the value of Vinny's talent, he thought it was worth a punt. He was a huge addition to the squad, even though he struggled with the strictures of modern-day training. His humour alone was worth his return.

After the draw, we felt we could settle the score and confidence was high for the replay. Even Vinny worked his way onto the starting fifteen after taking the place of the luckless Ian Robertson. Our demeanour was justified. We played them off the park in the first half, moving sweetly and notching up a six-point lead at the break. I now had one hand on a trophy.

Urban legend has subsequently established that there was a major bust-up in the Dublin dressing room at half-time. There wasn't. We remained calm, merely urging caution and warning against complacency. The only animated voice was mine. As I opened the door to lead the team back out into the tunnel, I slammed it again, turned to the players with an eye on Carr. 'If anyone decides to go through the motions over this next half hour, whip him off Tommy. Let someone in who wants to win this fucking thing. Don't give these fuckers an inch lads. NOT AN INCH!'

Before I could regain my breath, Kildare had scored two goals, wiped out our lead, taken my one hand off the Leinster trophy and given me a swift kick in the bollix. In ninety seconds we were reduced to a group of bewildered incompetents. We managed one solitary point in a wretched second-half performance. Failure now shrouded the Tommy Carr era. Failure was now etched on Dessie Farrell's captaincy. I didn't hide behind the excuse of transition or decline. I take every championship on its merits, go out to win. On Saturday evening, 12 August 2000, that possibility seemed more remote than ever.

Of course family life should have provided a haven from the attendant pressures of the mounting Dublin failures. It didn't. Rather I looked on it as another problem, not a release. In the past I had thrown myself into the particularly lively social scene that accompanied the Dublin team. Now an almost professional commitment was required just to play, meaning I was often gone up to six times a week. I had little time for anything else. Throw in the sacrosanct gatherings after big games and it meant I was missing in action for long periods, never really taking stock of where everything was going.

I did enjoy the social life initially. I didn't really feel any remorse or guilt at the time, but that would change. Club and county provided ready diversion, but somehow much of the *craic* masked the deep personal disappointment that accompanied each setback. I never understood this. I ploughed on regardless, feeling that the gnawing sensation that underpinned everything I did was a positive thing that would ultimately lead to glory and happiness.

Despite our lack of success, Carr was granted a two-year extension to his contract, a big relief for all of us. We couldn't escape the fact that the advocates for change were gaining strength, but the panel was tight and we believed that a breakthrough would come. One thing that helped our solid team spirit was the Spanish training week. As preparations became more professional, a week of warm-weather training was seen as a valuable team-building exercise. Most of the top teams now include it in their schedule. After a hugely enjoyable trip to Malaga in 2000, the venture was repeated in 2001 and it turned into an epic trip.

Spain gave us all a tiny glimpse of what life as a professional footballer must be like. Nothing but training, sleeping, eating well, good facilities, no intrusions, having a laugh and a little bonding in the local nightclub, or the 'Knicky Knacky Knoo' as our haunt became known. We were given a couple of free nights, but the strict curfew was broken on a number of occasions by a variety of cliques. Vinny made the breakout more than most.

Murphy's way of handling himself was a real inspiration. He abhorred the po-faced attitude now prevalent in players but, rather than being disruptive, his carry-on acted as a foil to the more serious heads. Carr was zealous about proper diet and discipline and Murphy was like his troublesome child, adorable yet hard work. I would also often drone on about diet. 'Lads don't forget yer pastas and yer carbos.' Vinny would always rubbish my advice. 'Farrell, a Ferrari can run on any fuel.' He put it to the test too, frequenting Fat John's fast-food caravan outside the Donaghmede Inn on a Sunday night.

Vinny was old school. One wonders if the game is now the poorer for almost excluding characters like him and the McNallys, Joe and Nipper. There's little doubt that the game as a spectacle is, in many ways, more thrilling now – it's certainly faster and maybe more intense. But you have to be almost anal to endure the sacrifices required, and the approach is airbrushing much of the character out of the game. It's also losing the incredible natural talent that certain players such as Vinny Murphy possessed. No sports guru is going to imbue most of today's dedicated athletes with the ability to field a ball like Murphy did. As someone who has embraced modern training and techniques, it would be hypocritical and sentimental of me to lament the passing of the old ways. Suffice to say, it was a lot more fun back in the early 1990s.

While we didn't run amok in Spain, a gang of us had been rumbled breaking the strict curfew on one occasion. We were supposed to be billeted in our bunks by midnight, but the players, with their captain at the helm, stretched it into the early hours. I was purposely rooming with teetotaller Wayne McCarthy to ensure his punctuality kept me on time for early-morning training. However, the one morning I needed him, after our nocturnal meanderings, the fucker slept it out. I got a call from Jim Gavin, 'Big Jim' as he was known, to get down to reception fast. Most of the players were still in bed and Carr was spitting fire. As I fell out of the bed roaring, hopping around trying to put on my socks and shorts, Karl Donnelly popped his head up between the two beds, oblivious that he was on our floor. 'What's going on?' he asked, with one eyelid struggling to open. 'Where am I?' 'Go into your fucking room and get your gear,' I said, trying pathetically to get my own act together. After the scalding I gave Wayne, I don't think he slept a wink for the rest of the week.

When, bedraggled, we all assembled in the lobby, Carr announced that we were to endure what he euphemistically referred to as a 'screw session', where he would run us into the ground. This was our punishment. Given the heat and the delicate state of quite a lot of us, we almost died from dehydration. Vinny was so chastened by the whole experience that his room-mate for the week, Paul Curran, arrived home after one of our permitted nights off to find Vinny sitting up in bed reading a sports psychology book!

While Carr's regime was tough, there was no shortage of comic relief. On a bus trip for a winter league match in Donegal, we stopped at a garage-café en route, where lads got off the bus to go to the toilet. A few went into the café and stocked up with some grub and arrived back in the bus with an array of burgers, crisps and sweets. Later that night, Carr scolded us at a team meeting. 'What kind of fucking jokers are ye?' he bellowed. 'Do ye think that ye can get away with that, going to play a match and loading up with burgers and buns on the way?' We struggled not to collapse with laughter. On the return journey, we made the same stop at the café. This time, the players were more circumspect about their purchases, Vinny included. He appeared back on the bus waving an apple and a banana defiantly in Carr's face. On reaching the back of the bus, however, he pulled out a sizeable stash of Mars bars, Twix and Maltesers from his trousers, yet again sticking to his dictum that a Ferrari can run on any fuel.

Vinny brought a great buzz back into Dublin, particularly during Carr's last summer as manager, and his two points against Offaly in the Leinster semi-final set up a final date with Meath. Once again we failed and, this time, I was enraged by our loss. We conceded a soft goal to Graham Geraghty early in the game and it left us on the back foot. We dominated for long periods, but were always susceptible to a sucker punch because we were essentially chasing the game all afternoon. Personally, I played well, but it was no consolation as yet another chance to get my hands on some silver went belly-up.

Carr probably would have been sacked were it not for the inaugural 'backdoor' which gave us a chance to redeem ourselves. It didn't feel like a lifeline at the time, as I had taken the Meath defeat pretty badly. I was desperate for some kind of redemption. It didn't make sense that the meticulous preparation and great loyalty in our ranks was yielding nothing. We knew our weaknesses, but somewhere, surely, we would get a break. An uninspiring, if ultimately comfortable, victory over Sligo pitched us against Kerry in Thurles. Some break.

After the Sligo game, I received the man-of-the-match award, which I really recall only because my son Frankie came onto the field afterwards and tried to chew the RTÉ microphone during the post-match interview.

We stayed overnight in a hotel in Horse and Jockey the night before the Kerry game and everything was very professional and ordered. This wasn't a routine league trip, there was the fussing that goes with a big game and I loved it. We all travelled to mass together, which was weird if strangely enjoyable, but it was Vinny, once again, who provided the welcome comic relief. He was sharing a room with Wayne McCarthy and, on the morning of the match, Vinny was towelling himself down after a shower when McCarthy called him over to the window. Outside, the actor and *Star Trek* star Colm Meaney, a big Dubs fan, was talking with a couple of fans. Vinny opened the window, dropped his towel and roared down to Meaney: 'Hey, beam me up Scotty!'

The first Kerry game was a chaotic passion play, from the moment our bus hit the heaving square in Thurles with the words 'the higher you build your barriers…' from Labi Siffre's anthem blaring on our sound system. We knew this was special.

But there is nothing like reality to rip the fucking heart out of romance. Two hours after searching for the 'something inside' myself, I suffered the ignominy of the most glaring miss of my career when I spurned an open goal from, well, a yard. After putting Séamus Moynihan on his arse to get the ball, it was a shocking miss. Collie Moran had done something similar; both chances would have stemmed Kerry's rampant assault. Eight points down in the second half, Vinny came on as a sub and turned the game with a goal in the sixty-second minute. As if proof were needed about the value of team spirit, we overwhelmed Kerry, and when Darren Homan fisted the ball into the net to put us a point up, it seemed that the one break I was praying for, for four years, had arrived. I never recall an atmosphere quite like it. Dublin's much sneered-at supporters were incredible. Then Maurice Fitzgerald's stroke of genius killed the moment. I think it was Nicky English who once remarked of his ill-luck, 'If I'd ducks, they'd drown.'

There was a tide of emotion in the aftermath of that incredible draw. It was not one I could readily join in. The sight of the open goal was framed in my head. The miss wrecked my performance, the miss wrecked our chance. Four years later, the sinking feeling recurs in an instant.

We'd lost our chance. Everything had turned for us and just as providence seemed to have cast a benevolent eye on the unlucky Tommy Carr, fate intervened. We prepared as well as we could for the replay, but giving a superior team a second bite was fatal. Confidence comes from victory, no matter what way it's achieved. Without a vital breakthrough, we were always vulnerable. After his dramatic spat with my old pal referee Mick Curley on the first day, Tommy was banished to the stand for the replay and, though we tried to use his punishment as motivation, we were emphatically outgunned by Kerry.

The Taoiseach Bertie Ahern came into the dressing room afterwards with John Bailey and commiserated with us. The sense of a united Dublin, even if it was fleeting, was sort of comforting. A little over a month later I would discover just how fickle any such thoughts were.

I remember giving a passionate speech in the dressing room afterwards. It was the end of an era, but little did we know that the curtain was about to be brought down.

'Lads, what I'm about to say got Paddy Cullen into trouble in his own speech in the Mansion House after we lost to Donegal in the 1992 All-Ireland. But I'm going to say it anyway. Ultimately, Paddy said that it was only a game of football and that there are more important things in life. While football was our lives for the past number of years, those words echoed in my ears because the one thing I see when I look around this dressing room today, as you wipe the tears from your eyes, is that this squad has something far more important. That is a true bond.'

Wonderful relationships developed during Tommy's reign. Surrounded by men like Curran, Sherlock, Gavin, Murphy, Connell, Homan, Andrews, Byrne, Darcy, Robertson, Moran, our manager and selectors and everyone else who listed in Thurles that evening, I knew we shared something unique, something special. It might not have come in terms of silverware and it might not come in words that are easy to relate, but it came and we all knew what it was and I'm thankful that football has given me the opportunity to share that feeling with some great people.

Sadly, despite the pledges of support, Tommy Carr was sacked less than six weeks later and that remarkable team bond was shattered. For four years, in difficult, disappointing circumstances, our loyalty never faltered, our resolve never weakened to try again – for ourselves, for each other and for Tommy.

Chapter 4

New Blue Rinse – 2001–2002

My public show of loyalty to the previous incumbent left my relationship with the new manager Tommy Lyons vulnerable, even if I didn't see it that way at the time. Once the fight to keep Carr was over, there was no point dwelling on the past and I was actually excited when I heard of Lyons' appointment just over a month later, on 5 November. His track record was good – All-Ireland club title with Kilmacud Crokes, Leinster and national league titles with Offaly – I was optimistic. After all, new managers bring fresh momentum. Trouble was I had never met him.

Our first encounter came over a cup of tea in Parnell Park prior to a team meeting where the panel was introduced to the new management – Lyons, Dave Billings (my old Na Fianna manager), Paul 'Pillar' Caffrey and Paddy Canning. I didn't feel in any way compromised by my stand on Carr and had gone on the record publicly calling for support for the new boss. Yet, as soon as I entered the room, I noticed Lyons was tracking me, watching who I was talking to, my reactions to what was said, my body language. He didn't come over to me, but I deduced from his gaze, rightly or wrongly, that he identified me as a troublemaker.

The subsequent meeting was standard enough fare: commitment, ambition, Dublin jersey. As a player entering the twilight of my career, I was obviously concerned about the manager's short-term plans, so I asked him was he aiming for success immediately or did he envisage a three- or four-year plan to rebuild the team. He didn't give me a straight answer. Leaving the meeting, I turned to Jason Sherlock and suggested that there might be a lot more contradictions ahead. It was only an observation, a hunch, it wasn't meant to be prophetic.

Shortly after the meeting, I got a phone call from Lyons who informed me that, given my litany of ongoing injury problems – knee ligaments, calf problems, groin strains – he would rest me for the league and reassess my situation later in the spring. I wasn't wholly comfortable with this arrangement, being isolated from a new-look panel, but it was the logical option and I accepted it. It meant I was excluded from the set-up during the formative months of Lyons' managerial reign.

It was hard not to feel that I was being kept at arm's length. As the conversation developed, I was pretty sure that my hunch was accurate enough. When the perfunctory part of the chat was dispensed with, Lyons brought up the subject of Tommy Carr's removal and why the players had remained so loyal. Did the idea of a public show of loyalty irk him? He told me that I had done 'one press conference too many', with obvious reference to my appearance alongside Carr in Jurys Hotel. 'I don't care if Ian Paisley manages Dublin,' I responded. 'If I felt he was doing a good job managing the team, I would support him.'

I explained that I trusted Carr and that the rest of the panel felt the same way. However, Lyons suggested that Carr hadn't shown much loyalty to Dublin by hastily agreeing to offer his services to Wexford footballers on a consultancy basis immediately after being sacked, particularly now as Dublin had been drawn against Wexford in their opening game in the 2002 Leinster championship. I laughed at this. 'Well, Tommy, he wouldn't be the first manager to move to another county for a few bob.' Lyons took umbrage at this quip. Perhaps he thought I was referring directly to his previous role with Offaly.

I didn't know or care whether or not Lyons was paid for managing Offaly. All I know is that I had struck a raw nerve. Managers *should* be paid. They are under enormous pressure to deliver, despite the nonsensical rhetoric that GAA officials and romantics espouse. For having to deal with the Association's politicos alone, they deserve payment and, of course, many are. But like a lot of things to do with the GAA, it's a grey area with little transparency and no official leadership or accountability.

The next day, I got another call from Lyons, who informed me that he only received minimal expenses during his spell with Offaly. I didn't doubt him for one minute, but his indignant response surprised me. Why was he so defensive?

Anyway, I was exiled for my own good, and he set about reshaping the Dublin team.

As someone who obsesses about fitness, I felt really weird not having the routine of early-season county training for the first time in nearly a decade. I vowed to remain diligent about my personal programme, determined that, when the call arrived to return, I would be prepared. I had no intention of drifting into retirement.

The new management made efficient use of the league, though given my sabbatical, I was largely unaware how Dublin were getting on, save for the odd report from Senan Connell, so I noticed a big change by the time I returned in April. The team had been reshaped: Alan Brogan and Ray Cosgrove were now first-choice forwards, Darren Magee was in midfield, Barry Cahill and Paul Casey were introduced to the defence, while Coman Goggins was appointed captain. There was a good buzz. The new players, in particular, had responded well to Lyons' promptings.

Lyons was very concerned about pace. He wanted the ball moved as quickly as possible to exploit the speed of his two key front men, Brogan and Cosgrove. Training was based around his idea of speed and movement, so hauling my creaking frame back into the mix at the end of April was never going to be that easy. I had to reacquaint myself with players, familiarise myself with the manager's game plan and then prove that I wasn't a physical basket case. Determination and experience were my allies, but my biggest enemy, injury, remained a constant threat. Still, for all the new emphasis, I was able to hold my own during practice games, even if I was chastised from time to time for actually slowing the ball up, regardless of the success or otherwise of my actions. On one occasion during a practice game in St David's, Artane, I picked up a ball from about thirty-five yards out, shielded it while shunting my young marker out of the way, and saw a definite clear run to goal. I took it, steered my way around the last defender and put the ball in the net.

'Dessie, what are ya doin'? You shouldn't wait for it to come to you. Move into the ball, keep it movin',' said Lyons.

'Do ya think so?' I replied. I bit my lip.

I eased my way into contention for a starting place on Tommy Lyons' first championship team to play Wexford in the quarter-final in Carlow, the same day as Ireland's World Cup opener against Cameroon.

In preparation for the championship, Lyons had taken the progressive step of employing the services of Dave Aldred, kicking coach to none other than English rugby's golden boy Jonny Wilkinson. Given our high-profile problems with free-taking and scoring, you couldn't fault Lyons' motives. In fact the manager was very organised. He was also by far the best manager I have ever experienced with regard to player welfare: we wanted for nothing and if Lyons could help any individual personally, he would do so. However, he never took a back seat. During one session with Aldred in UCD, my left knee had become badly swollen. Lyons approached me to check it out. 'How's that knee gettin' on? Throw it up there till I have a look at it, I know a thing or two about dodgy knees.' He grabbed my right leg, raised it and, after examining the joint, announced. 'Ya know, it doesn't look too bad.' I lifted my head. 'That's the wrong knee Tommy.' I suppose it was an easy mistake to make, as my right leg wasn't great either.

Shortly before the Wexford game, my knee flared up again (the bad one, as opposed to the other, not-so-good one). Lyons had stipulated that he would not play any injured players and wasn't keen on painkilling injections, so I had to make the decision myself to approach our doctor, Pat Duggan, for a shot before the Wexford game. Lyons didn't approve, nor did he want to know. I took the shot and survived seventy minutes in a spluttering two-point victory over a resilient Wexford. Ironically, I was one of the best of a bad lot.

Struggling to train flat out with my knee problems, I was dropped for the next round, a tasty clash with Meath in Croke Park; so often the defining point for a Dublin season. I was told that the management were concerned about my ability to last seventy minutes, so they felt it would be prudent to keep me in reserve. I disagreed. I always disagreed with any reasoning that left me out of the equation, even if I was carrying an injury. I believed in playing through injury, which, I know, contradicts the trust I place in sports science. But I hate being peripheral; I want to make a difference. If I come on as a substitute, I can't be sure I'll get to the pitch of the game, really make an impact. I'd rather start.

Mind you, if I wanted a genuine excuse, I had one. Surgeon Ray Moran told me the week before the game that there was nothing he could do for the knee, that it was a touch of the 'Paul McGraths'. Curran was also out with injury, while Sherlock failed to make the team even though he had played a crucial late role after coming on against Wexford. Both of us, however, were fit enough to play.

The mantra before the Meath game was very encouraging. So often in the past, we had paid a heavy price for starting slowly against Seán Boylan's side, so we vowed to get stuck into them from the off. Trouble was, I would be sitting on the bench while this approach was being taken, replaced in the starting line-up by Johnny McNally. I had played in the last seven championship meetings between the counties, so I found it hard to swallow. I tried to remain positive, but if ever proof was needed that a team game like football is really driven by individual ambition, then this was it. I would have to grin and bear it.

Victory over Meath was something of a personal triumph for Lyons. It was the first time we had beaten them in seven years, and we succeeded this time largely due to Ray Cosgrove's two goals and a consistent midfield display by Ciarán Whelan. Fortune had favoured Lyons' brave decision to recall Cosgrove. The manager had also capitalised on his investment in young players who now had a precious Royal scalp to help build their confidence. Meanwhile, I made a cameo appearance for the last ten minutes, managing to exchange as many pleasantries with Meath's Cormac Murphy as I could in the short space of time. I continually drew his attention to the scoreboard. What goes around…

The success was sweet, regardless of my reservations. The newly completed stands in a sun-drenched Croke Park had provided a unique backdrop for the game and added to the sense of excitement now permeating Dublin's summer following. Having made the calls and reshaped the team, Lyons stood at the vanguard.

My struggle to earn a starting place against Kildare in the Leinster final mirrored the approach to the Meath game. Every time I pushed myself, the knee flared up, so I remained slightly out of step. Paul Curran, on the other hand, was named at centre-back for the final while Jason was, remarkably, rooted to the bench with me. Of the other remaining veterans, Jim Gavin and Declan Darcy, there was no first-team reprieve, so I had to curb my cynicism a little and trust the management's call. To be fair, they called it right. Although we never quite put Kildare away – we only won by two points in the end – Brogan, McNally and Cosgrove scored 2-9 between them, essentially winning our first provincial title since 1995 in the process.

Both Jason and I were introduced late in the game (for ten minutes again in my case) and I immediately felt knackered. This is one of the reasons I hate coming on as a sub – it's sometimes impossible to get to the pitch of the game. Jason agreed with me afterwards, although he had shown great hunger, winning one vital ball and shipping a heavy tackle in the process. His exclusion gnawed away at me as did some of the aspects of our performance. Curran was called ashore early in the second half, although he was really paying the price for our problems at midfield.

Normally a very reluctant substitute, I rose in unison with the blue hordes in the crowd of 78,000 when we scored our two quick-fire goals, scores which helped exorcise the pain of the 2000 final. As Lyons inhaled the adulation that accompanied our success, I remained on the peripheries. But I was happy. Our journey would continue and I would get another chance.

For many long-serving players like Paddy Christie, Darren Homan and Senan Connell, it was their first medal. It ended a painful period in Dublin's history and Lyons had delivered it. He made a number of hard calls and deserved his day in the sun. He indulged in a bit of proselytising: filling Croke Park; the biggest gig in town; Dublin, the Manchester United of Gaelic football.

Still no one was complaining, except Curran, who was furious, when we later met in the Sunnybank, by the manner of his withdrawal. He knew he shouldn't have been hauled ashore, that the problems lay elsewhere on the field. To be fair to Lyons, he apologised to Curran at the next training session, an unusual step for a manager to take. However, he was dealing with one of the finest players ever to wear a blue jersey.

We were drawn against Donegal in the quarter-final on the August Bank Holiday Monday. It wasn't the worst name out of the hat and thankfully I remained sufficiently injury-free so I was disappointed when, once again, I was named on the bench. General preparations for the game had gone reasonably well until an eleventh-hour illness struck down Lyons who was rushed to the Blackrock Clinic. Pillar Caffrey took the reins on the sideline and, although I wasn't overly enamoured of Lyons' dressing-room talks or immediate pre-match routines, the younger lads in particular felt his absence. Still we survived, just about. Cosgrove's two confidently taken goals saved us as Donegal pressurised with a late rally led by Adrian Sweeney, who caused us all manner of problems at the back. I did twenty minutes this time after replacing Senan and, while my impact was minimal enough, I stayed injury free and brought myself into contention for a starting role.

The replay should have been a point of departure for me that season. I was moving better than at any other period, had properly nailed down a position at corner-forward and, from the outset, with Lyons back on the line, Dublin cruised through the game. But as if upon every silver lining there hangs a cloud, I was hammered by Donegal full-back Eamon Doherty as I slipped the ball to Cosgrove for our first-half goal and he made shite of my shoulder. I re-emerged for the second half after treatment but I was replaced after a couple of minutes by Sherlock. The way I saw it, it wasn't because of the injury. I didn't look to be taken off, I was fine to play on. I gave Lyons a withering look as I left the field, something that was picked up on camera and spotted a week later by the lads during our video analysis and greeted with howls of laughter.

We strolled through the remainder of the game, a facile victory which was celebrated with a dubious lap of honour. This annoyed me. I couldn't help think we were delivering the wrong signal. After all, surely we were now only one step further towards our ultimate target – an All-Ireland title? If I was annoyed, Jim Gavin lost the plot altogether. I don't really know how the celebratory lap came about – several of us were already back in the dressing room when it took place. But when Gavin saw the lap on a television adjacent to the dressing room, he stormed back in, throwing bandages and water bottles around the place. 'What in the name of Jayzus is going on? You'd swear we'd won something.'

Later that year I learnt, first hand, that Armagh captain Kieran McGeeney had taken great pleasure in watching the Dubs celebrate their quarter-final victory. Most teams need little or no extra motivation to beat Dublin. Now we'd packaged a nice little video for our semi-final opponents.

It was interesting that the improvement in our performance coincided with Lyons' return after his brief illness. His energetic support was vital at this point, particularly for the players he had personally brought along. He now faced his biggest test, a battle-hardened Armagh in the semi-final. We had assumed the mantle of favourites and, worse still, I knew only too well just how single-mindedly effective Armagh's pivotal leader, McGeeney, my Na Fianna club-mate, could be.

Given the stakes involved, Lyons surprisingly avoided any in-depth tactical planning prior to the game. I was itching to devise a game plan to counter their obvious strengths and apparent weaknesses, but we stuck to our routine. It was only at the last minute that I was detailed to line out at centre-forward to mark McGeeney. Lyons was right. He reckoned that it just might occupy McGeeney's mind sufficiently to negate his powerful influence. What the manager didn't realise was that I had damaged my calf muscle on the Thursday night before the game and couldn't sprint. I rushed to my own physio, Alan Kelly, or 'The great AK' as he is known in the trade, who informed me that the muscle wasn't actually torn: good news. However, it was a complicated setback that would hamper me considerably: not so good. I couldn't lift off the ball of my foot. I could only actually move flat-footed and, every time I'd tried to extend my calf, I could feel it about to tear. Just to compound matters, I also needed a painkilling shot into my injured shoulder before the game. Sounds implausible? I'm not kidding. I will do anything to play.

I was pretty daunted lining out against McGeeney on one leg but, strangely, Lyons' plan worked to a point. Regardless of my minimal influence on the game, the Armagh captain kept one close eye on me, which meant he couldn't deliver his trademark full-court press. However, after I was switched off McGeeney into full-forward, he started to control the game. Our sideline probably felt they had to act to curtail Armagh's growing influence on the game. It backfired, though. Not only did McGeeney start to dictate, I dropped a great ball from Sherlock which could have unlocked their defence. Ciarán Whelan had just revived us with a spectacular goal and, once again, I had made a high-profile mistake that might have determined the final outcome. It is one of those blunders that has haunted me since. Good hands are supposed to be my hallmark.

We remained in touch until Ray Cosgrove ran out of luck and saw his last-minute chance to equalise come off the upright. Surprisingly, Declan Darcy made his first appearance of the campaign in the last few minutes. It looked as though he had been introduced as a free-taker. However, Cosgrove stuck to his guns and took the kick. After his shot rebounded, I got the last hand on the ball as my calf eventually went, while my good leg cramped completely. I could barely get off the fucking field.

The biggest gig in town was over for another year. As with Tommy Carr and Mickey Whelan, the little bit of luck had deserted the latest Dublin manager. A dream final date against Kerry remained just that, a dream.

For me, the nightmare had already begun.

Chapter 5

Mind Yourself

A potted history of Dessie Farrell, 1988–2002:

Nurtured by two selfless parents and a caring sister, he became something of a sports prodigy as a teenager, first coming to prominence in 1988 after scoring 8-9 on the way to an All-Ireland final in his second of three years as a Dublin minor. Christened 'Little Boy Blue' in the newspapers. Left school with a good Leaving Cert. Played hockey for Leinster and Ireland, hurled and kicked football with the Dublin under-21s, and graduated to the senior football ranks under luckless manager, Gerry McCaul, in 1990. Progress halted when he ruptured his cruciate knee ligament in a club game and was told he'd never play again. Played within six months and was back on the Dublin team under new boss, Paddy Cullen and his successor, Pat O'Neill. Played in his first senior All-Ireland final in 1992, lost out to Donegal, his mother's county. Won four Leinster championships and, eventually, in 1995, an All-Ireland. Named an All Star the same year. Hit his peak as Dublin's star began to wane under Mickey Whelan. Got married to Noreen, had son Frankie then daughter Emma. Became Dublin captain under Tommy Carr, 'Busted' in the Sunday World, *won nothing, missed an open goal against Kerry. Upset the Dublin club traditionalists by aiding in the acquisition of outside players for Na Fianna. Won three Dublin championships on the trot, 1999–2001. Trained as a psychiatric nurse, worked as a nurse, left nursing, became a medical rep, left it. Appointed head of the Gaelic Players' Association. Could have retired when Tommy Lyons came along, didn't. Endured a strained relationship with the manager and won another Leinster medal...*

Enough? You would think. When the dust settled on our relatively successful 2002 season under Tommy Lyons, everyone assumed that was it for me. 'Any thoughts of retirement, Dessie?' Reporters concluded with the same question, taking the boots out of my hand to hang them up as we spoke. Easy story, easy headline, easy soul-searching interview. I could have gone and dished out the usual trite waffle about having 'no regrets' and moving on with great memories. I did have regrets. I didn't want to retire.

I was struggling with Lyons' style of management. He liked to play mind games with players, keep them in the dark at times, put them on the back foot, ironically, in an effort to keep them on their toes. I was an experienced player, but he had problems with some of the old guard. I know I wasn't captain any longer, but I couldn't understand why he didn't make a greater attempt to harness our experience. He embraced new ideas about training, yet at times opted for the old–fashioned practices. He contradicted himself sometimes. He also milked the publicity that surrounded his job. He was too public, a trait traditionally looked upon with suspicion in Dublin.

I was also trying to contend with serious injury and I was up to my eyes with the burgeoning GPA. But I have a recurring nightmare; I'll retire from Dublin and they'll win the very next championship. Even worse, they will fall short and I might have assisted in some way. It may be daft, it may not be plausible, but it's honest. Look at Colm O'Rourke; retired in 1995 after a hiding only to see his county win the title a year later. Having lost out on so many occasions, I wanted another chance to try and satisfy that lingering, unfulfilled desire.

Honest though my ambition was, it certainly wasn't prudent. My obsession with chasing another elusive All-Ireland was to have serious ramifications off the field and, in the winter months that followed that 2002 football season, my life spiralled out of control.

It had been a long time coming.

The night we won the All-Ireland final, 18 September 1995, I proposed to my long-standing girlfriend, Noreen Mulry, who I'd met and courted while working in St Brendan's Psychiatric Hospital. Given the sequence of prior near-misses with Dublin, it had become something of an ongoing promise – should we ever actually get our hands on the Sam Maguire, I would pop the question. I did. We married in Paris on our own a year later. After our son Frankie was born – I was the typical proud father, overcome with emotion at the whole wonderful experience – I commenced my new family life blissfully unaware where I was heading. After all, ambition meant winning championships, pretty much nothing else.

Life wasn't easy. Noreen and I worked opposite shifts in the hospital. When I wasn't working, I was usually training, playing, travelling, meeting, plotting, convalescing or socialising with other players. I don't know exactly when things started to go pear-shaped; there was probably no starting point. Suffice to say I was pretty much a selfish bastard from the outset. I accepted Noreen's endless help and largesse. She did absolutely everything she could to accommodate my ludicrous lifestyle. In return, she got to share in the relentless pursuit of my ambitions. Some trade-off. I loved my wife, I loved my child, but everything at home got thrown onto the altar of Dessie Farrell's ambition, where it could be sacrificed at any moment.

Mercifully, life has battered sense into me subsequently. But my conversion came at a heavy price.

I will never try to justify selfishness, but I remain at a loss to understand how any young, talented sportsman who aspires to achieve success can do so without some sacrifice. Maybe some can cope better with the conflicting demands. I don't think it's coincidental that many young players nowadays forego personal relationships, even career development, in an attempt to achieve success on the football pitch. During my tenure as captain, from 1998 onwards, demands on the Gaelic football field increased significantly. The knock-on effect for me was that I started to view domestic life not as a haven, not as a constant or an escape, but rather as another distraction from my primary aim – success on the field. I believed, naively, that anything that got in the way of football was to be avoided, so I reneged on some of my responsibilities at home.

I was twenty-six years old when we were married; Noreen was four years older and considerably more mature. I was a big fish outside of the house, but I was just about keeping my head above water at home. I became resentful.

Few of my friends were married, and none seemed as tied down as I felt. From the time I became Dublin captain in the late spring of 1998, a pattern began to emerge where Noreen was taking responsibility for our son while I managed to achieve the almost impossible: to get even more involved in football. With every championship setback, I grew more frustrated with myself, with my injuries, with my increasingly elusive goals. I enjoyed the responsibility with Dublin, but I shirked it at home. Rather than accepting the strain that is normal for new parents, I started to erect barriers. After our second child, Emma, was born in 2000, things became even more frenetic.

I ploughed on regardless, but it was easy for me to ignore reality. Go training three nights a week with Dublin, meet Saturday morning, play a match on Sunday, have a few jars that night, go to work on Monday and start all over again. When Dublin was out of the championship, Na Fianna filled the void immediately and, when there was no Na Fianna, there was always hockey. When there was none of the above, there were always drinking sessions to make up for the weeks or even months of abstinence. And then there was work. As if I didn't have enough on my plate, I decided in 2002 to accept the role as chief executive of the GPA, a twelve-hour-a-day task to get the fledgling players' body off the ground in the face of incredible intransigence. It was a risky move, as I had given up a very successful job as a pharmaceutical rep, a position in which I had been progressing nicely.

Noreen picked up the slack or, should I say, shouldered most of the burden. The more absent I became, the more she immersed herself in our children's welfare. I doted over both my kids, when I was around to dote, but my relationship with Noreen deteriorated into a blame game. We never seemed to have time together and, when we did, we fought. It was an endless series of unanswered questions. Where had I been? Where was I going? Why was I never around?

I paid little or no heed to the problem, nor did I ever discuss my domestic difficulties with anyone. I was refusing to recognise the emerging crisis, as I twisted everything around to justify my side of the story.

Maybe if my affair was only with Dublin football, I could have worked things out. It wasn't. Feeling detached in what was by now a shattered relationship, I started an affair with another woman. My disregard for Noreen was now complete. She didn't know, not at first at least. Not being content with being a demanding, selfish bastard, I was now a unfaithful, deceitful, selfish bastard who, when he wasn't spending all his time with Dublin, was spending whatever free time he could muster with another woman.

It was the ultimate cop-out. I digested all the excuses for my actions, keeping any guilt firmly at a distance and out of harm's way. I had concluded that my marriage was doomed, without contemplating exactly what that meant. In the dressing room, I lectured lads about honesty and I preached discipline. At home, I lied, cheated, made up stories, stretched training sessions. Few, if any, of my friends knew what was happening.

To ease the pressure on herself so she could cope with two growing children, my wife had begun to job share. At first she didn't know that I was cheating on her, but her suspicion was aroused by my increasingly erratic actions as well as my steadfast refusal to try and sort out our marital difficulties. Aware that our relationship was going down the tubes, Noreen pleaded with me to sort something out. I ignored the pleas.

Meanwhile, as I was single-handedly dismantling my marriage, my obsession with being a successful, winning captain with Dublin had come to naught when Tommy Carr was sacked. It was a defining moment, because it weakened the blind resolve that was powering my life. My hand was always on the tiller, controlling my actions, for better or worse. When Carr went, I lost something and it cast me adrift. I had surrounded myself in a fog of my own making. The jolt of no longer being Dublin's main man, the realisation that regret had become the dominant aspect of my sporting life, left me somewhat rudderless.

Noreen found out. Maybe I always wanted her to; I had considered for a long time that we were on a road to nowhere. But it was only then that it became clear to me just how much I had gambled. She had done everything she could for me and for our children. I had stolen her dignity. The kids were no longer toddlers, their beautiful young personalities were developing. What the hell was I at?

I panicked. The fact that I might lose everything, including the children, dawned on me. Noreen said she was thinking of moving back to Roscommon with the kids. When would I see them? Would I become a 'McDonald's' dad? I had a horrific vision of driving down the country on a Friday night to be with my children for a few hours on a Saturday. I sank into a mire of guilt. In what seems like a fairly tokenistic gesture now, though I never meant it to be, I asked Noreen could we address our problems. Too late. I was now trying to close the stable door. The horse meanwhile, was in the next county. I had missed my opportunity to save the most important thing in our lives by a considerable distance.

I never properly came to terms with what happened. I didn't want anyone to get hurt, but in reality I was only compounding the problem. What I know is that my wife was blameless. I hadn't resolved the contradictions in my own life. I mean, the idea that I might be lonely and without a partner horrifies me, yet I was prepared to lose the very person whose love for me, in difficult circumstances, was beyond doubt.

I had to accept that my marriage was essentially over, although I continued to live at home. I carried on as best I could. Na Fianna had been thrown out of the 2002 Dublin championship, so there was no winter diversion from my domestic travails. The GPA was growing rapidly and I threw myself into work and tried to put my fears behind me, which was almost impossible. The preceding number of stressful years had been leading to this situation: the drink-driving shame, the constant failure with Dublin, the loss of captaincy, injury, the loss of a solid relationship with my manager, the challenge of a new career. Now, marital breakdown.

The experience dragged me into the darkest corner of my life. Faced with the torment of losing my children, I despaired. I was suffocating with guilt, with anxiety. Every time I looked at my children, I was overwhelmed with the fear of losing them. I became aware of the harm I'd caused and realised that, no matter what, I had failed them in some regard. I didn't feel I could turn to anyone. What would they say? It was my fault, my mess – only *I* could sort it out.

My despair spiralled out of control. I awoke each day burdened by an oppressive weight. I cried myself to sleep every night. I embraced my children every night as they slept, hoping my sobbing wouldn't wake them.

I was a failure. My greatest fear in life had come to pass. A failure. I had lost all perspective. I couldn't cope any longer. As my depression deepened, my mind was a constant blur and I felt I had reached a dead end.

When was this going to go away? When would it be over? How would things work out? Not knowing the answers to these questions only added to the impending doom. I was no longer in control of my own situation. Underneath the calm exterior I was portraying, there was a crippling torment, one that would not subside. The more I tried to think clearly, to understand my predicament, the more confused I became. I didn't know how to repair the damage; truth is, I couldn't. Instead of addressing problems as they arose, I was quite prepared to let them fester, turn a blind eye. Things will sort themselves out, I thought. They didn't. The tunnel got darker and narrower. There seemed to be no way out.

Despairing completely, I struggled to sleep. When I did eventually collapse, exhausted, my reprieve was short-lived, as I would awake in the small hours, staring blankly at the ceiling. The fear and stress of my situation engulfed every waking hour. Sometimes I would pace the kitchen floor until dawn, trying and failing to find a way of hauling myself out of this crisis.

Other times, I would sit in the car and drive aimlessly around the city. In my darkest moments I even considered ending it all, wondering would it make everyone's lives easier. The outcome terrified me, yet the thought that I could end this remorseless misery held some grisly appeal. People in such a situation often have fleeting, suicidal notions. However, in my case, while it started like that, these notions became more profound. All of a sudden, I was giving the idea of ending my life more and more consideration. I was in big trouble. I needed help. If only I could bring myself to confide in someone, then there would be a chance of reversing the spiral. But I was afraid – horrified and ashamed that I, a Dublin footballer, a man, a father, with everything in the world going for him, was unable to cope.

I've no shame now in recounting these awful feelings. Stress, fear of failure, the pressures of marital break-up involving children can tip the most well-balanced individual over the edge. The idea that my football career, the backbone of my life, would soon be over, only exacerbated my depression. I needed help, and I needed it quickly.

On a cold February morning, I awoke in a panic at about four o'clock in the morning. Bewildered, I dragged myself down to the kitchen and put on the kettle. I sat with my head in my hands, crying. Physically, the whole ordeal had taken its toll. I had spent a number of weeks trying desperately to train, as if it might wrestle me from my stupor. I had lost weight, but not from the training. I wasn't eating, I felt constantly nauseous and a burning anxiety was tearing my guts out. I rose from the kitchen chair in anger, disgusted at my wretched situation; how I'd completely lost control. I went upstairs to try and steal another hour's sleep. Before lying down, I looked over at Emma and Frankie, sleeping peacefully, and the rhythm of their breathing relaxed me. I lay down beside them and whispered a promise to them in their sleep: I would seek help the following morning.

The next day, I contacted a counsellor and booked an appointment. After putting down the phone, I felt the first weight lift.

Why hadn't I spoken to someone previously? I needed to get so much off my chest, but couldn't. I felt I couldn't confide in anyone. Why was that? There were so many people that I knew I could count on to support me in difficult times, but yet I chose to suffer in silence, to try and sort out my own problems. Why could I not have spoken to Noreen? Well, our situation prevented me from doing that. What about my parents, whom I could, without question, call on for help with anything that life might throw at me? Anything except this. I think I felt I would be letting them down by succumbing to such problems. Mostly I had only ever given them reasons to be proud of me, but what would they think now?

Vanity prohibited me from even thinking of telling my friends.

I was trapped. Dessie Farrell was a leader on the football field, a leader of men. I wasn't supposed to have problems, only solutions.

One of the great lessons I had learned in my psychiatry training was the importance of encouraging effective communication, but when difficulties came to my own doorstep, I was too proud to talk to anyone. My reticence only compounded my condition. As a psychiatric nurse, I had spoken to countless young men who were crippled with a depression brought on by unfettered expectancy, by a society that only paints men in black and white, as winners or losers. My advice was always the same: talk to someone, share the burden, it's nothing to be ashamed of.

I should have been all too aware of the complexities of the troubled mind, but even though I knew what to do, I couldn't bring myself to do it. Only the traumatic experience of being faced with the ultimate darkness made me acquiesce and open my heart.

I was really nervous about counselling, worried that people would find out. I was fearful of the stigma attached to mental illness, but as soon as I started to discuss my problems, the bleakness of the previous few months slowly evaporated with every conversation, with every new day.

As a young, ambitious man, my predicament was certainly not unique. Unfortunately, society finds itself incapable of grasping the reality of how vulnerable young men can be, choosing instead to either ignore it or stigmatise the sufferers. Contrary to the popular belief that suicide only affects those with psychiatric illnesses, most people who act on their impulses have had no previous contact with any healthcare professionals.

It may seem surprising, but the worst effects of my depression weren't long lifting. No sooner had therapy been arranged, than I started to feel a massive relief from the oppression of the previous number of months. Over the next period, I completely refocused my life. My children would now come first. After all, it was the thought of losing them in the first place that brought my problems to the fore. I would not let all the attendant pressures of my work and football distract me from my primary commitment to them.

Ironically, shortly after I had come to terms with my own situation, the GPA became involved in a suicide-awareness campaign called 'Mind Yourself' in the North Eastern Health Board region, which targeted vulnerable young males. Dermot McCabe, Kieran McGeeney, Peter Canavan and I were all quoted in the literature with the express theme of encouraging individuals who were experiencing difficulties to seek help from their GP or other relevant groups. For me, there was poignancy about my involvement in the campaign. No one knew what I'd been through, but I was so happy to help encourage troubled young people to take that first crucial step.

It has been very difficult for me to relate this episode of my life. Yet I know that, in the first instance, my problems were compounded by silence. If I suffered from asthma, diabetes or any other serious medical condition, I wouldn't have any hesitation admitting to it, nor would I have any difficulty talking about how I was coping with such illnesses. So, for me to exclude from this account reference to such a turbulent period in my life would be to succumb to society's prejudice, to give in to the dangerous stigmatisation that persists. It would do a disservice to the people who are trying desperately to make society aware of the huge problem facing young men in particular.

If, in the long term, my story of emerging from a trough of despair can help others to seek help, then it will have been worthwhile.

Noreen and I may have now taken separate paths in our lives, but no matter what challenges lie ahead, our children will remain my constant focus. I have lost an extraordinary partner and I must live with that, but I can now control the distractions and desires that blinded me for nearly a decade. There is an order to my life and, hopefully, I will never again allow things to get out of hand. I manage my time and commitments carefully to ensure that the balance always favours those who are most important. My experience has taught me that ambition – and failure – often leave little room for rationality and must be kept in check.

The whole episode has changed my outlook on life. But I was one of the lucky ones. I had my children and my family. Through all the despair, I detected a glimmer of hope, a chink of light that enabled me to reach out and seek help – an act that may have prevented a more drastic deterioration in my condition.

The hour before dawn is always the darkest.

In 2003, over 10,000 people attempted suicide in Ireland.

Chapter 6

The Saddest Gig in Town – 2003

There was no miraculous cure, but at least now I had a structure: one that enabled me to cope, particularly with the bad days. No matter how busy I was, I would find time for my children every day. My relationship with them became paramount. I wanted it to develop in the fullest way possible and have a meaningful impact on their young lives, not just at weekends or holidays, as unfortunately happens with many working parents. I immersed myself in their lives and, slowly, I hauled myself forward. There was no improvement in my relationship with Noreen, at least not initially, but there was an acceptance that it was over and, in time, we would move on.

Thankfully, the oppressive feelings of guilt also dissipated. I accepted the reality that marriages fail and that I now had to deal with that failure in a way that would guarantee our children's welfare and happiness. It worked. In fact, the more time I spent with my children, the more I craved their company.

I accept how extreme this must appear; that I had to endure such a terrifying experience to realise what many lucky parents accept from the outset. But I refuse to view it this way. I'm just so relieved and thankful that I eventually reached this level of awareness. Accepting the hand I was dealt is all I can do.

It was a liberating couple of months for me. I felt as though I had arrived somewhere. Life was no less hectic – in fact, it was busier than ever – but it had a purpose now that I could simply not envisage some months earlier. Even though I had assumed further daily responsibilities, I felt freer.

So it was with a lighter heart that I faced into the new season, waiting to see if Tommy Lyons would invite me back onto the Dublin panel after the National League. He did, eventually, though later than he had the previous year. To be honest, given what I'd been through, I was thankful for the break, but as the championship loomed, my old desires burned as strongly as ever.

I don't really know where I conjure up the enthusiasm from. I should have copped what was unfolding. The wheels were starting to loosen on the Tommy Lyons bandwagon from the start of the league in February 2003. A high-profile league match against All-Ireland champions Armagh in Croke Park backfired when Dublin got a hiding in front of 51,000 people. The manager had spent the previous summer talking about selling the game to the people of Dublin and the promotional appeal from such a fixture was immense. But the defeat by Armagh kind of put the kybosh on any further promotional work (a similar fixture against Tyrone a year later was kept to Parnell Park). I wasn't involved, but I digested everything Lyons said in the aftermath of the Armagh game, including the suggestion that Dublin had 'overachieved' the previous summer. Whatever truth lay in his statement, he shouldn't have said it. It rankled with the players, many of whom were already tiring of Lyons' abrasive style. From where I was, it seemed that Lyons was only too happy to surf the wave of success while it lasted. What if it didn't last? Would he look for scapegoats?

While I was trying to put my life together away from the Dublin set-up, Lyons also oversaw a deal between the panel and the new and short-lived *Dublin Daily* newspaper. Although there was potentially an attractive financial package on offer for the squad, it was, in hindsight, ill-conceived. Profile is generally not a problem for Dublin players, even through the lean times. Now they were exposed on a continuous basis, committed to the constant distraction of giving interviews, even if they were anodyne quotes. It's worth repeating that no county needs further incentive to beat Dublin.

After rejoining the Dublin panel in late spring, I damaged my calf as soon as my training intensified and the injury was to rule me out of our first championship game, an easy victory over Louth. The win may not have helped everyone's perspective. Easy championship victories tend to unleash an irrational hype in the capital, so there was stupid loose talk of 'going one step further' and winning an All-Ireland. Lyons decided to change his winning hand for our next clash with Laois, the turning point in his tenure. Without offering any particular explanation, he made three changes in personnel and four on-field switches. He also named five Kilmacud Crokes players in the starting fifteen. As Jason Sherlock and I were both injured and Senan Connell was dropped, there was now no Na Fianna player in the line-up, which led to a strain between Pillar and his former players on Mobhi Road.

I was furious. I knew this was complacency at its worst and complained to all who would listen in the run-up to the game. For years I had seen how seriously men like Paddy Cullen, Pat O'Neill and even Tommy Carr had treated Mick O'Dwyer. Now smarting from his Leinster final setback with Kildare, this was a perfect chance for the astute Kerryman to get one back on Lyons. Dublin walked straight into the trap.

Lyons had introduced an edict that any player who hadn't trained by the Saturday a week before a game was deemed unready for selection. For the Laois game, both myself and Sherlock fell into that category, even though both of us were pretty close to full fitness. Lyons later made an exception to this rule for Alan Brogan, who lined out despite not being able to train the week before a game. I couldn't understand why he bothered with such approaches.

The morning of the Laois match, knowing I wouldn't be playing in Croke Park, I trained with Na Fianna and came through a full session unscathed. Sherlock wouldn't train with the club as he was holding out a remote hope that he might get to play some part of the game for Dublin. The panel was still thirty-strong, and he was convinced that, if things really went pear-shaped, Lyons would call on him. I told Jason that I didn't think it would happen, but he still togged out.

I was convinced there would be difficulties ahead in that game. We did not give Laois, a side managed by Mick O'Dwyer, the respect they deserved. Lyons was trying to keep the Dublin players on their toes, switching things around to avoid complacency. But he missed the point. And, while Dublin had no luck on the day, missing a succession of decent chances, Lyons didn't seem to have allowed for the possibility of the game slipping away from him. In the end, Laois won and Jason Sherlock was not called upon.

Having basked in the limelight for the past twelve months, Lyons now had a new task. Dublin had been beaten unexpectedly and, as I headed down the tunnel, I was intrigued to see how our manager would handle this scenario. He tried to pick the team up and was quite magnanimous in stating that he did not have all the answers. But he then shocked us by giving the panel permission to go out and enjoy a drink. Lyons, who was a strict disciplinarian, had been very anti-drink since his arrival, even scolding Paul Curran and Senan Connell for having a few jars after a league game on the one occasion they were caught trying to sneak a couple of jars in an obscure pub on the outskirts of town.

However, at that juncture in the dressing room, prior to the draw for the back door, we were scheduled to play our first qualifier the following Saturday. The manager claimed to embrace the standard rules of sports science, and drinking six days before a serious game wasn't clever. I raised my eyes up to heaven when I heard him, but I didn't want to say anything because I didn't think it was an appropriate time for a stand-up row. However, Darren Homan, perhaps seeing my reaction, told Lyons straight out that he felt drinking at this time was inappropriate. Lyons disagreed, reminding him that it was he who called the shots, and that was the end of it.

I ignored Lyons and approached the players individually to tell them to avoid drinking. I had no authority to do that, though I always felt that experience must count for something. It wasn't my job. After all, Ciarán Whelan was the captain, but I felt that ignoring Tommy's instructions was probably the lesser of two evils. Later in Jurys Hotel, where we were gathered for some finger food, most of the lads abstained. Events had overtaken us by the time we had regrouped, as our qualifier against Derry had been rescheduled for a week later than the rest of the games. Still, most of the lads avoided drinking and those few who decided to have a jar were asked to take it easy. The fear was that a big drinking session would develop, culminating in a late-night visit to Copper Face Jacks, and that it could tear the arse out of our preparation.

The next day, I got a phone call from Lyons who said he wanted to meet me. I asked him why and he said he had a couple of issues with my attitude over the weekend. We arranged to meet in the Skylon Hotel on the Tuesday night before training. I was convinced I was going to get my marching orders, though I didn't intend to make it easy for him. I wouldn't be intimidated.

Firstly, he brought up the drinking issue and bluntly told me that he was the manager and, as such, was entitled to make these calls. I countered, saying that his decision went against the grain. How come he was so anti-drink throughout the league campaign and then prepared to let players drink six days before a championship match? We didn't know at that point that our game had been rescheduled. Lyons reiterated his statement and then added that he had deliberately given lads the permission to drink so he could determine their attitude. If they drank, he felt, they would be showing a lack of discipline and responsibility. I was gob-smacked. Did he genuinely think I'd buy this? Needless to say, he never dropped the players who drank that night.

The battle lines were now clearly drawn. I felt I was now fighting for my future. Neither of us would budge. Lyons proceeded to accuse me of trying to undermine him from day one. I disagreed and told him again that I didn't care who managed Dublin as long as we were successful. My assertion that I wouldn't let personalities get in the way may have rung hollow, but I was being genuine. Time was running out for me and playing for Dublin meant too much.

We agreed to disagree. Despite having the distinct impression that he wanted rid of me, I wasn't going to make the decision easy for him. I reiterated my desire to play and that I wasn't prepared to let a personality clash deter me from that goal.

I left his company not really knowing where I stood; there had been no resolution. He never mentioned training that night, so I made sure I was up at the venue early and was on the field doing some shooting practice by the time he arrived, thereby letting him know that he didn't bother me. In the trial match the following Saturday, I lined out with the 'B' team, marking Paddy Christie. I managed to grab a couple of scores and lay off a few more, so I was transferred onto the 'A' team, where it was easier again to make an impression. Mind you, after the switch, Lyons told me to go in centre-forward, the only position in which he could envisage me starting, as he didn't feel I had the speed in my legs for the inside forward line. The strange thing about this notion was that, up until then, the inside forward line was the only place Lyons had ever played me.

I was selected to play against Derry in Clones the following Saturday and Senan Connell was also back in the starting line-up. We travelled to Clones on the Tuesday before the game for a run-out on the pitch and I could barely move with stiffness after a couple of hard practice games. On the bus back to the Nurenmore Hotel, where we were stopping for food and a team meeting,

Lyons told me that I had looked like an 'old man'. He compared my gait with the freshness I had shown on Saturday. I just grunted, but I knew he was right. It was becoming increasingly difficult for me to put in intense sessions back-to-back with little time for recovery in between. For all my experience, I couldn't really confide in him and felt as if I was always on trial. I wanted to be able to tell him how I was without endangering my place on the team. I wanted him to trust me. I wanted to tell him that I knew what was best for my own body without feeling I was compromising myself in some way. But I couldn't.

There was a bit of soul-searching at the meeting. Why had we lacked desire against Laois? If we were serious about our ambition to win an All-Ireland, why had Mick O'Dwyer's team shown greater hunger? Lyons claimed, correctly, that the lads were deluding themselves. They *thought* they were working harder, but they weren't. He also added that we had become predictable and were 'too nice'. The last criticism stuck in my craw. I don't think Tommy Lyons ever managed to balance his desire for discipline with the need for cuteness when, inevitably, a bit of rough-housing arose. His ambiguous outlook in this regard would surface again against Armagh in Croke Park.

Some of the players also spoke at the meeting and said the usual self-critical stuff, but it was hard to see how our whole mindset could be changed after one charged meeting.

In the dressing room in Clones, on the day of the Derry match, I was then held up as a paragon of virtue. 'You could all take a leaf out of Farrell's book,' Lyons announced. 'Look how much he has to lose, putting his body on the line.' It was truly bizarre; you never knew what he was thinking.

Things went well against Derry and it turned into a bit of a Na Fianna roadshow. I scored an early goal, Connell grabbed another and, just to complete the day, Sherlock popped up with a third. I was awarded the man of the match, and Lyons eulogised about my contribution. However, a couple of days later, he told me that there was a huge element of luck involved with these things.

So there it was. I thought I was being dropped from the panel, *persona non grata*, then I was the exemplary figure, the star of the show, only to finish up being the lucky chap. That was Tommy Lyons: always the mind games. He played them from the start. When I returned to the panel after my extended break, he questioned why I had put on a few extra pounds, despite the fact that I had explained that I had been on a weights programme for the previous five months to build up leg muscles to protect my knee. I had to tell him it wasn't fat, it was muscle tone, and that it had been prescribed for me by his own medical team. 'Get the calipers and do it properly,' I asked him, referring to the tool used to measure body fat.

Unfortunately, our success in the Derry game really only papered over the cracks and we were derailed against Armagh in the following round. Once again there was no real plan. The forwards were gathered together hours before the game and told to keep switching markers to prevent Kieran McGeeney from settling. After a short while, it became obvious that this plan was too difficult to implement in an ad hoc way; it needed to be practised on the training pitch, not just thrown in at the last minute.

The mistakes made by Lyons during that game have been well documented: the perceived sign of weakness shown by stopping his players from running down the tunnel alongside the Armagh men at half-time; taking off centre-back Johnny Magee after our keeper, Stephen Cluxton, had been sent off; criticising Cluxton after the game. As far as I was concerned, Lyons had gone far enough. I was fed up with his style, fed up with his attitude, fed up with his homespun psychology and fed up with what I perceived to be a flawed approach. Having endured the most strenuous comeback of my career only to see it come to no avail. I was enraged. We were out of the championship and I wasn't getting any younger. If, as he said, I was putting my body on the line, then he'll understand why I acted the way I did subsequently.

The night after the defeat, a lot of the players gathered in The Carpenter in Carpenterstown for a drink and the mood was decidedly rebellious. Players didn't like the tension in the squad and were fed up with Tommy's style of management. I decided to try and take control of the situation and act on what I saw as an impasse. Some of the players I spoke with had serious issues with Lyons and I knew of others on the squad who shared a similar view. Yet he had another year left in his contract. I was only acting because of what I had heard and, despite what some people felt – even some of the players – it wasn't a solo run. We organised a meeting for the senior panellists on the Tuesday night in

The Burlington Hotel. However, in the interim, Paul Curran, who was working as a columnist with the *Evening Herald*, had informed the sports editor, Dave Courtney, that a coup was being organised by the players. By chance, I found out that the story was about to be splashed on the back of the paper and pleaded with Courtney not to run the story as it would, unintentionally, kill it if he did. Thankfully, he held off, but word filtered out nonetheless, spooking the already frightened players in the process.

At eight o'clock that night, I arrived in the room we had put aside in The Burlington. However, only five of the eleven players contacted had turned up – me, Jason Sherlock, Senan Connell, Johnny Magee and Stephen Cluxton. We received a phone call telling us that the other six were sitting in a car parked outside the hotel, worried that the whole thing was a stitch-up by the newspapers. They were sure there were photographers present to snap them. I assured them that it wasn't the case, so a bizarre kind of stand-off ensued. Obviously these players were here to do something, but were scared of recriminations. Darren Homan then arrived to mediate between the two groups and, following a brief conversation, we decided to call it off. There was no point continuing if lads didn't have the belly for it. We decided to adjourn to the bar, thinking that the rest of the lads were not going to turn up.

Over our first drink, we concluded that it was no wonder we couldn't achieve anything on the field if we lacked the stomach off the field as well. Emotions were now running high, but before we'd even finished our first pint, we got another call from the other group who told us they had gone to a pub in Baggot Street. Among this gang were our current captain, Ciarán Whelan, our previous skipper, Coman Goggins, Paddy Christie, Peadar Andrews and Collie Moran. We decided to join them in Baggot Street. You could have cut the atmosphere with a knife when we arrived. I was seriously pissed off, and the lads knew it. Whelan explained that they didn't want this whole affair carried out in the papers and that news of the *Evening Herald's* aborted splash had confirmed his fears.

After skirting around the issue for a while, we got down to the dirty business. It didn't surprise me that we took up where we had left off. Everyone spoke and the mood was almost unanimous. Lyons was the problem. Only Paddy Christie disagreed. He felt that it was the players' responsibility for their own performances and that Tommy Lyons was being used as a scapegoat. I commended Paddy for being strong enough to go against the flow and assured him there would be no hard feelings no matter what transpired. So we put it to a vote. Did we feel something needed to be 'done' about Tommy Lyons? The result was 'Yes', by a 10-1 majority.

Now, though, we had to consider our options. Should we go to Tommy and tell him how disgruntled we were and look for changes? Or should we take the nuclear option, tell the county board we would no longer be playing under this manager? We pretty much ruled out option one because we didn't think Lyons would be amenable to such an approach, maybe another manager, but not him. Option two seemed a runner, yet when the players considered the enormity of such an unprecedented move, they hesitated. That hesitation was to prove critical. Though we decided to plough on, the plan was already unravelling without unanimity. Before leaving the pub, we agreed to inform the younger members of the panel of our moves and arrange a meeting of the entire squad. I was to phone one half and Ciarán Whelan was to phone the rest.

It seemed a pretty clear course of action to me, but it needed a unified core leading the way. There were literally hundreds of phone calls, yet we seemed to get nowhere – simply a mishmash of half-hearted conversations. Within a day or so, I found out that a few players had been told I was looking for the job myself, which was nonsense. I don't think Whelan was anywhere near as gung-ho about the whole idea as I was. This irritated me greatly at the time, believing that if we didn't succeed in our coup, it would be another fucking year wasted. Later, however, I would come to understand Whelan's reluctance. I was nearing the end of my career, while he had a lot more to lose.

The following day, I was contacted by Tom Humphries from *The Irish Times*. My first thought was 'Will I be the next Roy Keane?' I declined to give an interview on the basis that if I was going to play a part in seeing this plan through, I would have prejudiced myself in the newspaper. It would have been counterproductive. The template was there for the players to act upon and, if they didn't, there was no point. It would seem like sour grapes from a belligerent player about to retire. Dave Billings, Lyons' selector, gave an interview instead and hinted that there may have been a breach in trust between the players and the management. I took this as a suggestion that it wasn't just the players who felt that Lyons had lost the dressing room.

By the time emotions had subsided, the attempted coup had fizzled out. Several journalists queued up to have a lash at Lyons, but in a way they were missing the point. I had contacted John Bailey, knowing that ultimately the county board would decide Lyons' fate. I informed him of the players' views on the situation, but it became apparent to me during subsequent conversations that he was unwilling to act. Bailey had, after all, gone out on a limb for Lyons. He had cast his vote against Carr, which had precipitated Lyons' appointment. How would it look now if he were to oversee his sacking mid-contract? It wasn't going to happen.

Within a week, heads were back buried in the sand and Lyons remained at the helm.

I was angry that as a squad we hadn't stuck together. I believed that, with one final push, it could have happened. I felt this lack of unity was indicative of our performances on the field. I was also angry that the players should have been put in this difficult position in the first place. Under Tommy Carr, the one thing our squad hadn't lacked was unity. What had Lyons done to us? Now we were fractured, no longer could we trust one another. The bond was broken. I knew in my heart it would take a miracle for that to be resolved as long as Lyons was at the helm.

I presumed I had played my last game for Dublin under him.

SECTION 2

Chapter 7

Child's Play – 1971–1981

Hanlon's Corner cattle market stood where Prussia Street meets the North Circular Road, a couple of miles north-west of Dublin's centre. A labyrinth of pens corralled thousands of animals from the city's western hinterland, bringing two Irelands together. Not far down the ring road, through the old village of Phibsborough and past Mountjoy Prison, the two Irelands also met in Croke Park.

Early in the 1970s the market at Hanlon's was dying, the last of the hooves dragged pathetically into a dusty scene resembling an urbanised Spaghetti Western. Soon, it would disappear altogether, entombed beneath scores of re-housed Dubliners. Around the corner lay Annamoe Park where, oblivious to history, I was happily staking my first claim on the young lives of my parents.

While the sight of a cow around the place at that time wasn't unusual, the sight of a kid playing Gaelic football was. Soccer functioned in the concrete confines of the north inner city. Further to the east lay the beating heart of the GAA in Dublin. Here, 'de Gaah', as it was known in Dublin, was nurtured in the Christian Brother academies of Scoil Mhuire, Joey's of Fairview and Ardscoil Rís, which in turn fed the mighty St Vincent's club in Marino. As the suburbs of Dublin began to stretch, the new residents, many from rural Ireland, injected life into hurling and football. In time, these clubs would grow to dominate the games in the city but, in the Seventies, they were infants nurturing an idealistic tradition which they felt was vital to their identity, vital to counter the impact that they perceived *Match of the Day* was having on their children.

Then there was Heffo. Then there was the revolution. Then there were the navy shorts.

Dessie Farrell

In 1976, as a 5-year-old, I watched Tony Hanahoe lift the Sam Maguire on television while blood poured from his swollen eye. I was no fan, I was a mimic. I wasn't happy to just run around the small living room in Cabra aping the Dublin captain with my plastic ball. I made sure I gave myself a good belt in the eye so I looked the part.

My father Seán came from Blackditch, Nurney, a couple of miles outside Kildare town, where he grew up with his sister Mary and two brothers, Pat and Michael. Football was very much part of their lives as youngsters. Tragically, we lost Michael to a brain haemorrhage in 1987 and he left a young family in his wake. Mary still lives in Kildare and remains a constant source of banter for me as she wears her Lilywhite heart on her sleeve. Pat lives in England, but visits home frequently for big matches. He was very much part of my experience during our All-Ireland triumph in 1995, as he was at my shoulder for the week-long celebrations afterwards. I was happy to have him there as well because I've always felt that it is a lonely life being exiled abroad from your extended family.

While my father was training to become a psychiatric nurse in St Patrick's Hospital in James's Street in the late 1960s, he met my mother, Anne Carr, at a dance. After a brief courtship, they married in their early twenties and I was born a year later on 25 June 1971. My sister Aisling arrived four years later. Almost from the cradle, sport became a common interest for the two siblings, helping to form a strong bond between us.

My mother Anne comes from the Gaeltacht townland of Crove beside the village of Carrick, which is nestled spectacularly between Ardara and Glencolmcille in south-west Donegal. She attended St Louis' Convent boarding school in Carrickmacross, County Monaghan and afterwards applied for teacher-training in Carysfort College, Blackrock. However, a failed compulsory music test blocked her path and she then spent a year training in St Louis' Commercial College in Kiltimagh before returning to Dublin where St Patrick's College in Drumcondra offered her a position in the college's admin section. As she says herself, she ended up on the wrong side of the counter. However, there was great pressure on her to earn a living as quickly as possible after her move, being the second eldest in a family of fourteen children. She had eight sisters and five brothers, two of whom, Séamus and Noel, were not much older than me.

My memories of childhood in Crove, where I spent my entire summer holidays, are precious. Séamus and Noel were brothers to me and the bond has remained unbroken to this day.

The area is stunningly beautiful, but besides football and music, they had little else. The barren fields yielded no sort of living and my mother's people have always been sustained by the stinking fish factory in Carrick. As a child, I was as oblivious to the surrounding hardship as I was to the native tongue.

For me, the memories are still very much alive: Cassie, my beautiful grandmother, doting over me as I wait, ball in hand, for the lads to arrive home from the factory, while uncle Proinsias fired out tunes on his accordion in the kitchen. Then, straight to the field at Andy Cunnea's home near the church, or even the meadow beside the house, where our nightly three-and-in games – often bloody affairs – commenced. The spectators, terraces of purple heather, echoed our screams from the banks of the surrounding hills. As autumn approached, I fretted that the fading evening light would scupper our play.

There were other notable events: going to see Séamus and Noel playing matches, Gaelic football training in Glencolmcille and glorious punch-ups with Noel, who gave me my first real tanking and nearly got flayed alive by Cassie for his trouble.

It could be a lonely place. As soon as the boys headed for work, little would happen unless another uncle or aunt was home on holidays to provide transport, when we'd go on a rare trip to the local town. The visit of the postman was waited upon with great anticipation, especially when I knew my mother's letter containing £5 was on its way. Work was expected of me and I often found myself footing and stacking turf for the reward of a bottle of tea and a jam sandwich. I would also help Proinsias thatch the roof and even tried my hand at sheep-shearing, though it's as well there was no inspector from the ISPCA present for my earlier efforts. Sport was compulsive viewing on the two television channels: showjumping, Wimbledon, golf, Olympics – all were contested out in the field. When RTÉ's offerings ended, games of cards would see us off to our beds.

My grandfather Frank died in 1983. My grandmother Cassie passed away in December 2003 after suffering terribly with Alzheimer's for several years. And, in truth, going back has never been the same without Cassie watching over us. Yet, I love bringing my son and daughter, Frankie and Emma, up to Donegal to meet their cousins and regale them with the wonderful stories of my youth. Their appetite for the tiniest details of my own childhood days fascinates me. It's good for the soul.

To talk about the influence Crove had on my football career alone wouldn't do justice to the enduring importance of this period in my life. The kinship of the Carr family has helped shape me, my character.

Back in Dublin, in 1974 our family moved from a modest flat on Goldsmith Street, off Berkeley Road in Phibsborough, which we shared with two of my mother's sisters, to our first house in Annamoe Park, Cabra. There we remained until the end of the decade when we shifted again, this time back down the North Circular Road to Grangegorman. As my father was a nurse in St Brendan's Hospital, he secured one of the 'hospital' houses adjacent to the institution. I was ten years old when we set up home at Marne Villas, a little cul-de-sac tucked away in the shadow of the hospital. A large wall enclosing Dublin Corporation's Cleansing Department provided an ideal flat surface against which I could practise hurling, hockey and football.

The psychiatric hospital in Grangegorman was seen as a scary place by the uninformed outsider – a chillingly dangerous institution, full of lunatics and lost souls. For me it was my back garden, my playground. If inner-city Dublin was starved of sport, street football aside, St Brendan's was an oasis. Football, hurling, soccer, bowls, pitch and putt, cricket, hockey, and handball: they were all catered for in the grounds of the hospital.

My father was a talented sportsman, although he may not have applied himself to any great extent. An all-rounder, he was a decent soccer player (they christened him 'the Ghost' due to his elusiveness), a Gaelic footballer and, significantly for me, a good hockey player. Although working in Brendan's, my father actually lined out with the St Loman's hockey team, a squad which was made up primarily of country men working in psychiatric nursing in the city.

'The Ghost's' claim to fame was a digging match with Heffo's hero Paddy Cullen during a junior football match between Brendan's and St Joseph's O'Connell Boys. The heat of the moment sustained Seán during the row with the Dublin goalkeeper, but when he saw Cullen's imposing frame standing outside the dressing room, he steeled himself for a bruising exit. Typical of the man, big Paddy disarmed him with a handshake. Cullen would enter our lives again nearly twenty years later when he handed me my senior championship debut for Dublin.

My father had a great passion for hockey and I followed. Every weekend, I scrambled along the sideline knocking a hockey ball around, glancing every so often to see how he was getting on. The tables turned when I started playing properly. I can never remember a time when Seán wasn't on the sideline watching me perform. Our relationship is one I have, perhaps, taken for granted and not fully appreciated. We have always been terribly close but neither of us have every really examined our bond or spoken about how things have worked out. Football never seemed to allow us that luxury.

My parents are still a central part of my life. They have gone to ridiculous lengths to support me and my family – even helping to form and sustain the GPA. They have shared every leg of my sporting trek and I hope that my impending retirement won't leave an uneasy void.

While my father nurtured my early interest in sport, my mother sorted out my schooling, sending me to St Vincent's CBS in Glasnevin. It was a pretty decent school at both primary and secondary levels and enjoyed a close relationship with the Na Fianna GAA club up the road. Vincent's really stood out because it was one of the few schools in Dublin with a swimming pool.

It was in first class in Vincent's primary school that a man named Peter Molumby first introduced me properly to Gaelic football. The game wasn't new to me, but this was my first outlet, my first chance to play with other kids and develop basic skills.

The great Dubs team of the Seventies was of course in full swing by that stage. Ironically, Kildare was the first team I saw playing in Croke Park – a country father thing. Seán would always take me to the Canal End terrace, so I have these obscure, sepia-toned memories of a goalkeeper named Ollie Crinnigan and a corner-forward named Mark Shaw (the latter became a real-life person years later when I came across him in a pub in Celbridge). I only occasionally saw Hanahoe, Keaveney and Co in the flesh during that glorious decade, but it mattered little as their influence transformed the game in Dublin. We now had heroes.

Thankfully, my father's passion for his native county was eventually superseded by his interest in his son's career with the Dubs. A kind of blue-whitening, I suppose.

71

Though Dublin were on the wane somewhat by the time I was really clued in to what was going on, their heroics still provided the backdrop to a pretty content first couple of years at school for me. I prospered in the classroom and on the football field. I had also begun to hurl, thanks to an early introduction from a teacher named Jim McKeever. I developed an enduring love of hurling, a love that really came to the fore when I was a teenager. I revelled in the speed, touch and reflex and I really loved plucking the ball out of the air, a skill that became my forte. Being from a county where hurling was the poor relation, it was inevitable that football would eventually eclipse my involvement in the game.

One sport which remained outside of the parameters of my official childhood in the early years was soccer, which, typically, wasn't played in a CBS. Thankfully, this rule was reversed by the St Vincent's teacher, John Horan, by the time I reached secondary level. It would be an enduring embarrassment if the school which boasts Irish international captain Kenny Cunningham as one of its most famous sons had denied him the right to play soccer. Kenny was actually a year behind me in Vincent's, and League of Ireland legend Pat Fenlon was a couple of years ahead of me in primary school. The school was, and still is, surrounded by some of Dublin's most important soccer nurseries, such as Tolka Rovers, Home Farm and Bohemians. Anyway, the ban didn't extend beyond the school walls and, between Donegal and Dublin, I played plenty of soccer. I even donned the colours of Home Farm for a period at the behest of Cunningham who had become a close pal. But my involvement was short-lived, eventually being overtaken by Gaelic. Perhaps the fact that I was a Swansea City supporter at a time when most kids followed Liverpool didn't help my progress. My contrary choice of team was based on a bizarre nationalistic premise that any decent young Irishman should back a Welsh team – our Celtic cousins – slogging it out in the English First Division. John Toshack was their main man and I was their main fan. Kenny later joined me on the Gaelic field before our paths split after playing minor together with Dublin.

Two visits to Croke Park for school finals provided the high points of my primary days. We fought two epic battles with Scoil Mhuire of Marino, the aristocrats of the game in Dublin, winning on the first occasion. I marked Ger Regan, a Vincent's clubman whom I later played alongside for Dublin. Another outlet for Gaelic games then opened up for me as a kid when a teacher, Fiachra Leahy, brought me up to the Na Fianna club to join the under-10s. Leahy and another teacher, John Horan, managed the team and, though we weren't much use, it was a good club with good facilities. Anyway, underage club structures were nothing like they are today, with little emphasis on coaching and development. The school was really the critical place for young footballers and hurlers with the Cumann na mBunscol competitions providing a proper, competitive arena. I have huge admiration for this organisation and particularly the teachers involved. Thankfully, the Cumann in Dublin is still in the safe hands of the excellent Jerry Grogan and his team. This period culminated for me with a place on the north Dublin schools squad.

My obsession had begun. And there was more.

Chapter 8

Hockey

I've always noticed how football commentators and journalists rush to say that I was a decent hockey player. I think they're secretly relieved that not everyone in the GAA is a fundamentalist die-hard; that there are a few broad-minded players with a catholic taste in sport. Of course, none of this is relevant in any way to the circumstances that saw me take up a hockey stick.

I love hockey. Maybe it's my recreational sport away from the annual, anal pursuit of trying to get myself fit and mentally prepared for Dublin. When I stop kicking, I intend to play it until my body cries 'golf only, you half-wit'.

Hockey happened largely because of the influence of watching my father battle it out for St Loman's.

It also happened due to a sequence of rather odd events. St Brendan's Hospital's hockey folk were awful precious about their manicured turf pitch, but were constantly plagued by a gang of local kids from Stoneybatter kicking football on it and throwing bricks through their dressing-room windows. Two club members, Mick Kavanagh and Mick Ryan, decided, rather prudently, that they would start up an underage 'Colts' hockey team to try and entice the same local kids to actually take up the sport. The idea to protect the pitch was simple: if you can't beat them, get them to join you. Shortly after moving to Marne Villas, my father heard about the Colts team and decided to bring me along for a trial where I encountered the same gang. As I was a kind of sports loner, one of the lads, Paddy Lynch, decided to have a go at me, an 'easy target' for the hard nuts from Brunswick Street and Eoghan Ruadh GAA clubs, or so they thought. I don't know what got into me or where I got the courage – I was genuinely a quiet, well-behaved ten-year-old – but after a scrap ensued, Lynch

74

grabbed me by the hair so I lifted the hockey stick and delivered a stinging clatter to his ribs. Despite our tetchy beginning, the whole Colts experiment worked wonderfully, with hockey taking off in inner-city Dublin for the first time.

However, this was no easy task. These were inner-city kids, mostly from the Stoneybatter area, blunt-edged working-class lads to whom the idea of playing hockey was pretty incongruous. Yet, as if to highlight just how ridiculous prejudice is in sport, the same kids took to the game immediately and, as adults, would eventually run the hockey club. Lynch and the boys remain good pals of mine to this day.

I loved the game and developed quickly. Needless to say, backboned by tough inner-city kids, we were adept at intimidating Southside boys from such exotic places as Blackrock and Ballsbridge. We were quite successful at underage level, probably because we always had a hard edge – all for the tempting reward of a mineral and a packet of crisps in Frank Ryan's pub in Queen's Street afterwards.

Because of the constant struggle to keep the Brendan's set-up going, the club eventually merged with our Phoenix Park HC neighbours and recently with Portrane in an attempt to pool our meagre resources and remain competitive in senior hockey. However, in 2005, we re-established our Colts programme for the first time in over twenty years and, hopefully, in time this will come to fruition just as it did for us back then. It's pure pleasure to give something back to this great sport and I'm only too delighted that I can share it with my children, Frankie and Emma, as my father Seán did with me.

After a couple of years playing with Brendan's Colts, I was selected on the Leinster panel for the inter-provincial series. Though I was only twelve years old, if I could make a mark at the inter-pros, I would have a serious chance of making the Irish under-14 set-up, an ambition that began to consume me and my father who travelled everywhere with me. However, my father constantly tempered my enthusiasm, warning me that hockey's own class and school prejudices might militate against my progress. I was an 'outsider', from a Northside non-hockey playing school; I wasn't necessarily of the right 'stock'. This could, he warned, shape the views of team selectors. He was right. In my first competitive outing for Leinster against Munster, I stood out in midfield, scoring a goal in our 2-1 victory. In my second match, against Ulster, I was withdrawn, a move which the coach didn't explain to me. Having been removed from the shop window, I was subsequently left out of the group of players selected for an Irish trial the following day. I was distraught. We had been stationed in the Roche's Park Hotel in Dún Laoghaire for the tournament and I vividly remember being embarrassed and close to tears about my omission and not being able to face my room-mate. On hearing the bad news, my father wanted to accost the coach and 'nail' him for his decision. I suppose I don't have to dig too deeply to source my competitive edge.

The following year I made the Irish panel after spending a season like a whirling dervish on the hockey field. Once again, I was to meet what I perceived to be prejudice. I was utterly convinced of my ability, that I was as good as they had. The training ground assured me of this. Yet our coach, a Northerner named Lenny McMillan who also looked after the Ulster team, didn't start me and chose only to introduce me as a substitute. I swore that, from that day onwards, I would not allow the Leinster and Irish managers overlook me. I didn't. I enjoyed inter-provincial and international hockey until the demands of the Dublin set-up became overwhelming when I was appointed captain by Tommy Carr in 1997. Nonetheless, I cherish very fond memories of my youthful hockey career. Using the adversity of my background as a motivating force, I bucked the system and won. It would steel me for bigger tasks ahead, when I would have no excuses.

I never dwelt on the pretty unique fact that I was a hockey-playing GAA man, although I didn't exactly highlight my 'other life' in the football dressing room. Being a Gaelic footballer and hurler certainly helped my hockey, as fear, or being 'windy' as we refer to it colloquially, wasn't really a factor. Unfortunately for many of my peers it was, particularly as we approached adulthood with the Irish under-18 squad and the ball started to move with increased venom. Ciarán Bolger, a brother of former Dublin footballer, Declan, was a team-mate of mine with Ireland and the pair of us always volunteered to flank the keeper for short corners. This is where the opposition get to hammer the ball goalwards, usually face high. However, as 'Gaels', Ciarán and I never gave a shite, and always stood up to the plate.

Incongruous, maybe? But the hockey memories are fond and enduring; I am particularly proud to have been a member of the Irish team that defeated England in a Home Countries' international in Coventry in 1989 and to have played on the first inter-pro team from my province to defeat Ulster for a very long time. And I'll never ever forget the half-time period during that particular contest when a team-mate decided to give a pep talk. 'Lads,' he bellowed. 'Let's get out there and beat these Protestant fuckers!' Not everyone fell around laughing. Small wonder, I was the only other Catholic in the Leinster dressing room.

I still play hockey, though my interest at the top level was eventually curtailed by the Dubs. Prior to that, however, I gave it one last serious lash by switching from St Brendan's to Glenane, a more ambitious outfit fed by players from St Mark's school in Tallaght. The move came about primarily due to the influence of businessman Terry Cooney, who was involved with hockey in Mark's, a great Dubs fan and a former Na Fianna player. Unfortunately, I didn't win anything at Glenane. In fact the club had a great year the season after I left. But it didn't tarnish the game for me and now that I'm poised to bring down the curtain on my football career, hockey may fill a void for a few years to come.

Buried beneath the glamour of a long career with the Dublin footballers, my years of playing hockey with Brendan's still hold a special place in my heart. I've been lucky to have played with many great players who defied convention to reach the top level in their sport against all the odds. This was simply remarkable.

Chapter 9

Teenage Kicks – 1981–1989

March 1987

'What kind of Jayzusin' effort is that?' I bellow across the field on Mobhi Road. Myself, Colm Burtchaell and Eamon Rainsford are having a puck around. Peter Jordan's standing in goals. Burtchie's just lamped the sliotar *out over the trees and onto the roof of a car out on the road. By the time I rescue it, it's halfway down to the river Tolka. When I return to the gates of Na Fianna, the lads are all making their way out, dragging their hurleys. 'Where are yiz goin'?' I ask. 'We're meetin' those mots we met on holidays, you know, the ones from Lucan. We're meetin' them out at their place at three o'clock.' 'What the fuck are yiz doin' that for? We're havin' a puck around. C'mon back in.' 'Puck around yerself Farreller, we're headin' out to meet the mots.'*

My window of wonder as a child only opened one way: onto the playing fields. This narrow focus was no bad thing. My memories are laced with excitement. My adventures started on a Saturday morning when I was tying up my boots for a day's sport; the sense of anticipation is something I still experience today. I was innocent, unworldly, my daily appetites never stretched beyond kicking a ball against the gable end of a house, pucking a *sliotar* in the grounds of St Brendan's, practicing penalties on the hockey field. When the action was lifted onto the competitive stage, my excitement became unrestrained. My urge to compete was relentless from a very young age and I had learned how to fight my corner before I was a teenager.

In a golden age before high-tech computer games, DVDs and digital TV, I just practised and practised without distraction. My father and, particularly, my mother, were fairly strict disciplinarians, so I didn't really act the maggot and, bar the odd fight or stone-throwing incident, I steered clear of trouble. I didn't smoke and I didn't touch alcohol until I'd left school. Drugs were widespread around my area, but it never even occurred to me to touch them. It wasn't that I was a prudish little snot, I just couldn't understand why anyone would want to do anything besides play sport. It satisfied me in every way.

I did fight like a demon with my sister Aisling, my only sibling, who gave as good as she got. As we got older, though, we grew very close as we shared the same obsessive passion for sport. Aisling played football and camogie for Na Fianna and represented Dublin in the former. She was also an excellent hockey player and was the perfect foil for me, on hand every day for a kick-around up in St Brendan's. I loved to go and watch her play and give her advice. My sister was a worrier, a strong trait on my mother's side of the family, so I would try and put her mind at ease before big matches, remind her of the various drills we had practised. Our close bond has endured even now that she is happily married to Fergal in Garristown with her gorgeous children, Ciara and Eoin.

The support of our parents was constant and, just as my father was always by my side when I played hockey, so it was with football and hurling. With Seán I could always gauge my progress. He would quietly let me know when I didn't measure up and was equally quick to qualify any short-term success. Looking back, he seemed to possess an intuitive understanding of the vicissitudes of sport; treating victory and defeat in an even-handed way. I always feared losing, especially in school championships, not because it represented failure, but because it meant the end of a tournament. It was the finality of losing that killed me, something particularly relevant to Gaelic games, where the principal competitions tend to be organised on a knockout basis.

There were consolations though. Heading into the summer months meant Donegal and, moreover, participation in the most ludicrously competitive seven-a-side soccer matches with my uncles and the locals. School disappointments weren't long being consigned to memory. My relations were all involved with the local GAA club, Naomh Columba, but it was the impromptu Gaelic games in Mín an Éirigh that linger in my memory. I fondly recall one particular outing when we brazenly challenged St Catherine's, a 'proper' soccer team from Killybegs, to a game. The pastoral scene was redolent of Paddy Kavanagh, a throng of ruddy farmers and fishermen egging us on, their voices echoing off the church walls. As it was our first match against 'outsiders', we played as if our lives depended on victory. We'd little to worry about as we stuffed the St Catherine's boys 13-0, a result somehow strangely etched in my memory. Happy days.

With so much going on, I suppose I could have been forgiven for losing touch in the classroom, but I always managed to keep my head above water. My mother had a big influence on me in this regard, watching my progress like a hawk. I had also forged a pretty decent reputation in hurling and football in St Vincent's by the time I went into secondary school. The reputation came thanks to Brother O'Sullivan who insisted on parading our successful Cumann na mBunscol side around the school after we had defeated Scoil Mhuire of Marino in the final in Croke Park while I was in fifth class. I was never hassled in the schoolyard and most of my closest mates shared a keen interest in sport. Unlike my mates, however, my love affair with sport remained undiluted long after many of their own passions had turned to the opposite sex. Long into my teens I remained like a grumpy 10-year-old boy who truculently refused to play with girls. I had a lot to learn.

Secondary school provided the real platform for me to develop as a footballer and hurler thanks in no small way to the efforts of John Horan, Mick Ryan (my Latin teacher) and Mick Frawley. It was here, rather than in Na Fianna, that I made the first big step up. After winning a Dublin Colleges' football medal with Vincent's alongside Kenny Cunningham, we went on to reach the Leinster final where we were pipped by Clane, a school team back-boned by future Kildare stars, Martin Lynch and Jarlath Gilroy. The following season we were again beaten in the Leinster decider, this time by Patrician Newbridge, another Kildare academy who boasted such young talents as Niall Buckley and Anthony Rainbow.

The relative success continued right up to the under-18 grade where we won a Dublin 'B' title in Croke Park against Haddington Road and I was marked by Pádraig Harrington, a handy footballer from Ballyboden and a fair man with a nine iron. Harrington talks fondly of our encounter and of the drubbing he received, but I think he sometimes neglects to mention, rather magnanimously, that he got injured early in the game.

Just as my friendship with Kenny Cunningham meant a crossing of paths with professionalism, so being reminded of my joust with Pádraig now acts as a kind of brush with a life that might have been. Of course I entertained no such thoughts then. The 'idea' of becoming a professional sportsman doesn't really enter the mind of a youngster during his developmental stage, at least it didn't when I was growing up. I suppose children today are bombarded by the private lives of the sports stars they worship in the media, which has probably stolen some of their innocence. We just wanted to be good, to play, and to compete. Unfortunately, I can only yearn for some sort of missed opportunity. I don't regret where sport took me and landing an All-Ireland medal in 1995 was an extraordinary feeling. But to say I've no regrets now would be bullshit. I would have loved to have earned a living for doing what I did best, where I could have applied myself completely without a nagging sense of something unfulfilled. Harrington exemplifies a life I would have aspired to. Now, watching this great sportsman in action only accentuates my regret, particularly so when I think of some of the treatment dished out to GAA players over the years.

If the sporting tapestry of my youth wasn't already a complicated pattern, there were two other strands running through my early years – hurling and soccer. I didn't achieve a great deal with the former, but probably enjoyed it more than any other sport. I played centre-back and midfield for the school team and was elevated to the senior ranks in the club when I was still a young teenager. There were notable highs, particular my bizarre excursion to Galway to play with the St Brendan's senior hurling team when I was only fifteen years old. I was on the street one afternoon after school, messing with a hockey stick, when a man named Willie Shanley, a great hurler from Westmeath, pulled up outside the house in his car and asked me were my parents in. He entered the house and moments later emerged and asked me would I like to play a hurling match with the hospital against Ballinasloe Psychiatric. In an instant I had my gear and was on the bus. St Brendan's boasted such hurling luminaries as Wexford's Martin Storey, so I was in awe. And I remained in that state when I realised that Tony and Ollie Kilkenny would line out for the opposition. I played the full match at corner-back and we won. The boys went on a fierce bender on the journey home and, although I didn't touch a drop, I didn't return home until half four in the morning. With school later that morning, my mother was not pleased.

In secondary school, I also played soccer under the ubiquitous John Horan. I won a Leinster schools soccer title with St Vincent's. We fought one memorable battle with St Mark's of Tallaght in a Leinster decider when I was in sixth year. We trailed by a goal entering the closing stages when I managed to squeeze in an equaliser, shipping a dead leg in the process from the Mark's keeper, Wayne Daly, another man who would join me on the Dublin panel some years later. We won in extra time only to lose the All-Ireland semi-final to Salthill on penalties. As we also lost a Leinster Gaelic football final to Newbridge shortly after our soccer setback, my school sports days are, just like my adult career, tinged with some regret but full of happy memories.

Looking back, it was school competitions and hockey that consumed my heart. My GAA club, Na Fianna, had been less important initially, but as I advanced in years, it became central to my development, providing the platform on which to get noticed as a Gaelic footballer or hurler by county gurus and the like. We didn't have very strong underage sides, but at under-16 level we started to compete and were unlucky not to win anything. In 1987, when I was fifteen years old, Horan asked me out to play for the club's minor footballers. In return, he promised he would organise a trial with the Dublin minors for me. You may wonder why I needed coaxing. However, I was so dedicated to the various school teams – teams that I felt were competing properly – that the club took second place. In fact, I never won anything with Na Fianna until I pocketed a Dublin senior football championship medal in 1999. Still, county ambitions could only be served through the club and luckily I was advanced enough as a younger player to stand out for Na Fianna.

And, true to his word, John arranged a place in a trial game for Alan Larkin's 1987 Dublin minor team. Larkin had been a member of the Dubs team of the Seventies, a sort of *Braveheart* figure, famed for his uncompromising play and his fearsome, hairy appearance. It was a daunting task – an early chance for me to scale a serious rung on the ladder, or to make a bad first impression. I can't say I was nervous, but I expected little. To my surprise, the trial went remarkably well and I managed to back up the performance that day with a couple of other handy displays in subsequent trials. However, I played poorly in the final trial and didn't expect to be included in the panel. I was wrong. A couple of days later my name appeared in the panel printed in the *Evening Press*. I had done enough. At fifteen, I was handed my first Dublin jersey.

If my success in making the 1987 panel sounded glamorous, cycling the ten-mile round trip to St Anne's Park in Raheny for training after school a couple of times a week soon took the gloss off the experience, particularly as I didn't get a look in when it came to the championship. I wanted to play: I wasn't at all happy to be a bystander, particularly as I felt I was good enough. I never factored in my age, the fact that I was much younger than most of the panel. Eventually I stopped attending the sessions, as I really felt surplus to requirements on a team that contained the notable young talents of Paul Curran and Vinny Murphy. It wasn't precociousness that influenced my decision, I simply had no interest in sitting on the bench. I didn't want to make up the numbers. Following my departure, however, Dublin reached the Leinster final and, prior to that game, I was asked to line out in a challenge match for Na Fianna's seniors. It was only when I reached the club that I realised the opposition was the Dublin minor team. Motivated by what I perceived to be some sort of injustice, I lined out at full-forward and scored 1-2 against the first-choice full-back. It didn't change the management's decision about my inclusion, but it laid down a handy marker for the future.

I made the minor panel again the following season in 1988. This time the set-up was managed by fellow clubman, the late Dinny Gray, and Mick Moylan, whose son Senan was a prominent player on the team. Brian Stynes Snr, also one of the management team, had the pleasure of watching his son Brian follow in the footsteps of big Jim Stynes, a Dublin minor star of 1984 who went on to become a successful Aussie Rules player. Significantly in 1988, the team was trained by Niall Fitzgerald who was probably the first real modern trainer I worked under.

Having made the starting fifteen, my first championship clash for Dublin came against Laois in O'Moore Park, Portlaoise, and it proved to be a real eye-opener. Captained by the dynamic Ger Regan from St Vincent's, we won the game with a convincing display. But it came at a price, as I was beaten black and blue. It was pretty evident after that Laois clash that my concept of 'looking after myself' would have to be reassessed. It was one thing to mix it in a schools match, a different matter completely when the stakes were raised on the county stage. It didn't faze me; it was rare for me to feel physically threatened by an opponent. I accepted that getting belts came with the turf and just got on with it.

We hammered Wicklow in the semi-final in the following game, securing a glamorous Leinster final place against Meath in Croke Park. As the senior team would also face the Royals on the same day, it meant a full house. This was my first big date in a blue jersey with all the trappings – a full Hill 16, Meath, and the eyes of a nation, or a province at least, upon us. And it couldn't have gone any better.

We won comfortably and I scored two cracking goals into Hill 16, one of which – a rasper into the top right-hand corner of the net – was mentioned on *The Sunday Game* that night. Everything fell right for me. You see, goal-scoring was my thing at the time – I stuck to the principle of aiming for the crossbar and hitting the ball as hard as I could, an approach particularly suited to minor level as the keepers were generally small. The 'aiming for the crossbar' technique quickly became redundant as players matured. I just wish I hadn't reverted to my youth when faced with an open goal years later.

Doubts and nerves seemed to be exacerbated with age; I recall going into the Meath match unburdened by either. I remember wondering during the game if any of the senior stars were watching me. I wanted to impress. I know I sound like a cocky little bollix, but I wasn't. I was just doing what I always did. I wanted to impress, to win. What I would subsequently learn was that innocent ambition, a drive to make an impression, to score, to win, was not enough to achieve anything at senior level. Harsh lessons lay ahead.

But they were for another day. After our shower, myself and our keeper, Derek O'Farrell, a good mate of mine from school and subsequently Na Fianna, headed up to the Hogan Stand to watch the Dublin seniors, chuffed with ourselves. Unfortunately for the minors, the seniors lost when Charlie Redmond fired a last-minute penalty over the bar, denying us kids the support of the legions of Dublin fans for our semi-final. Before we faced Galway though, we had to play New York in an All-Ireland quarter-final. Over the years, such fixtures have been added to various competitions to keep the ties strong with the GAA diaspora in the States. Years later I would come to know this community well, travelling to play football in New York on several occasions.

Our minor quarter-final was a bit of a one-sided affair, and I managed to bag four goals, but things didn't go as well for me the next day out against Galway. Nonetheless, we won, which meant that I would line out in an All-Ireland minor football final, with a championship tally of 8-8 under my belt.

Talk started in the papers about possible records being set if I could bolster my tally on the fourth Sunday in September. I didn't. As often happens with 'good' stories in sport, my high-scoring feat came a cropper when I only managed a point in the final which we lost to a better Kerry team. We probably overdid the tactic of lamping high balls into our big full-forward, Senan Moylan, and paid the price. So, 25 September 1988 marked the first day of many that ended with me leaving Croke Park in a pretty dark mood.

Still, regardless of how cruel it may seem to come so close to the prize, it's always better to fall at the last than crash at the first. The 1989 season taught me that. My minor career with the Dubs extended to a third season, but it ended abruptly last time out when we exited to Kildare in the first round.

I had stayed back to repeat fifth year in school on Horan's advice, primarily because of sport and the fact that I was young enough to do it. It worked out really well because my best friend Stephen Francis and school goalkeeper stayed back also, which meant we were now in the same class as our other pal, Kenny Cunningham. Kenny also made the Dublin minor team in 1989, lining out at corner-forward against Kildare. An extended run would have been a nice addition to his notable career as a professional soccer player and Irish captain. Kenny was a good Gaelic footballer and extremely intelligent on and off the pitch. He always seemed to know the right thing to do, a great trait in a player. Jim Gavin, who was to become a staunch ally in the senior squad, was also part of that minor set-up.

Anyway, in the wake of that narrow defeat, my father, being a Kildare man, got a lot of stick from his fellow county men in the stand that evening in Newbridge. It tested his love affair with his native county. From that day on, his allegiance was to his son and his adopted county.

My parents were now Dubs.

Chapter 10

Fortune's Sharp Adversity – 1990–1992

I left school in June 1989 with a decent leaving but with no particular ambition outside of football. College seemed like the ideal environment, a place to arse around when I wasn't playing or training, which wasn't very often. So I accepted the offer of a place in Kevin Street Technical College and decided I was going to become an electronic engineer. Having never really researched what the course was about, I eventually realised that it wasn't for me, so I switched to medical laboratory science. During my short spell in Kevin Street, I squeezed in an All-Ireland Freshers' 'B' football title when we defeated UCD in Croke Park. Ciarán O'Hare, who became a good friend of mine and later a Dublin colleague, played on the same team. Outside of sport, I hated college life. For some reason the *laissez faire* attitude of a third-level college didn't sit easy with me and I set my sights on doing something different.

Some years earlier my father had developed chronic back problems and was forced to go on long-term sick leave from St Brendan's, which halved his salary and put some pressure on our family life as Aisling was still at school. So I quit Kevin Street after first year and enrolled in St Brendan's to become a psychiatric nurse, following in my father's footsteps. Looking back, I suppose I was justifying my decision to leave college in some way, as we probably would have managed regardless. But I was moving to more familiar territory. Being accustomed to the hospital environment helped me settle in immediately as did the fact that student nurses were paid during their training.

It was in Brendan's that I began to socialise properly for the first time. Like many of the service professions, there was a culture of hard drinking, something that was accepted as it provided an easy escape from the grim reality of the day job. As soon as I joined the club, the barriers that had

86

sustained my naivety as an underage sportsman quickly crumbled. Not that I let drinking impinge on football – I was still way too serious to allow such an intrusion. Suffice to say, I was up and running as a proper 'youngfella'. At last I started to develop relationships with girls and, after spending a period dating a girl from Na Fianna, I eventually crossed paths with Noreen Mulry from Roscommon, a nurse in Brendan's, who would later become my wife.

Against this backdrop came my elevation to the Dublin senior football team. Shortly after starting in Kevin Street, Na Fianna notified me that I had been invited by Dublin manager, Gerry McCaul, to join the squad for training in Parnell Park. I was kind of expecting the call given the three years I had under my belt as a minor, but the national league was already underway when word came through. I can't say I was completely fazed by the prospect. After all, my mate Derek O'Farrell was already the Dublin reserve goalie, so I wouldn't be heading to training alone. I also had a youthful belief that if I could get my hands on the ball, I would score goals. Simple philosophy. How I yearned for that same belief years later when doubt and uncertainty started to perforate my thoughts. I don't really know why confidence diminishes with age. I suppose doubts develop due to setbacks, due to weaknesses, due to the increasing complexities of adult life. Later, of course, experience compensates, but players still hit their peak in their mid twenties when the combination of experience and confidence is most finely balanced. For me, as a young player, belief in my ability was a carefree thing. It was also a vital component if a young player was going to make the step up to senior level.

On a shitty, wet Tuesday night in November 1989, I entered the dressing room in Parnell Park and sat down on the bench alongside the heroes of the Eighties – Barney Rock, Kieran Duff and Joe McNally. It was daunting. Yet, in addition to the respect for the men around me and the apprehension I felt, my own desire burned intensely. Later in my career, I realised just how conspicuous a newcomer could be in the dressing room surrounded by the cliques. You stuck out. Little was said to new kids; they were made feel pretty anonymous. Thankfully, both Rock and Duff broke the ice with me and welcomed me to the fold, which was more than a lot of the others in the room did. I just kept my head down and got on with it.

McCaul was a serious man and he was undoubtedly determined to make up for a disappointing All-Ireland semi-final exit to Cork earlier that summer when events had overtaken his talented side in Croke Park and they had let a seven-point lead slip. He met me outside briefly before training and welcomed me along. No *plámás*, no bullshit. Little did I know then that our relationship together as player and manager would be severed before it even had a chance to develop. He impressed me greatly during the short spell I spent under his leadership and, while it would be hard for me to accurately assess his ability, given I was a starry-eyed teenager, the older lads on the panel like Mick Galvin and Keith Barr swore by him. McCaul's knowledge of football was excellent and he was highly respected by the panel. He was a man of few words, but he communicated his ambition well on the training ground. His sessions were horrifically cruel. Physically, Dublin were a match for anyone in the late 1980s. Unfortunately for Gerry, Meath were the top side in the country, perhaps the greatest Meath team of all time. And they were peaking. Playing the Royals and, on occasions, beating them, was a big achievement for Dublin. McCaul also brought on a lot of good young footballers like Barr, Galvin, Eamon Heery, Vinny Murphy and Paul Curran – the basis of Dublin's domination of Leinster some years later.

The Sunday after my first training session with McCaul's panel, I travelled with Dublin to play Armagh in the Athletic Grounds. Four minutes from the final whistle I was sent in as a substitute for my senior county debut. I ran on to the field, brimming with confidence, convinced that I could get a goal and level the game. 'Just give me the fucking ball,' I kept repeating to myself. However, there was little ball and no dream start. We lost the game by four points. Ironically, Kieran McGeeney, a talented 18-year-old defender from Mullaghbawn in South Armagh, lined out that day. A decade later, our paths would cross in a Dublin nightclub and we'd end up spending the latter years of our careers as club-mates in Na Fianna.

I may have been a confident teenager, but I didn't kick a ball in a competitive match with Dublin for the rest of the league. Not a look-in. Seated on the bench, I feared that I wasn't part of McCaul's grand plans for the summer. It was hard to fathom why I would play four minutes of a league match and then not appear for the rest of the competition. I don't think the manager planned to keep me out of the limelight, but I craved the chances that players like Alan 'Nipper' McNally, Leo Close and David Delappe were being given during the league. He had to give me an opportunity sometime.

Dublin began the run-in to the championship with a series of challenge games and, early in May 1990, I was handed a corner-forward berth in a friendly against Monaghan in Scotstown. This was my chance; I was determined to take it, to prove myself to McCaul. And I did. I stood out from the off and ended up scoring 1-4. It's funny, but recalling such a rewarding experience sounds brash when isolated from the endless preparation and ambition that enabled it to happen. I never stopped practising, training and imagining. Succeeding in making my first big mark, impressing the Dublin manager and my team-mates – this was what I lived for. 'Just give me the fucking ball.' If I had been racked with doubt, if I hadn't believed from the start that I could play for Dublin, I couldn't imagine that I would have ever made the initial step-up. Leaving Monaghan that summer's evening, I had few, if any, doubts about my ability. I didn't expect to have to confront those particular demons for a long, long time. I was convinced I would play for Dublin in the championship that summer, I would score for Dublin in the championship that summer, and Hill 16 would get to know me that summer. 'Just give me the fucking ball.'

Four days later I was told I would never play football again.

The Wednesday after my heroics in Scotstown, Na Fianna played St Anne's in a Dublin senior football league match in Mobhi Road. I was operating at wing-forward and, early in the second half, I was going around my marker, Gerry Heaslip, when he threw out his arm and swung around my neck. My left leg planted in the ground as my body turned and my knee just snapped. I collapsed in agony. I had completely torn the posterior cruciate ligament in my left knee, which is different than the more common anterior cruciate injury (which, later in my career, I would tear as well). Essentially, when the posterior goes, it goes for life. There is still no operation for this injury. Just for good measure, I also suffered a grade three tear in the medial ligament. I was taken to the Mater Hospital and scoped the following morning. The doctor on duty then called by to see me to discuss the prognosis. To this day, this is how I remember his insensitive message. 'You're the footballer, aren't you?' he asked, peering at me from the side of the bed. 'I am,' I replied sheepishly. 'I'm afraid the injuries to your knee are really bad. There'll be no more football for you. In fact, you'll probably have difficulty walking up the stairs.' Maybe he was preparing me for the worst, but he ended up terrifying me. Thanks be to Jayzus I had a dogged, resilient streak in me. If I hadn't, my tangle with the blue jersey would have ended up a mere flirtation.

I hobbled out of the Mater on crutches the following day and was strapped in a cast for three months. This was 1990, when they strapped you in plaster from toe to hip, just to ensure that every muscle wasted away. I had no idea whether I would ever be able to raise a gallop again. It was depressing stuff. Later the same evening, after leaving hospital, my father brought me up to Parnell Park where the Dublin team was training. I just wanted to show my face. I met McCaul outside who sympathised warmly with me. 'You'll have a long career with Dublin, Dessie,' he concluded. It meant a lot. A couple of players nodded, their eyes quickly turning away as if their glance would reveal what everyone was thinking. As we drove out through Donnycarney, I swore to myself I would not let up until I was back.

I started my rehabilitation immediately. Literally. As soon as I was back in the house I started doing sit-ups and press-ups. I was still in Kevin Street at the time, so I finished up my exams before heading off on a family holiday in the sun, where I managed to lose a load of weight due to the amount of exercises I was getting through each day. As my mother was working in St Pat's in Drumcondra, I had access to the gym in the college and, as soon as the cast came off, I started to build up my leg with weights. I had suffered serious muscle wastage during the three months. Nowadays, of course, athletes who suffer knee-ligament damage undergo a rehabilitation process before they are even operated upon so as to avoid muscle wastage.

Injury not only cost me any chance of an early championship call-up for Dublin during the summer of 1990, it also erased me from the picture the following year when, under new manager Paddy Cullen, the Dubs played out the incredible four-game series against Meath. I watched that particular drama unfold from the Hogan Stand, wondering if I could have made an impact; if I would have survived in such a cauldron. In fact, during my exile to the stand, my desire to become part of this theatre – to play for Dublin in front of 65,000 people – actually intensified. As I left Croke Park on the final day of the Dublin-Meath saga, I vowed that the next time the Dubs took to the big stage again, I would play my part.

Needless to say I went back to play with Na Fianna before my rehabilitation was complete at the end of 1990. I did myself no favours. I struggled terribly because I had lost mobility. What I didn't lose was determination, and the words of the doctor that night in the Mater Hospital drove me through a difficult year in 1991. Hurling also helped and my elevation to full-back on the Na Fianna senior hurling team made an impression on the county's under-21 selectors. The manager, Tom Quinn, father of current Dublin footballer Tomás Quinn, brought me into the side in 1991 and I captained the team until Kilkenny beat us in the Leinster semi-final, a game in which myself and Adrian Ronan ended up getting sent off.

Although I was still visibly struggling with my knee in early 1991, I had been selected for the Dublin under-21 football team under another former Seventies' star, Bobby Doyle. My involvement with both under-21 teams helped enormously to restore my confidence. The fact that I could still make something of an impact while operating at a percentage of my ability gave me great heart. However, I wasn't quite there yet. My graph may have been rising slowly throughout the year, but my stock fell after a trial match for the seniors against Louth early in the autumn. Though I scored 1-1 in the first half, a second-half blunder saw me taken off. Worse still, I heard nothing from the selectors afterwards. I would have to wait.

Thankfully, my exile didn't last much longer. Over Christmas, word was sent by the Dublin selectors to Na Fianna that I was to attend training again in the New Year. The nagging pessimism that had plagued me since the injury was now lifting. 'You'll never play football again.' Back on the Dublin panel, I knew my chance had arrived to shove those haunting words back down that doctor's throat.

I liked Paddy Cullen immediately. He was a warm, engaging character with real Dublin charm. He took me under his wing the moment I arrived at Parnell Park. In fact, I remember our first quiet chat, when he made sure I knew what my elevation to the Dublin senior team really meant. 'Dessie,' he said, 'I've heard all about you. I've been told Dessie Farrell did this and Dessie Farrell did that. Son, this is the real thing. This is your opportunity.'

Paddy was very different from Gerry McCaul. He was a colourful man, full of chat and rapport. Paddy's strength was his man-management skill. He was a great man to settle a team in the dressing room. He was also flanked by a very talented management team in Pat O'Neill, Jim Brogan and Fran Ryder. O'Neill was really the motivator on the team. Brogan organised everything, including tactics, while Fran Ryder was an excellent physical trainer. We also had great characters like the 'Trapper' Dalton whose loyalty and commitment to the Dublin team was extraordinary. Every player will have a different perception of a manager or a management team, but it's hard to argue with the balance of the set-up back then. It couldn't have been any better in my opinion. But a traumatic All-Ireland defeat and one flippant remark exposed fissures that weren't apparent to me at the time. Just as was the case with Gerry McCaul back in 1990 when I first joined the Dublin senior panel, my time with Paddy Cullen would be short.

Having been presented with my 'opportunity' by Paddy and his selectors, I now of course had to go and seize it. My first outing under the new set-up was in a challenge game against Clare in Ennis early in the New Year where, after coming on as a sub, I managed to score a goal. This ensured my name was in the hat for a national league fixture against Mayo in Castlebar shortly afterwards. The Tuesday night before the Mayo game, Paddy Cullen named me at corner-forward in the starting line-up. My full competitive debut for the Dubs. And, true to my philosophy at the time, I scored a goal against Mayo. Obviously I have fond memories of that day in Castlebar, but what sticks out most in my mind was Paddy's hilariously colourful speech before the game when he spoke of men on tractors and the importance of keeping them in their place. 'Lads,' he implored. 'We're Dubs, we need to take our guns from our holsters and blow these culchies away!'

The next league game against Tyrone presented a problem for me. I was again selected to start, but it clashed with a holiday abroad that I had booked months in advance with my friends. Typical of the man, Cullen took me aside for a 'word'. He explained the importance of the game, not as a fixture, but for the development of the Dublin team and for the development of Dessie Farrell. He also offered to fly me out on the Monday to catch up with my friends. I stayed, played against Tyrone in Croke Park, scored my goal and flew out for my holiday the following day.

The relief and joy of making the breakthrough onto the Dublin seniors marked an end to a pretty harrowing period in my young life. Serious injury leaves a footballer in a very lonely place, particularly back in those days when you had to rehabilitate yourself without help or any proper supervision. The lack of a professional approach left many footballers and hurlers on the scrap heap; they were consigned to history because of the lack of support and willingness to carry them through their recovery. How many good players were lost to the game because we were so far behind the times? Things have changed somewhat, but nowhere near enough. Only certain counties are willing to follow-up on treatment for serious injury and to assist players in their rehabilitation. Others seem far too concerned about the cost of such help and, with a conveyor belt of youngsters coming through, are prepared to ignore the individual's well-being. I wonder are we, in the GAA, the worst offenders in this regard or is it the case in all sports?

With two years of torment behind me, I was now ready to take my place on the big stage. The championship.

Chapter 11

Little Boy Blue – Championship 1992

Crash Landing – Leinster Championship Debut

As soon as I joined Paddy Cullen's senior squad, I held a naive belief that my step up to senior football with the Dubs would be automatic. Drafted in from Bobby Doyle's under-21 side, given a couple of runs in the national league and a few platitudes from the manager, I assumed I would line out in the championship. Reflecting on my confidence now, I realise how deluded I was. Without the benefit of experience, it never dawned on me that I could have been one of the many young players to have kicked football with Dublin during the league down the years and never seen a minute's action during the senior championship. Now, I know I was lucky. I got my chance immediately.

Young players don't ever really take stock of their situation. Most cling to the foolhardy assumption that their graph will continue to rise. Perhaps this is why so many young talents, when faced with rejection and adversity, drift from, rather than rise to, the bigger challenge. Some rectify that later in their careers by making the cut with their county again but, quite often, they're damaged goods. The fact that my own long-held ambition to play for Dublin was now tenuously linked to a serious injury went over my head. Blind trust in my ability probably stood to me.

The first round of the 1992 Leinster campaign was a meeting with Offaly in Tullamore on 31 May. Fellow under-21 player Pádraig Doherty and I were named in the starting fifteen while another underage team-mate and good friend, Pat Gilroy from St Vincent's, also made the senior squad and was pencilled into a midfield pairing with Paul Clarke. Hardened by the traumatic experience of the 1991 four-game saga against Meath, Dublin were fancied to see out most of the summer, especially because the Royals had already been ambushed by Laois. Preparations had gone well for me considering my previous travails and I was pretty sure I could hold my own. As a rookie, I didn't really understand the different cliques on the senior team yet. Sure, there was a noticeable division of territory in the dressing room, a sort of Northside–Southside split, though there were exceptions to the divisions. I suppose it was a pretty intimidating place and young lads were certainly not fussed over. There were a lot of high-profile players like Keith Barr, Eamon Heery, Charlie Redmond, Paul Curran and Gerry Hargan – strong characters both on and off the field.

But there was no shortage of high jinks either, with Curran and Barr being the architects-in-chief. If there was a bit of new gear going, or a chance of a kit-bag, you had to swoop pretty quickly to get your quota. I often sat down to tog out for training only to realise that the toes were cut out of my socks or the arse out of my shorts. Women's knickers would also occasionally end up sitting proudly on the top of your Dublin gear.

I just kept my head down and didn't open my mouth. My playing colleagues of a more recent vintage might find that hard to fathom given that most of them have had to endure my opinions *ad nauseum*. I knew my place.

Before long, I would incline towards the Northside crew that socialised in Hanlon's pub – Mick Galvin, Mick Deegan, Charlie Redmond, Keith Barr *et al* – but not, mind you, before I had established some sort of credentials on the playing field.

The dictum of my earliest days with the Dubs hadn't changed – give me the ball and I'll do something with it. Yet, to follow that maxim, I had to contend with a talented bunch of footballers that, almost to a man, liked to run with the ball. In Vinny Murphy we had one of the country's hottest talents, an unrivalled ball-winner who nearly always went it alone. Certainly, if I was to make a name for myself in my first senior championship, I was going to have to do it on a pretty meagre diet of possession.

I don't recall any particular fuss leading up to the game, despite the fact that it was going to be my senior championship debut. There was nothing like today's media focus back in 1992. Now, it is customary for every new Dublin player to be thrust into the spotlight, analysed and rated, before he's even kicked a ball in anger at the top level.

However, if the run-up to the game was low-key, an incident on match day would more than make up for it. I remember my father dropped me down to the county board offices, then in Belvedere Place, near Mountjoy Square in Dublin's north inner-city. I hadn't been too nervous; I had managed to sleep and have breakfast, but it was a dank morning, something that left me on edge. I hooked up with fellow rookies Derek O'Farrell and Pádraig Doherty on the bus, which took off from Mountjoy Square and headed down Gardiner Street. As we pulled away from the lights, a car sped through the junction and ploughed broadside into the Dublin bus with an almighty clatter. If the prospect of my championship debut hadn't fazed me earlier in the morning, I was pretty uptight now. My first reaction to the shock was; 'Will we make it to the game? Will we have to concede the match? Holy Jayzus, will my first big day in blue end in Gardiner Street?'

There was pandemonium. Hard to believe, but in a pre-mobile phone world, management and officials had to scurry off to telephone boxes to summon another bus while the players sneered and scoffed, primarily to conceal any edginess. Meanwhile, seventy miles west, the Dublin hordes were gathering in the pubs around O'Connor Park and word wasn't long filtering to Tullamore that the Dublin bus had been involved in a crash. Afterwards, I learned from my friends and club-mates that, with every mile between the capital and Kilbeggan, exaggerated stories of injury and even death permeated Dublin fans, making our eventual safe arrival in Tullamore all the more satisfying.

What was probably most pleasing of all, however, was the start we enjoyed against Offaly. The game had been delayed by ten minutes, but our truncated preparation didn't give me time to dwell on the match and, after a brisk change in the dressing room, a quick briefing from Paddy Cullen and a rousing spur from Pat O'Neill, we took to the field. I lined out top of the right in a full-forward line with Vinny and Pádraig. Charlie, Jack Sheedy and Niall Guiden manned the line outside us. The ball was thrown in, Paul Clarke caught it, lamped it forward and Doherty connected on the rain-soaked surface and stuck it in the net. Less than twenty seconds into my senior championship debut with the Dubs and we were a goal up. Despite losing Keith Barr to a hip injury after only ten minutes and the referee getting an awful belt in the head in an accidental collision, we didn't suffer unduly. Another goal from Redmond killed off the tie and we ran out comfortable winners 2-17 to 1-9. Despite the propensity of a lot of our players not to pass the ball to the inside forwards, I managed to get some decent possession and scored two points to mark my championship debut. Offaly never really troubled us and the players who had suffered the heartbreak of losing a historic joust with the Royals twelve months earlier took the first step on the road to redemption. Or, so they thought. Unattached to the established dressing-room parties, I didn't participate much in the banter afterwards, but I do recall fondly the words of encouragement from Mick Galvin who, peering through the steam in the showers, told me I'd done well. Words can be very hollow in football – you know yourself how you did. But when they're sincere, that's as good as it gets in the game. It's really when you leave the dressing room that the bullshit starts.

Following his hip injury, Keith Barr, by then a pivotal figure on the team, had been whisked off to Tullamore Hospital immediately for an X-ray. However, despite the best intentions of the hospital staff, Keith refused to wait for results because he wanted to rejoin his team-mates on the bus journey home. As time went on, I could understand Keith's desire to hook up with the lads so quickly. The social life that surrounded the Dublin team in the 1990s was something else for a young man. Sunday's championship outings were usually followed by a golf outing to Royal Tara on the Monday and a feed of drink in Hanlon's pub (for the Northsiders) that night. On the Tuesday, Fran Ryder would run us into the ground to atone for our lapses, but unbeknownst to the management, a sizeable portion of the squad would then descend on Bad Bob's, a sort of American-themed nightclub in Temple Bar. Tuesday nights were best of all.

Socialising wasn't as frowned upon as much back then and there were fewer spies to talk about a night's *craic* the day after. Despite my reticence for any proper stepping out, I wasn't long finding my feet with this gang. Remember, before the weekly inter-county league campaign and the back-door system in the championship, our schedule was nowhere near as hectic. There was recovery time if you had the mind to pull the reins in, which most of us did. Anyway, you'd be found out soon enough if you pushed it too far.

With my championship debut out of the way, it was nearly a month to our next engagement, a clash with Wexford in a swelteringly hot Portlaoise on 28 June. Though we struggled for long spells in this game, a Vinny Murphy goal and a strong finish saw us home easy by 1-18 to 0-11. I started once again, grabbed another brace of points and should have been pretty happy with my progress. However, something happened that day that marked a nagging low point in my early career and, in truth, has left me sour ever since.

During that summer, as well as being a rookie in the senior football ranks, I was still a member of the Dublin under-21 hurling team that I had captained the previous year under Tom Quinn. After our defeat to Kilkenny in 1991, the management team had requested that they keep the squad together for training and challenges because so many of them were still eligible for 1992. However, the county board response was to question whether they would be appointed or not the following season. On principle, they refused the job in 1992, which left the under-21s without a manager. Self-proclaimed hurling enthusiast and county board chairman John Bailey took charge of the squad and, despite the *ad hoc* nature of the arrangements, we managed to defeat Wexford with fourteen men in the Leinster championship quarter-final. I lined out in midfield for that game and scored the equaliser before Mark Molloy from the Commercials club grabbed an injury-time winner. In the face of adversity, we had landed ourselves in a Leinster hurling semi-final against a highly-fancied Offaly team spearheaded by Brian Whelahan and Johnny Dooley. Buoyed by our victory over Wexford, the Dublin under-21s bonded. There was a lot of good young talent in the squad, players like Ger Regan, Conor McCann, Liam Walsh and Seán Power. We genuinely felt we could give this game a real rattle, reach the final and maybe actually win the title. I remember being truly excited at the prospect.

There was one big snag, however – the final was fixed as the curtain-raiser to the Dublin vs Wexford senior football game in Portlaoise on 28 June. Having personally played such a significant part against Wexford in the hurling semi-final, I was pretty sure that Bailey would have the game rescheduled so that I could line out for the hurlers. Right up to the week of the game I waited for confirmation of the change. It was only at training the week before the game that John Bailey informed us that they would go ahead with the scheduled fixture. I realised that I would have to miss out. Would Tipperary, Cork or Kilkenny have settled for such a scenario? This has always stuck in my craw and I have never been able to stomach the lip service that's paid to hurling in Dublin ever since. I'm sure the pre-eminence of football took the blame, but Paddy Cullen had allowed me to line out in the previous round. Despite the presence of a true Dublin legend, Lar Foley – who had agreed to help us out for the day – the Dubs lost the semi-final to Offaly 0-14 to 0-12. The fact that many of that Offaly team, players of the calibre of Brian Whelahan, Johnny Dooley and John Troy, went on to leave their mark on the top stage, made the experience all the more harrowing. It also marked John Bailey's card in my book. I don't know whether it was in his domain to get the match rescheduled at the time, but I've seen games switched for lesser reasons. For over a decade, Bailey has made a series of proclamations about how Dublin would make the hurling breakthrough at senior level, yet a Walsh Cup is all the county has to show for his trouble. Thankfully, there has been good progress made recently at underage level, but harnessing underage talent requires careful appoint-ments and the establishment of a content camp. Despite years of blueprints, think-tanks and a succession of managers and gurus, we have actually regressed at senior level. The row in the summer of 2005 between the county board and the senior hurling panel marked a new low. With every repeated pledge by Bailey that hurling in Dublin will eventually reach the top table, my thoughts turn to that June date in 1992 and what might have been.

Thankfully, at the time I had the welcome distraction of an imminent date in Croke Park against Louth in the Leinster SFC semi-final on 12 July – my first championship outing in Croker with the seniors.

The week before a championship match we rarely did much in the way of physical training; something that never sat easily with me. Similarly, at home, nothing would ever seem right for me in the lead up to a game. I was what was known colloquially as a 'piss mire' on such weeks, moping around like an antichrist. In time I would refer to it as my 'PMT', my pre-match tension! Contrary to accepted wisdom, I always felt I should be doing something, practising at least. I found going out for a kick around in the ball alley in St Brendan's, or with my sister Aisling, would settle my head a bit. Probably not the most scientific of approaches, but it's something I would continue to do pretty much throughout my career. Discipline the week of a game, though, wasn't an issue with me. I never countenanced drinking before a big game and, thankfully, I never had any difficulty sleeping or eating. The morning of a game, I would always head out for a short cycle to loosen up.

As Croke Park was still Dublin's home-league venue in 1992 there were never any special travel arrangements, not even for the championship. Dublin players made their own way to Jones' Road. So when the big day arrived, I hopped into my father's old Ford Fiesta for a spin down the North Circular. En route, Seán actually stopped in Delaney's Pub in the Smithfield Markets so he could drop in tickets – and finish off a pint – while I sat in the car outside for a few minutes. I would amuse myself by watching the excited Dublin fans making their way to Croker down North King Street, oblivious to their corner-forward earwigging in the Fiesta. It all seems a bit quaint in today's professional environment, but I remember being relaxed and Seán helped greatly in this regard by telling that if I got the ball, I would do the right thing.

I wasn't overly nervous, just a little tense. Dublin's dressing room was buried in the bowels of the old Hogan Stand, situated under the point where the Hogan met the Canal End terrace, just into the left as you headed for the tunnel and out onto the pitch. I glanced at the tunnel before togging out to face Louth. At that point, my stomach stirred.

Our dressing room in Croker was where the various factions in the camp became properly defined. The dominant characters stripped off down the far end, as far away from the management team as possible. Heery, Curran, Barr, Galvin, Redmond and veteran Mick Kennedy inhabited this group. Jack Sheedy, Paul Clarke, Davy Foran and Gerry Hargan also seemed to have established patches. Our captain, Tommy Carr, never really hooked up with anyone in particular bar maybe Jack Sheedy. Tommy seemed sort of aloof to the rest of us at the time, but he was a good leader. As for the peripheral players and newcomers, we were forced in beside Paddy Cullen and his selectors. You knew your place. Yet I can recall the tension of the occasion ebbing as I glanced around the room. These were big, strong men who believed they would win; a comforting notion to a new recruit. I already knew just how strong-willed some of these footballers were from playing backs and forwards in Parnell Park. They didn't hold back then and they wouldn't do so now.

Yet, for all that, we were almost ambushed by Louth. They had a good outfit in the early 1990s, backboned by players like Seamus O'Hanlon, Ken Rooney, David Mulligan and Stephen Melia. Up front, Colin Kelly and Stefan White packed a real scoring threat. In fact, a goal by White just before the break put us on the back foot and we trailed by a point entering the last six minutes until Heery pushed forward to grab the equaliser. A late flurry of points from Galvin and Sheedy saw us limp home, 0-15 to 1-9. The introduction of Davy Foran, who replaced Pat Gilroy in the second half, probably turned the game. Once again, my tally was two points and I remained busy. I was keeping my hand in. More worryingly perhaps for Dublin was the amount of wides we accrued. Wasted chances would haunt us in time.

New Rivals, Old Enemy – Leinster Final 1992

Having survived the Louth scare, we secured a Leinster final date with Kildare. I had missed the first instalment of Dublin's new rivalry with their provincial neighbours in the 1991 national league final but, essentially, the bad blood had increased with Mick O'Dwyer's arrival on the scene. Prior to that, Kildare hadn't really threatened Dublin for nearly two decades. Micko was a real adversary, as I would learn, harshly, many years later. Now, heading for our provincial final outing on 26 July 1992, I witnessed, for the first time, a change in Paddy Cullen's attitude. I also saw the determination in his fellow selectors, particularly Pat O'Neill. This was personal to them. O'Dwyer was an old enemy, their yardstick. For a fortnight before the game, our management delivered an expletive-charged mantra – that their old nemesis O'Dwyer would not be allowed to come back to haunt them. Kerry must have been indelibly marked into the psyches of the Seventies' men who managed us, because I remember distinctly playing an 'A' vs 'B' game up in St Vincent's ground in Marino prior to the Leinster final when, out of the blue, Cullen started dancing around the sideline and shouting at us on the pitch. 'Ha, Jayzus lads, Kerry have been beaten in the Munster final – by Clare!' I wasn't sure whether his delight was at seeing the old enemy embarrassed or whether it was the perceived boost to our own chances of winning the All-Ireland.

The Kildare match was intense. Croker was jammed; O'Dwyer's enthusiasm had swept Lilywhite fans to headquarters in their thousands.

Beforehand, I remember the dressing room had a distinct edge to it. Our marksman, Charlie Redmond, retched in the toilet, as he did before most big games, while O'Neill stoked the fire in our bellies with some kind of mad story about horses on the Curragh, and, well, turning the Lilywhites into horsemeat! Mick O'Dwyer was never far from their lips and Kildare would now pay the price for their high-profile appointment. I don't recall being scared – it was almost hard to be. I mean, Heery, Barr, Sheedy, Hargan and Carr were pounding the floor with their studs, waiting for that door to be opened, waiting for the arena. Remember, there was no warm-up area in Croker in those days, nor did we meet anywhere for a stretch beforehand, so the tension wasn't released until the door of the dressing room was flung open. 'Do your job,' I repeated to myself as we tore up towards the Hill, one of the truly great, butterfly-in-the-stomach inducing feelings for a Dublin footballer.

There is some amount of nonsense spoken about Dublin fans. Their support through the championship has always been fantastic. Why it is always questioned by our country colleagues? The 'Where-were-they-during-the-national-league?' brigade. Well, they're no different from any other county. Do Cork fans flock to see the Rebel footballers during the league? Do Kerry? Does anyone for that matter? If the bloody managers and players didn't always take it seriously, why on earth would a fan? Hill 16 is a fabulous spectacle and was an awe-inspiring backdrop for a Dublin footballer. Unlike the country towns and villages, city folk don't necessarily have the same bond with clubs and parishes. They relate directly to the Dublin county team, which should be encouraged and respected by GAA people in the city.

Kildare flew out of the traps and it took us a while to settle, but we gradually got a foothold in the game. The pace was frantic, but an incident after about twelve minutes into the game changed the course of the contest and killed Kildare in the process. I went deep looking for a ball and shipped a hefty late tackle from Glenn Ryan. Jack Sheedy immediately sought redress. Within seconds there were blue jerseys arriving from all angles. Keith Barr made a beeline for Kildare centre-forward Tom Harris, who fled the scene with considerable haste. Meanwhile, wing-back Eamon Heery – oblivious to the fracas – had dashed forward to score a trademark point into Hill 16 with his left foot and was jogging back to take up his position. However, a sideways glance revealed the goings-on to Heery and, without breaking stride, he turned 45 degrees to bolster Dublin's standing.

A lot of my team-mates had soldiered long and hard against Meath. You stood your ground and were expected to – by the management, by the players and by the fans. When the dust settled against Kildare, the sheer scale of the brawl, which lasted about three minutes, left referee Brian White unable to identify any particular culprit, so he merely booked two of the initial combatants, Redmond and Rainbow. Shortly afterwards, Sheedy kicked a free from his own half up as far as Redmond who was out on the '40'. Charlie perceptively saw Barr thundering forward from the half-back line and fed him with a delightful hand pass. Nothing could stop Keith in full flight and he finished an incredible move by drilling a fabulous shot to the corner of the net from twenty yards away. We led 1-10 to 0-4 at the break – worth the late tackle.

In truth, we were pretty awful in the second half and Kildare kept chipping away, but our defence was resolute enough to see Carr up the steps of the Hogan Stand to lift the Leinster trophy.

I had played well being marked by 'Sos' Dowling and was pretty satisfied with myself that evening. With a first senior medal secured, disappointment seemed an unlikely prospect in the near future. You could taste the buzz in the capital as we did our celebratory rounds over the next couple of days; a heady feeling knowing you're centre stage.

Under The Weather – All-Ireland Semi-Final 1992

The novel All-Ireland semi-final pairing with new Munster champions Clare and their manager, John Maughan, was previewed as a one-way ticket to the final for Dublin, so there was much cautionary lecturing and gnashing of teeth up in Parnell Park. Yet, the Sunday prior to our meeting with Clare on 23 August, the whole Dublin squad had travelled to Croke Park to watch Donegal scrape a 0-13 to 0-9 victory over Mayo in the other semi-final. It was one of the worst games any of us had ever witnessed. With Clare and Donegal standing in our way, no one could dispel the notion of a handy All-Ireland. It's cringing now to think of us filing out of the game laughing and joking. More cringing still is the fact that it was suggested that the Dublin panel in 2004 travel to headquarters to watch one of the qualifier double-headers. Thankfully, some of the senior players declined and the idea was shelved. If you don't learn the lessons of history…

With things looking decidedly rosy for Dublin leading up to the Clare match, I spoiled my own party by damaging a quad muscle in my left 'kicking' leg. I had to use my right foot in training, not always the prettiest sight, but I survived nonetheless. Then, during the week of the game, my problems were compounded when I went down with the flu. On the Thursday night, Paddy Cullen told me I would have to undergo a fitness test with fellow-panellist Chris McCormack from St Pat's in Palmerstown on Saturday before I could be assured of my starting place. This test, of course, concerned the quad muscle. I never dreamt of telling him about the flu.

On the Saturday, I nipped up to St Brendan's before heading to Parnell Park for the fitness test, just to see if I could manage. I couldn't kick a ball and couldn't sprint full out. Things looked bleak indeed. It was a miserably wet morning, which helped my case when I was eventually put through my paces later on that morning. Soaked in wet gear, I was able to keep tabs with Chris and kind of spoofed my way through the session, helped by my team-mate who knew the score. Worryingly, that morning session left me in rag order later that night. Running a high temperature and nursing a vicious cough, I had to get out of bed and change the sheets, and eventually just grabbed a quilt and went to lie down on the couch in the front room. And there I still lay late on Sunday morning with the All-Ireland semi-final merely hours away. In fact, I was still on the couch when the minor match between Meath and Cork appeared on the television. My father couldn't stick it any longer. 'Dessie, we have to ring someone and let them know how you are.' An hour later I arrived in Croker with my gear over my shoulder. Togged out, played, set up a goal and scored a point with my weaker foot in a fairly comfortable 3-14 to 2-12 victory for us. All-in-all, I was pleased… Or blessed!

The papers started to take notice of my role and the *Evening Herald* ran a piece with Seán Boylan talking about how I was measuring up to the task. 'Little Boy Blue' read the quaint headline. Enough to send shivers down the spines of future opponents! Hardly. I got away with my duplicitous actions, something that I would repeat again later in my career. I often wondered, though, should I have been so economical with the truth. Dishonesty with a manager can cost a team a game or certainly concede valuable ground to the opposition. Yet I always seemed to be able to battle through the pain barrier, a trait that probably exacerbated many of my injuries.

Vinny Murphy ran amok against Clare. He caught a ridiculous amount of ball and scored 2-1 in the process. Already our target man, this performance sealed the tactical approach for the final in the minds of our management team: hit it long and often to Murphy. It was pretty easy after the event to dismiss the tactic as somewhat one-dimensional, and the shortcomings in our approach to the final have entered the folklore of Dublin football, but on the strength of Murphy's incredible ability, you could hardly have blamed anyone at the time. As corner-forwards, Mick Galvin and I lived off scraps, which of course we were happy to do if successful. It only became an issue when we lost.

The hype of Dublin reaching their first final since 1985 papered over a lot of the cracks in our displays. We really weren't playing that well. Experience and strength were shunting us along. Countering complacency remains one of the most difficult jobs in management. No manager wants to stifle confidence, nor can he shield amateur players from the excitement within a county.

Model Preparation – All Ireland Build-up 1992

I was oblivious to much of the now well-documented flaws in Dublin's approach to the 1992 All-Ireland final and using hindsight to deliver judgement on our preparation would be a little rich coming from 'Little Boy Blue'. In fact, my own personal situation approaching the decider wasn't great, what with family relations descending on the capital to support Donegal. Yes, parts of the lead-up to the game were shambolic. Complacency had probably set in and, worse still, this had become evident by the camp's behaviour. I don't think anyone in particular was to blame; changing times had stolen a march on everyone involved. It was a new experience for most of the panel.

Firstly, there were no management strictures placed on any of the peripheral events that were subsequently blamed for our performance. There was the chance of a few bob modelling clothes for Arnotts and appearing on a local radio station for a big laugh. Players, unused to this kind of notoriety, despite the enormous crowds they drew, jumped at these fatal distractions. There were loads of small things that, looking back, seem daft. I mean, we all had to troop into Arnotts in Henry Street individually to collect our clothes for final day in the full glare of a bemused public. Puma boots were delivered to training sessions and we even had a guy call to Parnell Park with a pair of Wrangler jeans for everyone.

I had my own distractions, which, of course, I should have avoided. How would I deal with the countless relations from Donegal? Despite their good manners and good intentions, you can still imagine how strained the conversations were with my uncles, trying to remain diplomatic and cordial, saying 'Would ye give us a chance at all Dessie?' I was on a hiding to nothing, and that was before the endless ticket demands. Worse still, I would be facing players in Croke Park with whom I'd shared my summers in Donegal kicking football. During those romantic days I spent in Crove, I had dreamt of playing in an All-Ireland final. I never imagined, however, that the realisation of my dream would be clouded by my mother's people standing in opposition. Her home lies in the heart of Donegal football country. Mairtín and James McHugh, Anthony Molloy, Noel Hegarty, John Joe Doherty and Manus Boyle: all footballers I knew as a child. The love and enthusiasm for the game around that area was one of the main reasons I took to football in the first place. It would be difficult to get my head around this match.

Paddy Cullen would eventually pay the price for many of the mistakes made prior to the game, but it should be noted in mitigation that their removal in subsequent years didn't automatically lead to an All-Ireland title.

For all the anecdotal condemnation in the wake of the All-Ireland, our preparation on the field seemed good. We were moving very well, brimming with confidence. A few minor injury scares to Gerry Hargan and Mick Galvin were dispelled in the run-up to the game and we seemed ready to accept our destiny. What we'd really accepted was a set-up.

Donegal manager Brian McEniff had done his homework on Dublin. We heard that Seán Ferriter had carried out a spying mission at Dublin training sessions on his behalf (not uncommon back then) and McEniff also employed in-depth analyst Gerry McDermott, who had compiled a video dossier of Dublin in action and a detailed report for each Donegal player on the strengths and weakness of his opponent. While Dublin's tactics probably didn't require much analysis, the one-dimensional nature of our primary plan might not have been so far off the mark had we actually fed Vinny Murphy with quick ball. It was really the laboured build-up that played into Donegal's hands.

Northern Exposure – All-Ireland Final 1992

The twentieth of September was a bright, warm autumnal day. I set off for my cycle up to the Phoenix Park and back down the North Circular, after which my father dropped me up to Na Fianna on Mobhi Road where, for the first time in the campaign, the Dublin team gathered. Seeing the lads assembled on match day signalled an end to my week-long pre-match tension. The emotional build-up rarely changed over the years; my grumpy 'PMT' would be replaced gradually with a kind of anticipatory excitement, followed by a euphoria on the pitch.

The dressing room on final day was pretty much as it had been all summer, if a little edgier. I remember a bit more jogging on the spot than normal. Our captain, Tommy Carr, spoke articulately and passionately. As usual, Charlie retched and Pat O'Neill raised the temperature, while Paddy Cullen spoke as if we were about to fulfil our birthright. Gerry Hargan sat on the bench staring into space and I recall Paul Curran telling him to 'liven up'. 'You look after yourself and we'll be alright,' came the trenchant reply.

We were on the back foot from the off that day. I was marked by Noel Hegarty. Anthony Molloy gave Donegal a firm foothold in midfield, Martin 'Rambo' Gavigan anchored their defence, while the McHughs ran at our backs with a fleet-footed defiance. Not that we didn't have chances to stem the flow. In training Eamon Heery had told me that, if I made an early cross-field run when he was in possession on the left wing, he would swing the ball over to me quickly. I had practised the receipt of such a pass in the ball alley and, sure enough, Heery duly delivered such a ball to me in the first half that left me with a sight of goal, but I got under the ball and my shot sailed over the crossbar. The commentators asserted that I should have buried it but, in truth, it was only a half-chance. Shortly afterwards, I was bundled over for a penalty, a dubious decision at best. Charlie missed it and our opponents grew in stature. It was one of those days. We chased the game, but never achieved parity, never managed to get the opposition doubting. Manus Boyle, fortunate to be in his side's starting line-up, delivered an unbelievable performance.

Vinny won a huge amount of ball, but the delivery to him was ponderous, allowing Donegal to bottle him up with two, and often three, players. His marker, Matt Gallagher, never kicked the ball in the whole match, but he got his hands in when in mattered and didn't let Murphy pass him.

In truth, I didn't get a great deal of possession. Donegal seemed to press relentlessly and Dublin's 'handy' All-Ireland disappeared in front of my eyes in a green and gold blur. There was no Sam for the Hill. Instead, Anthony Molloy from Ardara took Sam to the 'Hills'. I had seen Molloy lift a Donegal under-21 championship trophy back in the 1980s when Ardara beat Aodh Rua of Ballyshannon in a replay in Fintra near Killybegs. The next cup I saw him lift was on the steps of the Hogan Stand that evening.

Bewildered, I slumped off as the September shadows were crossing the field but, before I reached the sanctuary of the dressing room, Brian Carthy collared me for an RTÉ Radio interview. I couldn't articulate my emotions, but conscious of my mother's people, I tried to be as magnanimous as I could be. Talking is the last thing you want to do in a situation like that.

Barely a word was spoken in the dressing room afterwards. Eyes, many tear-stained, were averted. Players shuffled out and went their separate ways before regrouping in Jurys Hotel that night where the band played 'Simply the Best', a song I can't stomach to this day.

The function was painful enough, but alcohol numbed the senses. Mick Galvin's wife Maura gave birth to their first child Mikey that night, which added a bit of perspective to the moping. I hit the wall at about four o'clock in the morning and, when Noreen and I reached our bedroom, we discovered another couple in our bed – the room had been double-booked. I lurched back down to reception, was issued an apology, and we were given another room. However, when I reached my new destination, there was yet *another* couple *in situ*, and this pair weren't as sedentary as the first! We ended up being upgraded to a luxury Jurys Towers' suite where, on arrival, we discovered our first mini bar. We rang sub keeper Derek O'Farrell who promptly arrived over and helped us drain the contents.

Four sheets to the wind the following morning, myself and Derek arrived late to the lunch across in the Burlington Hotel. In the lobby, my mother and father were speaking to Donegal captain, Anthony Molloy. My strong emotional attachment to his homeland made me somewhat envious when I saw him until I met up with the rest of my team-mates who were well in the process of their second healing.

Our subsequent duties later that evening were excruciating. We were paraded on an open-topped bus down O'Connell Street flanked by a handful of fans. People heading home from work looked on in bemusement. No one could have contrived a more apt metaphor for the precarious nature of being a Dublin footballer. After that trip, we were guests at a civic reception hosted by the Lord Mayor in the Mansion House.

Tragically, the night before, a Donegal fan had been killed in O'Connell Street and, in those circumstances, Paddy Cullen spoke at the reception of our setback as being really only 'a game of football'. His words didn't go down well with some of his fellow selectors and some of the players. I remember Eamon Heery being incensed with Cullen's philosophical acceptance of the whole final defeat. Sadly, Paddy's attitude probably hastened his departure as manager. But that was Paddy. He didn't get worked up in the same way as others. After all, this is the man who, before a big game in Croke Park in the Seventies, stood at the end of the tunnel smoking a cigar alongside a very tense John McCarthy, or so the story goes. Macker asked him how on earth he could be so relaxed. Cullen smiled, opened out his arms and replied: 'Macker, aren't all these people here to see me?'

Tempers were frayed, fuelled by and large with drink, and harsh words were delivered for a few hours in the Mansion House. Charlie Redmond even announced an impetuous retirement such was his disappointment. Yet anger turned to a kind of maudlin sentimentality as we settled into the tiny Dawson Lounge for a sing-song later that night. On hearing some of the classic Dublin ballads, the first real tears of disappointment were shed. It was then that it dawned on me what had happened, what we had left behind us in Croke Park the day before. The enormity of such an occasion is easily lost until it's too late.

I didn't quite understand the dynamics of the management team at the time because I was so young, but suffice to say that Pat O'Neill was the dominant personality. He would later replace Paddy as manager, while trainer Fran Ryder and selector Jim Brogan would remain. Bobby Doyle, our monitor in the stand in 1992, also became a selector. Collectively, they blossomed as the management team which would eventually deliver the big prize.

I really liked Paddy Cullen. I liked his candour and was sorry to see him go. His flamboyance was pleasant to be around and he had a deep-felt belief in Dublin football and in his players. I often wonder how relations turned out afterwards between Cullen and his former selectors.

Seven months later, Dublin would gain a modicum of revenge by landing the national league title, beating Donegal in a replay. A crowd of over 59,000 showed up, the biggest attendance ever at a national league game. However, my personal ghost had come back to haunt me. In a hockey match later that winter, I tore my medial knee ligaments again. I missed the latter part of the league and only made the bench for the league final. As it always was in my career, the present was tense and the future imperfect.

Chapter 12

Tunnel Of Love – Championship 1993

Unfortunately for the Dublin team, particularly between 1992 and 1994, the panic button was pressed too often at the critical stages of our most important games. What happened? Well, in my opinion, players started performing as individuals: over-carrying, attempting long-range efforts for scores, giving away needless free-kicks – trying too hard, if you like. Steeled by the setbacks in 1991 and 1992, no one wanted to shirk responsibility, but instead of doing the simple things well, we ended up wasting golden opportunities. We were beaten by better teams on the day, but I've always tried to figure out *why* they were better on the day. Over a long period we were by far the most consistent team in the country. But why did some of our rivals swell with self-belief when, conversely, we seemed to go to pieces?

The Dublin panel was cliquish, even disparate at times. This fragile make-up put pressure on individual players, which is why, I believe, they tried to go it alone, to prove their worth to themselves and their colleagues. The All-Ireland final against Donegal revealed this. Had we been more united as a bunch of players, maybe we mightn't have been as selfish in possession of the ball; we might have thrown it around a bit more and added more variety to our game. Nonetheless, we had the consolation of a holiday to Florida in January of 1993 – a fantastic trip, full of golf, booze and high jinx.

Despite the hit we had taken after losing to Donegal, we still didn't doubt the class we possessed. Our consistency led us to victory in the national football league final replay in 1993 when we earned our revenge over Donegal, despite having our captain Tommy Carr sent off early in the game for a kick on Brian Murray, a transgression for which he would pay a ludicrously heavy price. Keith Barr and Charlie Redmond were suspended – they had been sent off during the first game, which was a draw – but Heery steered us magnificently to victory, while forwards Niall Guiden and Martin Doran shone up front.

I watched that game from the substitutes' bench, having just returned to the panel from my latest knee injury lay-off. Despite my selection in the subs, I was well off the mark and would really remain so for the whole of the 1993 season. I remember selector Bobby Doyle asking me to warm up during the replay. He said they were thinking of throwing me in at corner-forward to 'mark' Barry McGowan, to negate his pace (McGowan was one of those Donegal corner-backs who never seemed to stop running). 'Are you up to it?' asked Doyle, peering at my heavy knee brace. My affirmative answer mustn't have masked my self-doubt, as I never made the field. I warmed up for half the game. The lads sneered at me afterwards, saying the Croke Park ground staff would have to re-sod the sideline after all my running.

I never told the management team that I had damaged my knee a couple of months earlier in a hockey match. Though I had received permission to play hockey, I fibbed to O'Neill and told him I had twisted it while practising in the ball alley. I wasn't going to risk any subsequent restrictions.

League champions once again, Dublin were rapidly becoming the most consistent team in the country. Better still, we'd turned the tables on Donegal, so there was great confidence in the camp that we could go on and make up for the All-Ireland setback of 1992.

Yet, observers felt that we needed to take Meath's scalp to properly exorcise the ghost of the 1991 epic. Drawn in the same half of the Leinster championship as the Royals, we would face our nemesis in the semi-final if we could overcome our first two hurdles. It was a liberating thought. However, Down and Donegal's successive All-Ireland victories had inspired another Northern pretender whose rising status was not yet visible to us on the horizon.

Despite the rehabilitation exercises I had to do while overcoming my knee problems, football wasn't an encumbrance. Life was pretty free and easy for me in the spring of 1993. I had moved into a flat with Noreen close to my parents' home in Rathdown Villas and to my workplace across the road. As a shift worker in the hospital, I managed to make all the time I needed for training and playing by swapping hours and shifts with other nurses. Night duty was a pain, but at twenty-two years of age, I could handle the hassle. My elevation in status with the Dublin team helped me to come out of my shell a little – not enough, mind you, to dilute my obsession with the game to any great degree.

The loss of Paddy Cullen as manager didn't register that greatly, as most of the same management team was *in situ*. The league success strengthened Pat O'Neill's hand in the eyes of the public, but he was acutely aware that he had merely replicated an achievement carried out by both of the previous incumbents. There was a more serious feel to his team sessions, essentially because he was a strict disciplinarian. Bravado was frowned upon, so the dossers on the panel gave O'Neill a wide berth. On a one-to-one level, though, he was quite understanding and accommodating. I was still very much at the 'keep your head down' stage of my development as a Dublin player, so my relationship with him was perfunctory, save for the constant discourse about my bloody knee. The next two years would see a much stronger relationship forged between us.

Much of the criticism following our All-Ireland defeat in 1992 had centred on the propensity of our defenders, particularly our half-back line, to attack incessantly, to the detriment of their defensive duties. O'Neill decided to tinker with our formations during the 1993 campaign to see if he could rectify these perceived flaws.

There were also quite a few new faces in the first-team shake-up, which ensured that I never whinged about my knee. In the wake of his sending off, Tommy Carr was handed a six-month sentence which, although it was reduced, only cleared him for the All-Ireland final should we make it. Gerry Hargan also retired, so these changes forced O'Neill's hand and an entire new full-back line emerged in Ciarán Walsh, Dermot Deasy and Paddy Moran. Deasy, though several years older than me, became a close friend on the panel. He was a straight, no-nonsense kind of fellow, and I admired him greatly as a footballer. He'd a great knack of assessing a situation and always weighed up the odds to his advantage. Coincidentally, Dermot and his predecessor in the full-back slot, Gerry Hargan, are married to two sisters. Both are also from the same club, Ballymun Kickhams, and the Ballymun tradition doesn't end there because our next long-term full-back, Paddy Christie, was also from the same club.

Dessie Farrell

On Tour – Leinster SFC 1993

Our first summer engagement in 1993 was against Wexford in Wexford Park on 23 May, which turned out to be a pretty dour non-event, memorable only for the fact that a Dublin fan fell through the roof of the Wexford dressing room. We certainly kept our feet on the ground following our 0-11 to 0-7 victory. I was back in the first team, but patently struggling with my mobility. The game marked John O'Leary's first outing as captain, a role he would continue to play even when Tommy Carr's suspension was eventually lifted, and one he wouldn't relinquish until Keith Barr took over the mantle under Mickey Whelan. It also marked championship debuts for Jim Gavin (with whom I had already become good friends) and Martin Doran. The fortunes of these two players would contrast wildly, with the former going on to play a key role in our All-Ireland success and the latter quickly falling from the dizzy heights of his league-final performance and drifting into footballing anonymity.

Two weeks later we travelled to O'Connor Park in Tullamore, where we hammered Westmeath 2-11 to 0-8. Keith Barr, who had been suspended for the first outing, lined out at centre-forward. Keith fancied the move, and managed to bag 1-2. Charlie Redmond's introduction as a sub for Mick Deegan cleared Barr to return to more familiar surroundings later in the game, but it marked the manager's determination to try and tap into what he believed were the natural instincts of some of his defenders.

The Fourth of July 1993 was an appropriate date for my first senior championship joust with Meath. The independence gained from ditching our greatest rivals in Leinster couldn't be underestimated. Seeing that this was our first championship meeting since the 1991 epic, the media hyped the game out of all proportion and there was a tense build-up to the clash, both on and off the field. As it transpired, it was a scrappy encounter. I was shadowed by Kevin Foley and my first opportunity to lay down a marker against our biggest rivals ended when I fluffed a good scoring chance into the Canal End early on, throwing a limp kick at the ball with my strapped left leg.

Meath held the upper hand in the first half as our tactical approach made no in-roads. Charlie Redmond played out on the '40', but Martin O'Connell kept him well under wraps. Jim Gavin roamed from corner-forward with Robbie O'Malley in tow to little avail, while Keith Barr, wearing No. 11, was wasted at wing-forward.

It was obvious at half-time that O'Neill's experimental line-up was not working, so after the break, Paul Bealin came in at centre-forward on O'Connell, Redmond moved into the corner on O'Malley and Barr returned to the half-back line in place of a young Dermot Harrington who was making his debut. The moves changed the course of the game. Redmond grabbed a smashing goal and we carved out a five-point lead. Typically, Meath clawed their way back as our repeated failure to finish games started to kick in. When Colm O'Rourke equalised at the death, it seemed as if another Meath-Dublin soap opera was about to commence. However, Curran, Barr and Heery kept probing and, for once, our persistence paid off. A ball broke to Redmond on the Hogan Stand side and, despite his kick being blocked down by Robbie O'Malley, he managed to move the ball to Jack Sheedy who fired over a fabulous long-range point to win the game. The moment was captured beautifully by an RTÉ camera behind the Canal End goal, which showed the rapturous Hill 16 greeting the ball as it sailed over the bar at the far end of the field.

It was far from a classic, but the relief and joy in the dressing room afterwards was palpable. It rang a bit hollow for me as my performance was once again inhibited greatly by my lingering knee problem. My attitude was to protect my place on the team by steadfastly refusing to let the injury affect my work rate. I continued to plug away in the corner, feeding as best I could on scraps of possession. No more, no less.

Leinster Final 1993

The Leinster final against Kildare on 27 July was billed as a grudge match, given the tenor of the previous year's encounter. Pat O'Neill continued tinkering with the line-up for the game, this time taking Eamon Heery out of the half-back line and throwing him in at right half-forward. His customary left half-back berth was filled by Paul O'Neill from Fingallians who had impressed in training. I wore the No. 11 shirt, but took up residence in my normal right corner-forward position, marked this time by Noel Donlon who would, some years later, go on to marry my cousin Deirdre in Kildare.

It was a blustery, showery day, one that wasn't conducive to decent football. Still, it couldn't excuse the dreadful thirty-five minutes' football that followed.

Kildare obviously felt the need to stand up to Dublin physically, so from the outset there was a lot of thumping and niggling. Kildare played Martin Lynch in front of their full-back line as a kind of sweeper, a fairly innovative move on Mick O'Dwyer's part. It worked well in the opening half. Playing with the strong wind, we drove senseless long balls into Lynch's arms, making no headway at all (Paul Bealin got our first point from play after thirty-four minutes). We led by three points to two at the break and Kildare looked poised to push for a historic victory.

Circumstances then changed dramatically and bizarrely. Jogging towards the tunnel at the Canal End for the half-time interval, Larry Miley ran into Jack Sheedy, the latter turning just at the last minute to deliver a robust shoulder into the Kildare man which landed him on his arse. Miley played up the belt, holding his face on the ground while consternation ensued around him and several Kildare officials remonstrated with the referee. On witnessing this, the Dublin and Kildare substitutes at the back of the group sensed a row and started to sprint for the gate. There was no row in the tunnel to start with, but because the late arrivals into that area thought there was, one erupted anyway.

I was just about to enter our dressing room when I turned on my heels and saw the mass of brawling bodies coming my way. By this stage, however, most of the first-team players were in their respective dressing rooms, which were immediately locked by officials who feared the worst. Two distinctive groups assembled at the junction between the two team areas, each beckoning the other to 'come and have a go'. No one refused the challenge, including me, and our manager wasn't shy about the course of action we should adopt. Johnny Barr was in the vanguard and I weighed in behind his considerable presence. Amidst the grappling, one Kildare sub got hauled onto the Dublin side of the battle lines, his tracksuit top reefed around his head in the process. He was a big lad, which stood to him as he endured a barrage of punches to the head before he was released to beat a retreat back through the Dublin players. One of the lads saw him off on the final leg of his journey with a hefty boot to the backside. There was absolute mayhem. I got a forceful thump in the ear and I couldn't be sure it wasn't one of our own lads that had delivered the blow.

The garda on duty in the tunnel was Dublin Seventies' star John McCarthy, who lost his cap during the affray and can recall one of the Dublin players kicking it at a Kildare player's face. Contrary to the folklore that was spawned by the row, McCarthy did try and bring some order to the events but was left to do it alone because all the green blazers and stewards appeared to have exited the area.

It was a maelstrom and the noise was deafening. Most of our team, including Eamon Heery and Keith Barr, had been locked in our dressing room by a steward who was hoping it might contain the melee. The players were literally kicking at the metal door, screaming to be let out. Studs pounded the concrete corridors outside and expletives reverberated around the walls. When the unfortunate and petrified official eventually opened the door to let us back in, he was nearly killed in a stampede as the caged Dublin players stormed out past him in a fury.

When we regrouped, our dressing room resembled a scene from *Apocalypse Now*. O'Neill didn't try and defuse the emotion either. Rather he channelled it. He put us on a war footing, explaining, perhaps critically, that only victory would properly vent our anger. It was a message we probably interpreted better than our less-experienced opponents.

Jack Sheedy stepped up to the plate on the resumption and, after shipping a nasty belt from Johnny McDonald, spearheaded a move that led to our first point, which I duly clipped over from the right corner of the Canal End. We hit six unanswered points as Kildare flailed at us.

Forced to come out and play with the wind, they could no longer contain us and Sheedy delivered a man-of-the-match display, while Charlie Redmond defied the conditions and punished Kildare's indiscipline with his placed-ball kicking. Mick Galvin made a noteworthy contribution after coming on as a sub until a niggling Achilles tendon injury forced his subsequent withdrawal. We ribbed him afterwards that it was really the belt in the snot he got from Davy Dalton that prompted his departure. Despite our dominance, however, there were undercurrents in our display that were dragging us down. Vinny Murphy, who started to liberate himself from the clutches of the excellent Dalton in the second half, was sent off for two stupid tackles on the bounce and we allowed Niall Buckley to chip away at our lead – once again displaying our inability to finish games. Johnny Barr, Galvin's replacement in the closing stages, restored our superiority, but it belied a scrappy finish to the game by

Dublin. We won 0-11 to 0-7, but should have been ten points ahead. Essentially, Redmond's kicking accuracy and incredible range backboned our drive. However, we still lacked variety in our play.

As the Light Declines – All Ireland Semi-Final 1993
Of the many disappointments I endured with Dublin throughout the 1990s, our semi-final meeting with Derry on 22 August ranks as one of the hardest to swallow. I could say at this juncture that, yes, we were beaten by a better team on the day and that I've no regrets. But I do. I've always looked for reasons why our performances didn't measure up. It's not that I don't accept defeat, or that I discredit the talent Derry possessed in that team – Anthony Tohill, Brian McGilligan, Henry Downey, Tony Scullion, Joe Brolly – they were a serious outfit. But we had victory within our grasp and had it prised from our fingers. We succumbed to a greater team performance at the critical stage of the game. Why?

Well, the way I see it now, we ended up playing as individuals again, particularly in the later stages. There were a number of factors that culminated in our breakdown. We lost our full-back Dermot Deasy after six minutes which, although significant in itself, forced an unsettling reshuffle. Mick Deegan came on at left half-back and young Paul O'Neill moved back onto Joe Brolly, Derry's flying corner-forward. Critically, Eamon Heery, so long one of Dublin's most dynamic half-backs, was left in the half-forward line. Unlike Kildare, Derry were a physically imposing side and they singled out centre-back Keith Barr for a lot of punishment. It was a measure of Barr's resilience and talent that he still delivered a powerful performance. In Tohill and McGilligan, Derry had two of the best (and the biggest) midfielders in the game and they dominated for crucial periods throughout the afternoon.

Tactically, I think Derry were superior. They seemed to have more options when it mattered. They reacted quickly and decisively with their substitutions and managed to bypass our half-back line by targeting Brolly as often as possible with quick deliveries. They varied it too. Their half-back line wasn't slow to seize opportunities to break forward: Gary Coleman, Henry Downey and Johnny McGurk all scored on the day.

In the heat of battle, mind you, it's often difficult to determine how various strands of a game might come together. Despite the early setbacks, a string of early wides and a fifteen-minute blitz from Derry, we clawed our way back into the match. Vinny Murphy won a lot of frees off his marker, Danny Quinn, and Charlie Redmond – described on the day by radio commentator Mícheál Ó Muircheartaigh as 'the man who has lost more weight than any other man in the world this year' in reference to the visible effects of Charlie's daily cycle from Ashbourne to Finglas – punished Derry with five points from placed balls. Pat Gilroy finished the half strongly, kicking two good points. We led 0-9 to 0-4 at the break, a pretty solid advantage under the circumstances.

What our strong finish blurred was the nature of some of our play. We registered seven wides in the first twenty-four minutes; many were shots from distance that came to nothing. As a corner-forward, it is very difficult to function with such a game plan. Murphy and Redmond frequently foraged deep looking for possession, leaving me inside as the only forward in the remaining third of the field. I spent much of the half running between the flanks and gesturing vainly with my hand.

Conversely, Derry's most effective tactic was hitting right corner-forward Brolly early with ball, an approach which yielded several frees. Unfortunately for us, Redmond's dead-ball expertise was matched on the day by Enda Gormley's. Not that the comparison should diminish Charlie's extraordinary contribution in that All-Ireland semi-final and throughout that period in Dublin football. One can only wonder at the difference a man like Redmond would have made to more recent Dublin incarnations.

In the Dublin defence, however, Paul O'Neill was patently struggling with Brolly's pace while our midfield was fitful. Derry manager Eamon Coleman didn't tarry when it came to switches and whipped off Quinn and replaced him with Karl Diamond midway through the first half. In turn, Tony Scullion went onto Murphy and blotted him out for the remainder of the game.

Still, only hindsight reveals the chinks in Dublin's armour. Sitting in the dressing room at half-time, we more or less told ourselves just to keep it going, that victory was already in our grasp, probably how most punters read the situation. Two minutes after the resumption, referee Tommy Sugrue gave Derry a ridiculously soft 14-yard free and suddenly the game's complexion changed. What followed was probably one of the best half hours of football for the neutral observer. It was an undulating journey punctuated by incredible scores and a shifting balance of power.

Brolly continued to torment Paul O'Neill, but by the time we switched Mick Deegan onto him, a lot of the damage had been done. The Derry corner-forward had built up a head of steam and continued to draw fouls from his new marker. Mick Galvin replaced O'Neill, prompting Heery's return to the half-back line. Our failure to nail down midfield meant our pressure was sporadic, but we kept our noses in front. Redmond's seventh point of the day put us 0-13 to 0-10 up, but instead of pushing for home, we withdrew into ourselves again, became a bunch of individuals trying too hard, trying to execute the difficult option rather than keeping it simple. We turned over way too much possession and Derry hit us with four points on the bounce. With five minutes remaining, Redmond levelled the game again and, when Keith Barr made a spectacular block on Damien Barton's goal-bound shot shortly afterwards, a draw looked a banker.

Yet Derry's finish was more purposeful. In the absence of a 'Plan B', we squandered possession and, when a ball broke to Johnny McGurk under the Hogan Stand, he struck an audacious point with his left foot over the closing Heery and over the bar. For the third year in a row, Dublin had failed when the big squeeze came on.

Despite the tinkering with our half-back line, it was patently obvious that our over-reliance on long balls into Vinny Murphy was a flawed approach, regardless of how more conservative our half-back line was. In the bleak aftermath, there would be yet more fallout as Pat O'Neill and his management team searched for solutions to our collapses in tight games. Was it tactical, physical, psychological? The search went on.

With such a sequence of defeats it's hard to credit that Dublin could go at it again with renewed purpose. But there was an arrogance about us that made us believe that we would be back. That was the annual conclusion drawn at the end of a few days' drinking.

Sadly, we lost Eamon Heery from the squad later in 1993 when he withdrew from the panel in disagreement with Pat O'Neill. A forceful presence in the Dublin half-back line for over six years, his absence would be sorely felt. There was anger and sympathy over Eamon's departure. It seemed to me that he had been sacrificed from his customary left half-back position to accommodate a player who had failed badly on the big day and who had drifted out of the picture subsequently. It would ultimately cost him an All-Ireland medal as he didn't return until after Pat O'Neill's departure.

Still, the value of the medal can sometimes be overstated. I have plenty of regrets over missed opportunities, even though I have won an All-Ireland medal. Heery's legacy to Dublin football is as valuable as any All-Ireland winner's, as he will always be remembered in the city as a great footballer. I even think a number of the young Dublin players I have played with recently are actually unaware that Eamon hasn't got a medal. They still gravitate towards him when they meet in company and there is something that every Dublin player and supporter identifies in Heery's defiance and approach to the game.

As the curtain came down on 1993, we brushed down our burgeoning reputation as chokers, ventured into the national league, and defeated the teams we were supposed to. Thankfully, I was emerging from the restrictive influence of my knee injury and starting to come out of my shell a bit.

We believed we would be back and set our sights on next year and the possibility of another road to redemption – for Dublin and for me.

Chapter 13

Life in St Brendan's, Grangegorman – 1990–2000

The backdrop to my early life didn't change much in the 1990s. The broad expanse of St Brendan's Psychiatric Hospital was my childhood playground, an oasis in a crowded inner-city which allowed me the freedom and space to kick football, play hockey and puck *sliotars* around. My father had earned his living from St Brendan's and, in 1994, after three years' training in the same hospital, I qualified as a psychiatric nurse and took up a temporary contract position there. My playground had become my workplace.

There was a great depth of interest in sport in the hospital and my involvement with the St Brendan's hurling, football, hockey and soccer teams helped my status in the place. They were good teams too. Wexford's Martin Storey was a psychiatric nurse in Brendan's at the time, so the hurling team was well anchored. In fact the hospital hurlers, even without Storey, won a Dublin championship in 1980.

My commitment to the Dublin football team in the 1990s was facilitated by my nursing colleagues as opposed to the hospital authorities. For my eight years in St Brendan's, I was a member of the Dublin panel and I don't think I missed more than one or two training sessions due to work. Without the largesse and support of other workers, this, of course, would have been impossible. Rostering arrangements were pretty rigid: one day on, one day off or, alternatively, a week of night work followed by a week off. It didn't always suit an inter-county career, but people looked out for me as much as they could, even if it was only keeping dinner for me after training or a match. With stricter work practices nowadays, no such latitude would be tolerated. As there was no official dispensation for time off, it was impossible to always have cover so, on occasions, I had to fork out and pay people to work for me, something I didn't mind too much because it meant not having to sacrifice my off-duty. Anyway, the expenses accrued were generally covered by the county board. I remember having to pay a nurse to cover for me on the day of the All-Ireland final in 1995. Although there was no shortage of people prepared to swap with me, there was no leave of absence available for football matches, regardless of their importance, a situation that, I'm pretty sure, is mirrored in a lot of jobs today. So much for the standing of our national games.

Handling full-time work is a fact of life for inter-county players. Strong self-motivation is needed to juggle the strenuous demands of football with the daily professional grind in the workplace. You accept it because that's what you do. You love football, but you have to work – a difficult juxtaposition, but a simple logic.

St Brendan's had been a massive institution, at one time housing up to 2,000 patients. It was a real university of life. By the early 1990s, with new developments in the approaches to psychiatric treatment, the population of the hospital had shrunk to about 300, but the experience gained in such a place was wide-ranging to say the least. In time, my relationship with nursing in general and, moreover, with the job would fall apart somewhat. There was an accepted change in the nature of patients admitted to the place, what was referred to in the hospital as a move from 'madness to badness'. Society was changing rapidly and drugs and criminality were becoming an increasingly prevalent factor in psychiatric nursing. Fortunately, I had an escape in football, although it was very hard to leave the job behind, dealing frequently as we did with great human tragedy.

But it certainly wasn't all doom and gloom, especially in my first few years as a nurse. I developed some great relationships, not just with my colleagues, but also with patients. My job entailed being moved regularly from one section to another. One week I would be posted on admissions, where people presented for assessment. The next I could be looking after patients in a high-security unit. My favourite duty was in the geriatric ward, Unit 10b, where I knocked particular *craic* out of some of the older characters.

There was no shortage of strange occurrences in Grangegorman. Night shifts could be interminably slow moving so, when you weren't busy, you tried to keep yourself amused some way. The male dormitory in the geriatric ward held about twenty patients and it lay adjacent to a large day room. One night, long before my time in the hospital, an attendant apparently decided to bring his Honda 50 into the day room to give it a good service during the slack periods of a night shift. He laid sheets of newspaper on the ground, wheeled in the bike and got to work. Anyway, at about four o'clock in the morning, he completed the job and, somewhat inconsiderately, decided to turn the key and see how the engine was ticking over. On hearing the engine, a couple of staff members arrived on the scene and, before long, everyone was taking spins on the Honda 50 around the day room. One old patient in the dormitory woke up to the commotion outside and started roaring abuse. He was indignant about the noise and steadfastly refused to go back to sleep or take any medication. When the morning staff arrived, he was still ranting and raving about 'a feckin' motorbike, I tell you, they were driving a feckin' motorbike around the place. What kind of bloody hospital is this?' The doctor was eventually summoned and, after listening to his complaints about the 'night rider', he decided that the poor fellow was probably delusional.

Another moment I recall fondly from my time in Brendan's happened one night when a patient was dying. The doctor was summoned to administer more morphine and it was accepted that the poor unfortunate had only hours to live. In such instances, staff would generally tiptoe around the dormitory, so as not to disturb the other patients. However, one wag in a bed down the end of the room woke up and saw the doctor tending to the dying patient. He sat up in the bed and, at the top of his voice, roared: 'Ah, when your time is up, your time is up, and no fuckin' doctor will save you!'

The same man, Vinny, who was from Limerick, became a good sparring partner for me in arguments and he was never beaten. He drifted from lucidity, where he regaled me with stories of life in the 1940s and 1950s, to wonderful hyperbole. 'Ye're all soft bastards now,' he'd proclaim. 'I fought Jack Dempsey and Joe Louis and beat the pair of them, landed Dempsey on his arse, I did. I also marked Mick Mackey in a Limerick county final in 1945. Not only did I keep him scoreless, but I scored 3-5 meself.'

I can still hear his hearty laugh, imbued with its joyous timbre, oblivious to his surroundings in Grangegorman. 'I swam the Atlantic, you know, Dessie.' 'Did you, Vinny? That must have been tough.' I'd reply, egging him on to colour his fantastic tale. 'Not only that, I swam it underwater. And I had to fight off three sharks along the way. I managed to cut the head off of one of the bastards and the other two swam away with fright.'

Occasionally residents could become cantankerous. The behaviour was often outrageous, but we were never judgemental. One evening, Vinny was seated at a table in the day room slurping through his evening 'goodie' from a metal bowl. Goodie was bread soaked in tea, a staple repast for ageing patients whose teeth weren't the best. Opposite Vinny, an elderly lady sat baying for her cup of tea. She was a really elegant woman, but quite the prig. 'Where's my cup of tea?' she wailed. When the domestic arrived, she offered the woman some goodie. 'I don't want goodie, I just want my cup of tea!' She didn't let up. 'Where's *my* tea?' Next minute, Vinny lifted his bowl of goodie and landed it straight on the woman's forehead. 'Will ya shut up, ye're crying for that feckin' tea since ya got up this mornin'!'

Two other favourites of mine were two elderly travellers, one of whom, Mikey, claimed that he had been 'King of the Tinkers' in his time, a title reserved for champion bare-knuckle boxers. The poor man was blind, scarred and very infirm, but his claim to fame wasn't doubted because if you didn't restrain his hands when you were dressing him, you'd pay a heavy price. One nurse, new to the unit, approached Mikey one morning to dress him, as he always slept in the nip. The nurse lifted him off the bed, oblivious to the need to restrain his hands and the next minute he was left prostrate across the dormitory floor with blood streaming from his nose. Mikey was a difficult patient. Used to the outdoors, he did what he wanted and often relieved himself in the middle of the day room or in the corridor, which caused consternation, especially when visitors were present. I'd great time for him, nonetheless. Mikey was a link to a past, a way of life that has been long forgotten by most.

I enjoyed taking patients out for trips, particularly when we joined others from Portrane, St Loman's and St Pat's for matches in Croke Park. There was a section of the old Nally Stand reserved for psychiatric patients and they kept the seats for us even up to the All-Ireland semi-final stages. The section was known as 'Woodbine Corner', referring to the brand of cigarette favoured by the patients. After games, we would usually bring a few of them for a pint on the way home, something that was remarkably fulfilling, as it gave us the chance to share in their enjoyment. The patients weren't always spectators at games either. On occasions, when we would be short of players on the hospital team, we would let some of the patients tog out to help us make up the numbers.

However, enabling patients to sample the normal pleasures that people take for granted could be a hazardous business. Every night, it was customary to take one elderly man on a particular ward down to O'Dowd's pub adjacent the hospital for an hour at teatime. He'd usually drink two pints, after which the nurse would bring him back. One evening, a staff nurse who was temporarily in charge of the unit dropped him down to the pub at five o'clock and returned to the office. Busy with other duties, it completely slipped his mind to collect the patient an hour later. At around eight o'clock, I was doing a head count on the ward before handing over to the night shift when I noticed we were a man down. Realising who was missing, I informed the staff nurse, whose jaw dropped. 'Oh Jesus, I forgot to collect him from the pub. Run down and get him, quickly. He'll be locked.' I took off in a sprint down to the pub where, on arriving, I heard this almighty crash inside. I entered to find the poor fellow being lifted off the ground, drunk as a lord; he had just upended a table full of glasses. The locals, who didn't know he was a patient, were helping him up when they spotted me coming to assist. 'Ah Jayzus, Dessie, is it yourself? It's all right, Dessie, it's all right, don't worry, we'll look after your Da.' My father was more than a little amused later when I told him the story.

Recounting funny tales and general good humour among the staff helped us cope with the pressures of the job, particularly when we worked in the high-security unit. While I was stationed at the hospital, they upgraded that particular area with new padded cells and reinforced windows and, after the renovations, the authorities boasted that they had created a 'safe environment' where patients who were violent as a result of their illness could do themselves no harm. The wing was scarcely opened a week, however, when one suicidal man managed to jump through a window on the second floor of the unit, landing on his back in the enclosed yard below. They feared for his life. He was a huge man of eighteen or nineteen stone at least, so when the ambulance crew arrived, they couldn't get the stretcher through the narrow corridors leading from the yard. Eventually, after some difficult manoeuvres, they got him to the ambulance. He was unconscious, so he was placed in a collar in case of spinal damage. All the while, a nurse held his hand, but just before they took him away, he squeezed the nurse's hand and beckoned him down. Given the gravity of the situation, the nurse braced himself for a dying wish, a plea perhaps to inform his family of how much he loved them. 'Nurse,' he whispered into his ear. 'Any chance of a fag?'

I carry a lot of special memories from St Brendan's. The wit and humanity of a lot of the people who worked there and, indeed, many of the people who lived there, helped to dilute the sadness of the place.

Unfortunately, though, my recollections will always be overshadowed by two tragic incidents.

On the night of 6 March 1997, I was working in the assessment unit. This particular part of the hospital stands opposite a row of houses called Orchard View, off Rathdown Road, just doors from my family home. Grangegorman owned a number of these buildings and they housed ex-patients, some of whom lived in high-support units with nursing care, while others fended for themselves in what were known as low-support hostels. In the past, these had been staff residences.

At about half-six in the morning, we were sitting in the office, chatting, when a night sister burst through the doors. 'They're all murdered. Murdered!' she shrieked, barely able to form the words as she struggled to catch her breath. We had no idea what she was talking about. I thought she might have been sleepwalking and might have awoken in shock. However, when she picked up the phone to the gardaí, the cause of her agitation was spelled out to us. Two elderly residents, 61-year-old Mary Callinan and 59-year-old Sylvia Shields, had been brutally stabbed to death and mutilated in the house opposite our offices. A third woman present in the house had escaped attack, although it transpired subsequently that the murderer had entered her room. This woman had taken her nightly medication and had been sleeping with headphones on, oblivious to the carnage that had been perpetrated. When she woke at six o'clock the next morning to make a cup of tea, she found her handbag at the bottom of the stairs with everything out of it. A windowpane in the kitchen was broken and the window had been opened slightly. Kitchen drawers had also been pulled out into the middle of the floor. She knew something was wrong, and entered Sylvia's room, where she made the horrific discovery. She ran from the house and called in to the high-support hostel a couple of doors down where she informed the nurse on duty who duly summoned the senior assistant chief nursing officer (ACNO). The ACNO bravely entered the house to witness the grisly tragedy for herself. She quickly dispatched her junior colleague to raise the alarm. Pandemonium ensued in the hospital. Several squad cars, ambulances and the fire brigade arrived at the scene as we tried to cope with the shock, which was now spreading in waves through the corridors of Grangegorman.

As dawn broke, the sheer frenzied depravity of the attack was emerging. The victims had been viciously hacked to death with a kitchen knife.

Sleep didn't come easy the following morning. I lay in my flat a couple of hundred yards from the crime scene, with a nauseous sense of foreboding. Brutal murder is upsetting enough from a distance. When the victims are two lovely, gentle souls known to you and the incident happens in your back yard, it is incredibly unsettling.

The following evening's night shift was a disturbing twelve hours. Working in the assessment unit, we were conscious that the murderer could well present to us for admission. The gardaí and senior nursing staff confirmed this frightening prospect. Now knowing the full extent of the murders, I carried a hurley stick to work and kept it by my side. There was an uneasy silence among the staff, still in a state of shock and incredulity. Later that night I gazed out the window of our office upon the house, cordoned off and flanked around the clock by a number of gardaí. The house remained under guard for quite some time because I remember several nights later peering out in the middle of the night and seeing a couple of gardaí kicking a football on the road to pass the hours.

If this harrowing tragedy wasn't bad enough, more disturbing still are the twists the case took subsequently, which raised questions of a massive cover-up. Three months after the murders, Dean Lyons, a 24-year-old homeless drug addict who was living rough in Grangegorman, was arrested in connection with the murders. Despite going through 'cold turkey' during the interrogation and suffering severe psychiatric problems, he gave a series of statements admitting that he had carried out the killings. However, his arrest was being hailed as a triumph. On 16 August, a young couple, Catherine and Carl Doyle, were brutally murdered at their home in Castlerea in Roscommon. The killing involved frenzied stabbing with a kitchen knife and it bore striking similarities to the one in Grangegorman. The following day, Mark Nash was arrested by gardaí in Galway. Later, while in prison after confessing to the murder of the couple in Roscommon, Nash proceeded to give a frighteningly accurate account of how Sylvia Shields and Mary Callinan met their death that night in Grangegorman. Nash even explained to detectives how he had spared the third woman in the house, a fact hitherto unknown to the general public. Yet Dean Lyons remained on remand in Mountjoy Jail for a further nine months before the charges against him were dropped. He received neither an explanation nor an apology at the time. Tragically, he took a heroin overdose and died alone in Manchester before Christmas 2000. Following intense political pressure, the gardaí issued a public apology to the family of Dean Lyons.

Nash, jailed in Arbour Hill for the Doyle murders, subsequently retracted his confession to the murder of the two women in Grangegorman. No one has ever been brought to justice for these heinous crimes and I can only imagine the ongoing anguish for the families of the victims and, indeed, for the family of Dean Lyons, who are still demanding a public inquiry. Gardaí recently conducted a forensic review of the Grangegorman murders in a bid to gather new evidence that might eventually lead to an arrest.

While this case remains unsolved, a black cloud will hang over Grangegorman for everyone who has ever worked or spent time there.

An incident between two former patients reawakened the horror of the Grangegorman murders. Paddy Askins worked as part of a rehab programme for ex-patients in the hospital cleaning and emptying bins and, although not a particularly likeable character, he was well known to most of the nursing staff. It is common enough for former patients to remain on in the hospital in some capacity, with many living in accommodation in the general vicinity. Driving back from a short break in Donegal one afternoon, I was listening to the radio when the newscaster announced that a Mr Paddy Askins had been charged with the killing of another former patient, Christy Meehan, who had been stabbed with a broken bottle during a drunken row in Askins' flat. I nearly crashed; I had been working with Askins the previous week. When I got back, I checked in with my colleagues who briefed me on the story. Askins had presented himself for work the morning after the murder, while Meehan's corpse lay in his flat off the North Circular Road. However, the landlord, who had been called to inspect a water leak, discovered the body in the flat. Gardaí apprehended Askins on his arrival home. They found him carrying black-plastic refuse sacks and a number of sharp knives.

Good humour, wit and high jinx sustained us. Pranks, usually played on unwitting general-hospital students on secondment to the hospital, were common. One extreme case concerned a poor young nurse from the Adelaide Hospital who, after being dunked in a cold bath, had to take off her unique polka-dot uniform and put on some dry clothes. In the absence of anything else, she dressed in stock-issue patient clothes, which were starkly hickey and could be spotted a mile away. On leaving the hospital, the prankster phoned the gardaí to inform them that a patient had escaped. There was hell to pay when the squad car arrived back at the hospital with the student.

Sympathy for patients often saw staff break the rules, albeit in a very minor way. One man on the ward suffered from late stage Karsacoffs, a disease of the brain similar to Alzheimer's, but caused by alcohol. Some patients were occasionally treated to a bottle of stout after tea and this old man was always pining for a sip. One ward attendant, feeling sorry for him, decided that it would do him no harm to give him a bottle, as he perceived the damage was already done. He handed the old man a bottle but, in the excitement of taking a swig, the stout went against his breath and he suffered a fit of coughing, almost turning blue in the process. The attendant, standing at the other end of the room, sprinted up to the patient and, while he grabbed the Guinness bottle from his hand, roared with fright: 'Give me that, some bloody alcoholic you were!'

I left St Brendan's in 2000. I liked my job and was recognised by colleagues as being pretty good at it but, in the end, I was sort of glad to get out. Despite doing what I believed was a decent interview, my application for a staff position had been unsuccessful. I learnt of my failure to nail down a permanent job shortly after the hospital had made a special presentation to me after winning the 1995 All-Ireland, so I remained on contract work. Fortunately, I had options. My profile as a footballer and my experience as a nurse appealed to the pharmaceutical companies, so I was successful in securing a job as a medical rep and spent the next couple of years on the road.

Understanding the difficulties inherent in working in a psychiatric hospital, I retain huge admiration for the staff in Grangegorman and the great quality of care they provide in extremely testing conditions. The experiences I shared with the patients, unforgettable moments, will endure no matter where my career takes me. Prime wisdom, it is said, comes from what lies before us in our daily lives. For anyone who's ever worked in a hospital, they'll understand exactly what that means.

I wonder what poor old Vinny from Limerick would think of it all.

Chapter 14

Decade of the Duds – Championship 1994

The Rare Auld Times

Painting a rosy picture of the past is hard to avoid as a footballer. The truth about the 1994 season was less flattering than my memories of the year. As an old Latin teacher of mine was fond of reminding his pupils, there is properly no history, only biography.

I have always clung to the belief that I played much better football in 1994 than the previous year, but I was still struggling to assert myself fully in championship football and was still feeding off a diet of scraps in the full-forward line. I know I was going better in training and I don't think my place on the starting team was ever in jeopardy. Yet my contribution on match day was only marginally better than 1993 and it would take another severe kick in the arse to move me – and Dublin – to the next level.

Thankfully that kick in the backside came in the very first game of the 1994 championship against Kildare. This outing would act as a rude awakening to a team that saw an All-Ireland title as the only just reward for their effort.

There was a surreal quality about the opening of the 1994 summer campaign. Firstly, we played Kildare on 18 June, the same day Ireland faced Italy in the World Cup in Giants Stadium, New Jersey. We were a real sideshow, a mere diversion from the World Cup hype. Secondly, the old Cusack Stand had been demolished, so we lined out in a building site in front of barely more than 20,000 people, less than half the attendance of our previous two championship jousts with the Lilywhites. Thirdly, there was a pub strike at the time, so there was a strange atmosphere around Croker as bewildered fans wandered the streets, cans in hand, many decked in green jerseys in anticipation of that night's encounter across the Atlantic.

Not that any of this had any real impact on the game. What affected that, more than anything, was the strong swirling wind that blew around the pitch, making it almost impossible to deliver any kind of quality. Kildare fans were particularly thin on the ground in Croke Park; the buzz that heralded Mick O'Dwyer's arrival was beginning to dissipate. Despite losing to them in an ill-tempered league match in Newbridge earlier that season, we were hot favourites to defeat them in the championship for the third time in a row. What followed was a fairly grim seventy minutes of football, significant, from a Dublin point of view, only for the changes in our personnel and formation. Playing with the strong wind, Kildare raced into a 0-6 to 0-0 lead. We couldn't get out of the traps and it wasn't until the introduction of Brian Stynes to midfield in place of an injured Paul Bealin that we managed to get into the game.

Brian Stynes had followed his older brother Jim out to Australia where he spent a number of years playing Australian Rules football. I had played minor with Brian in 1988 when he was only sixteen years old. A tall, rangy player, he had incredible energy and, though it took him a short while to readjust to Gaelic football, his impact on the team was immediate.

Another significant move saw Vinny Murphy moved out of the full-forward line for the first time in years. He was now placed at left half-forward where his aerial prowess could be employed for kick-outs and where management hoped he would also act as provider rather than as a score-getter.

For a brief while against Kildare, I played in Vinny's old position at full-forward, where I got little change from Davy Dalton who, although a veteran, was still a powerful full-back. Charlie Redmond manned his customary left corner-forward berth, but Niall Guiden lined out in the other corner. Tom Carr had returned to the line-up, but was now placed on the '40' in what would be his last starting role in a Dublin championship team. His suspension in 1993 was a bloody disgrace and it's accepted that it marked the beginning of the end for our former captain. Yet the evidence from his performance against Kildare a year later doesn't really bear this out. I remember he got a bit of stick after the game with some pundits hinting that he was finished. But he worked very hard that day and had a critical hand in our first few scores. A couple of wayward kicks seemed to obscure his worthwhile contribution.

Martin Lynch ran amok in midfield in the first half. Graham Dunne, Noel Donlon, Denis O'Connell and Lynch all hit the target before we'd drawn breath. Then Stynes came on and started to win possession. Redmond grabbed our first score after twenty-two minutes, a typical fifty-yard punt into the wind. We scrapped away and built ourselves some kind of a platform. I managed to score our last point before the break, which was set up by Carr, and we trailed 0-8 to 0-3. The dressing room remained positive, despite the awfulness of our display. None of us believed we could actually be beaten by them. With the wind in our favour, we felt it would only be a matter of time before we broke Kildare's authority.

Researching this particular game only confirms the oddness of the whole occasion. The match took place on a Saturday and RTÉ televised it live to bolster their bumper World Cup package for the day. Injured Irish striker Niall Quinn and team assistant Mick Byrne delivered the half-time analysis live from the States where they were gearing up for the Italy match. Both concurred that Dublin would turn it around.

And, they were right. Nearly. We overhauled Kildare's lead in the closing stages of the game when Vinny Murphy scored an amazing point after fielding a ball over Dalton's head to put us 0-10 to 0-9 ahead. But there was another twist on that most surreal of days. We squandered chances to extend our lead and Kildare snuck back in with two more scores, the last point coming from sub Ken Doyle right on the stroke of full-time. We were gone. Thankfully, John O'Leary didn't see it that way, and his clever, quick kick-out caught Kildare napping. When Johnny Barr won the ball and delivered it up field, who else but Redmond was on hand to equalise from thirty-five yards out in injury-time with his eighth point of the day. 0-11 each.

The usual dressing room ribaldry was absent afterwards. The *olé, olé craic* would have to wait until later that evening. What we couldn't conceal was the smug sense of knowing that we had sickened Kildare. We'd gotten away with an inept performance. Better still, it acted as a warning, dispelling any further danger of complacency.

The pubs may have been on strike, but this only seemed to add to the buzz around the city that evening and there was certainly no restriction on our entry to a pub in Smithfield that evening where I watched the Ireland match with my best mate, Stephen Francis.

Take Two

Despite the fact that this Dublin team had been on the go for some time, the management were still searching for a formula that would produce more fluency after our inept display against Kildare. It was decided that Mick Galvin would replace Murphy, though the former was placed at full-forward. After his rescue act on the first day, Stynes was handed his first championship start alongside Paul Bealin in midfield, with Jack Sheedy moving onto the '40'.

Galvin made a huge difference. His work on and off the ball added variety to our play as evidenced by the number of early scores he set up in the replay. Unlike Redmond and Murphy, he didn't try for a score himself with the same frequency, although you couldn't fault his finishing. What he lacked in speed off the mark, he made up for with guile. After moving Murphy outfield for the drawn game, dropping him altogether was a big move for manager Pat O'Neill. He had been the county's principal ball-winner in the forwards since the late 1980s and it was the first sign that management were thinking of varying their tactics. However, in 1994, it was merely a hiatus for Murphy, who managed to work his way back onto the starting fifteen with a fine display later in the campaign after coming on as a sub against Meath.

We blew Kildare away in the first half of the replay on 3 July. With Galvin and Redmond leading the way up front and Stynes, Bealin and Sheedy dominating the midfield area, we carved out a 0-11 to 0-2 half-time lead. I enjoyed a much better outing this time and I think the significance of Galvin's influence on my own performance can't be ignored. Yet, for all that, we had a terrible wobble just after the break when a Niall Buckley penalty brought Kildare back into the game. Shortly afterwards, Bealin was sent off for a second bookable offence and, before we knew it, it was 0-11 to 1-5. Then I won a breaking ball down near the old Nally Stand and set up a one-two with Galvin, who was tripped by Dalton in the square as he was bearing down on goal. Charlie struck a perfect penalty low to the keeper's right and we were back in business. We defied our numerical disadvantage with some really fluent football and kept Kildare on the back foot for the remainder of the game. Only for Niall Buckley's strong performance after moving to full-forward, we would have been out of sight. We finished up 1-14 to 1-9 winners.

The two meetings with Kildare helped Pat O'Neill and his mentors to establish a settled line-up. With the exceptions of a few tweaks up front, a pattern was emerging in the starting fifteen. In the absence of Eamon Heery, Mick Deegan had nailed down the No. 7 jersey, while Stynes was now a first-choice midfielder.

A week after the Kildare replay, we played Louth in Croke Park in a similar type of game as we opened well, endured a wobble early in the second half, and finished strongly. We led 1-5 to 0-2 at half-time thanks to a goal from Charlie. However, our lead was whittled back shortly after the break when Eugene Judge capitalised on a rebound off the crossbar and flicked a Louth goal past John O'Leary. Buoyed by that score, Louth closed the gap to a point. O'Leary then proved why he was still considered the best keeper in the land with a point-blank save from Stefan White. The save spurred us on and we rattled off a succession of points to win the game 1-15 to 1-8. I grabbed a couple of points in a more industrious performance while Niall Guiden and Mick Galvin bolstered Charlie's contribution with some great finishing from play.

Royal Pardon

The Leinster final against Meath on 31 July turned out to be a mirror image of the previous year's encounter. Typical of games between the two counties, it was a tense, dour battle set against the backdrop of a simmering packed house. Time has enhanced Dublin vs Meath clashes due to the 1991 epic series, but they were rarely classic exhibitions of football. What they lacked in quality, however, they made up for in effort and drama, and the 1994 meeting was no different.

Both sides tore into one another again and this time I had to contend with Colm Coyle's cosy attentions. I didn't fare too badly in that I won a good share of ball off him, particularly in the first half, but I wouldn't have been one of the main protagonists. The big battle of the day centred on Keith Barr and Colm O'Rourke who fought like dogs for possession. Paddy Moran was another Dublin player who always rose manfully to the Royal challenge and, on one occasion in the first half, he put his head into a collision with O'Rourke where most people wouldn't have driven their car. Bernard Flynn caused big problems for Dublin early on with his ability to find space and he probably would have rocked us back with a goal only for John O'Leary, who ran nearly thirty yards from his goalmouth to haul him down.

Stynes continued his noteworthy introduction to senior championship football, not only giving Dublin an important foothold in midfield, but also getting forward and grabbing a vital point in each half. Meath led by 0-5 to 0-3 at the break and they would have been further ahead if a young Trevor Giles hadn't found Hill 16 so intimidating when lining up his placed balls. Our hand was strengthened considerably after the break with the introduction of both Paul Clarke and Vinny Murphy. Clarke and Stynes edged Dublin into a 0-6 to 0-5 lead when Murphy pulled down three great balls around the middle and helped put Meath on the back foot. O'Rourke, uncharacteristically, missed two good chances and I matched his carelessness by wasting an opportunity to extend Dublin's 0-8 to 0-6 advantage. Then a mistake by Meath keeper, Mickey McQuillan, handed us a match-winning advantage. Charlie Redmond curled a free from under the Hogan Stand but, while the kick hadn't the necessary legs to go over the bar, the ball squirmed through McQuillan's hands and into the net. I added a point to put us 1-9 to 0-6 in front, an unassailable lead against most opposition.

However, Meath's resilience was an unquestionable attribute in the 1980s and 1990s and, sure to form, they clawed their way back, firstly with a point from Brendan Reilly and then with a fantastic individual goal from wing-back Graham Geraghty who, panther-like, got the jump on Niall Guiden and travelled about eighty yards before deftly finishing to the Canal End goal. PJ Gillic added a point and, *déja vu*, Meath were a point behind Dublin with two minutes left in a Leinster championship decider. It's funny how fortune does the rounds. Meath were awarded a free about fifty-five yards from goal, right at the death. Gillic and O'Rourke seemed to get locked in a discussion over who was going to take it and I remember thinking that had to be a good sign. Gillic was entrusted with the kick and I recall, vividly, staring at the crowded Canal End terrace for the first indication of the ball's trajectory. The crowd remained static. 1-9 to 1-8, we had beaten Meath again for our third Leinster title on the trot.

I walked back into the dressing room expecting a lot of whooping and hollering. Instead there was restraint. Underlying the deep satisfaction of getting another one over on our closest rivals was the fact that, for the Dublin players who had played in the four games in 1991, a hundred victories over Meath couldn't really erase the trauma of that defeat. A one-point win for the second year in a row was hardly dancing-on-their-grave stuff. After all, we had surrendered the unassailable lead. There was also a grudging respect for the opposition that took the edge off the obvious animosity we shared towards each other.

Years later, many of the players from both sides became pretty good friends, which I suppose is the beauty of sport. Still, Meath as a team will always raise my hackles despite my fondness for most, if not all, of the players I soldiered against.

False Dawn

Our reward for dispatching the neighbours was another novelty show All-Ireland semi-final, this time with Croke Park first-timers Leitrim. Their historic Connacht championship success under John O'Mahony earned them a 21 August date with Dublin and generated even bigger hype than Clare had two years previously. Fabulous as the occasion was for Leitrim and neutrals alike, it was never going to be a contest. Unlike 1992, Dublin were now a battle-hardened outfit bearing the scars of three solid years on the road. It wasn't cockiness – Dublin were as short as 1/10 favourites with the bookies.

After arriving in Croke Park that day, most of us sat pitch-side, watching a talented Galway minor side defeat Dublin. Little did we know at the time that Galway youngsters Michael Donnellan, John Divilly, Declan Meehan and Paul Clancy would all go on to win senior All-Ireland medals. The Dublin team also had its share of players destined for the step-up, including Ian Robertson and Ciarán Whelan. However, the one man playing who was destined to make an immediate impact was Jason Sherlock, an impish forward from my own club who had already forged a fledgling reputation on the soccer field and on the basketball court.

Less than an hour later, Leitrim were greeted onto the Jones' Road turf for the first time with a tumultuous din and, as we assembled for the pre-match parade, you could sense the novel excitement. There was a palpable feeling of something historic. Yet any sympathy or romance evaporated when Leitrim broke away from the parade before we reached Hill 16, a ploy carried out by

Derry a year previously. I suppose it was a psychological gesture to Dublin supporters, an 'up yours' kind of thing. I always considered the parade a daft imposition anyway, so it didn't faze me unduly. When you're keyed-up for a big championship game, after months of training, the last thing you want to do is to saunter around after a band or, for that matter, stand jogging on the spot waiting for them to depart at half-time. I often get the impression that the Artane Boys Band means more to some GAA officials than the players do.

Leitrim started positively, looking nothing like Croke Park debutants. We looked anything but 1/10 favourites as the water was being tested in the first five minutes. We were also missing Paul Curran who had been ruled out with a fractured cheekbone and his place at wing-back was taken by the versatile Paul Clarke. I was marked initially by left corner-back Fergal Reynolds, although Joe Honeyman was subsequently shifted onto me. Ironically, Reynolds later became a rep for the Gaelic Players' Association and a good ally of mine. Another irony of course was that, some years later, Leitrim's captain, Declan Darcy, would play alongside me when I captained Dublin.

Jack Sheedy had returned to the Dublin midfield after a quiet enough Leinster final on the '40' and he took a while to impose himself on veteran Mickey Quinn. Seamus Quinn, still an under-21, stood out from the off at fullback and cut out a lot of ball destined for our full-forward trio.

However, a sequence of passes between myself and Charlie Redmond close to the Canal End goal ended with Charlie planting a fairly easy goal past Leitrim's diminutive keeper, Martin McHugh. My hand pass to Redmond was questioned after the game, but I maintain that I got a clean strike on the ball. Regardless, the goal stood, and although Leitrim didn't lack for gallantry, they never regained any superiority afterwards.

Before half-time, Mick Galvin landed the goal of the season, completing a sweeping move that had started in our fullback line with Dermot Deasy. Deasy fed Paddy Moran on the 21-yard line at the Hill end. Moran drove a long ball out to the wing on the Cusack Stand side, where Galvin picked it up about fifty yards out. He played a one-two with Niall Guiden before passing on to Mick Deegan who'd raced forward in support. Deegan slipped it back to Galvin who thumped it to the roof of the net from sixteen yards out. Just as well he didn't miss as myself and Charlie were in better scoring positions inside!

The second half was a procession. Despite a Leitrim goal by Colm McGlynn, we continued to pull away and, in hindsight, the facile nature of our victory did nothing to steel us for the ultimate challenge on 18 September. I had the run of the corner and my performance earned me a sport-star-of-the-week award from the *Irish Independent*. I was particularly pleased with the award because the annual ceremony held by the paper gave me a rare chance to meet top players and athletes from other sports. Anyway, players may feign cynicism about awards and tokens of recognition but, deep down, they appreciate them.

Paul Bealin, Tom Carr and dual player, Liam Walsh, all got a run after the break against Leitrim and the game was to mark Carr's last championship action in a Dublin shirt. I concluded proceedings with a goal after latching on to a long ball from Clarke, which sealed a 3-15 to 1-9 win. Funny how time plays tricks, but I had an image in my mind for years that I nearly got decapitated in the process of finding the net. Closer inspection reveals a mere tap in the face. There is no history, only biography.

Down, Down To Hell

Unfortunately, it's difficult to put a spin on the cruel reality of what happened in the 1994 All-Ireland final against Down. This was a pure disaster for Dublin.

It all seemed so promising in the afterglow of our semi-final. Our build-up was smooth and focused. Belief was strong that the failures of the past would be rectified if we all respected our responsibilities. The fact that we were playing the aristocrats of Ulster football, by then clearly the dominant province, was drilled home. Respect for the opposition wasn't in question. O'Neill and his selectors were all too aware of Down's strengths and, in particular, the threat posed by Mickey Linden, arguably the most potent forward of that time. Linden's blistering pace would have to be countered.

However, we lost our corner-back Ciarán Walsh – the man in line to mark Linden – through injury, in circumstances that still rankle with the Dublin management. Three weeks before the final, the Dublin championship quarter-finals were scheduled to take place. Fearful of losing players to injury, O'Neill contacted county chairman John Bailey requesting a postponement of the fixtures and, understanding the frustration of the clubs, the Dublin manager even offered to meet with representatives of the eight club teams to state his case. Bailey assured O'Neill that the games would be put off until after the All-Ireland. However, the next day, O'Neill heard a radio bulletin announcing that the Dublin club games would in fact be going ahead. He was furious and felt seriously let down by the senior county official. Obviously, Bailey knew where his priorities lay, but he didn't even afford Pat the opportunity to talk with the clubs involved. O'Neill read the riot act to the chairman and told him he didn't want him anywhere near the squad in the future.

O'Neill's worst fears were realised when Walsh injured himself playing for St Anne's and was ruled out of the final. The knock-on effect of the injury was to have a huge bearing on the All-Ireland. O'Neill and his selectors now had to make alternative arrangements. Paul Curran, who had himself just recovered from injury, was detailed to mark Linden.

O'Neill's judgement was shaped primarily by a league match in Newcastle earlier in the year when Curran had moved to corner-back to mark Linden and succeeded not only in negating the Down man's influence, but actually going on to kick two points himself.

I concurred with management that it was the best plan. Curran had marked me in training for three weeks and his pace and ability to play you from in front seemed perfect for the task in hand.

The preparation for the final was the best I had experienced to date. I was beginning to communicate my feelings to management and I remember going for a kick around with Mick Galvin and selector Jim Brogan up in St Oliver Plunkett's ground off the Navan Road the week of the game. I told Brogan that I felt Down were a manufactured team and thus were vulnerable. He agreed, though in hindsight our interpretation of what we perceived to be Down's 'flawed' system was incorrect. My confidence was confirmed in a letter I sent to Stephen Francis in Boston, dated the Wednesday before the final, where I stated that I was optimistic I'd have a medal in my arse pocket before the weekend was out. Behind all the optimism was probably the fragile belief that we couldn't self-destruct again.

Psychologist Tom Moriarity was also harnessed by management to assist with the collective mindset and, while this wasn't to everyone's liking, it seemed a positive move given the nature of our defeats the previous two years. Sports psychology was in its infancy in Gaelic games and we had only really begun to experiment with it that year. Yet psychology came to the fore when we met in Parnell Park the day before the final for a squad meeting. Brogan delivered an evocative slideshow that included images of the Sam Maguire, All-Ireland medals and the like. It sounds a bit twee, but when you consider the fuss that was made of Armagh manager Joe Kernan's apparent half-time performance in the 2002 All-Ireland final – where he produced his jersey and runners-up plaque – then it doesn't seem so quaint. Had we won the 1994 decider, I'm certain you would have seen slideshows up and down the country.

Something happened after the show that still resonates with me and many of the players to this day. After the management had briefed us, they left the room and allowed us to speak among ourselves. As the players' meeting developed, everyone felt obliged to speak and the language became more and more passionate, with each contributor digging deeper into himself to articulate the collective desire to win this game. A huge amount of emotional energy was discharged at that meeting. In fact I remember rushing to the car without speaking to anyone afterwards because I had tears in my eyes. I wasn't alone. I discovered, subsequently, that many of the other players felt the exact same way. Had we lined out for the final there and then, I don't think any team would have beaten us. Problem was, the game was twenty-four hours later.

The team talk in the dressing room the following afternoon was much more muted and players seemed slightly on edge after their outpourings on the Saturday. Heavy rain started to fall about an hour before the game, which seemed to add to the uneasiness. The conditions would also have a huge bearing on the outcome.

I lined out at top of the right as usual where I was marked by Paul Higgins, a strong corner-back and a good reader of the game. Down's physical presence was substantial. Superior strength was an advantage we enjoyed over most opposition, but we were on the back foot that day, particularly on a heavy pitch. We started brightly enough, but two missed chances early in the game allowed Down to take the initiative and grab the first score. The circumstances surrounding that first point were to effectively shape the course of the game and have remained painfully vivid in the memories of Dublin supporters since. A ball was played towards Mickey Linden who was situated in the corner of Hill 16 and the new Cusack Stand (half of which was opened for the final). Paul

Curran read the situation and, as a wing-back, instinctively got out in front to try and intercept the pass. However, he slipped and the ball broke inside to Linden who set up midfielder Gregory McCartan for a point. Considering most of the talk in the build-up to this game centred on the Curran-Linden duel, the incident had a seriously unsettling effect on Curran, who was considered by many to be our finest player. Over the next fifteen minutes, the harder he tried the worse things got. Linden got the upper hand and won a series of frees and grabbed an early point himself.

Initially, we kept in touch. Jack Sheedy moved to midfield and broke forward for a point that left us trailing 0-5 to 0-3. Then Curran and Paul Clarke got sucked into a tackle on our 21-yard line. Both ended up on the deck while the ball was broken to their two respective markers, Linden and James McCartan, both of whom had a clear sight of John O'Leary's goal. Linden calmly slipped the ball to McCartan who rounded O'Leary and tapped into an empty net. It was a serious body-blow. In a tight match on a heavy pitch, it was ball-breaking to concede such a score. Clarke was moved onto Linden while Curran was released to the half-back line.

While the switch may have been too late, we had our chances. Niall Guiden made a surging run forward and clipped a fisted point over the bar to leave the score 1-6 to 0-5. However, I was standing on the edge of the small square with a free strike on goal. Had he slipped it to me, well, who knows? Ironically, in the second half, Guiden found himself free in the square when Charlie Redmond could have played him through on goal, but instead the latter had a shot for a point blocked down. I suppose Guiden did what most Dublin forwards did at the time: scored when they had the chance. It's hard to criticise a player for doing just that, but the older I got the more I realised that the winning of tight games often lay in a player's ability to make an accurate, split-second decision, either to take or sacrifice a handy point or pass to a colleague who may be in a position to try for a goal. There is no time to weigh up these opportunities; instinct and experience provide the only guidance. We've all made the wrong call at times in tight matches. Suffice to say, at that juncture, a point didn't stop Down in their tracks.

We retired at the break 1-8 to 0-7 in arrears, not an insurmountable lead, but the game hadn't really swung in our favour for any decent spell. The spine of

Down's team, particularly in their defence, was dominant. Brian Burns and Barry Breen marshalled Mick Galvin and Vinny Murphy well. I was fitful, getting on to the odd ball, but I didn't really escape Higgins' clutches.

We changed our sodden jerseys at half-time for dry ones and faced into Hill 16 to try and wrestle control of our destiny. Little changed initially in the second half, although Paul Bealin's introduction for Pat Gilroy bolstered our midfield somewhat. I managed a point, but Down kept their advantage and with the score at 1-12 to 0-9, it looked like we would limp to defeat. I was moved briefly to centre-forward while Murphy was thrown back into his old stomping ground in the square. I felt liberated out there. I got on the first two balls that came my way and set up a score. Then Seán Cahill came on for Galvin and I was shoved back into the corner. It did not seem to make sense.

For the remaining twenty minutes, Down didn't score again. At last we took charge at midfield and started to drive at them and, for a period, it looked like they would fold. Redmond and Cahill closed the gap, but our efforts were generally haphazard. In fact, our sequence of missed chances, wrong options, spilled ball, and snatched opportunities is woefully hard to digest, even a decade later. We resorted to individual effort, trying too hard. The only thing collective about our performance was the malaise.

Then came the final hammer blow. Eight minutes from time, we trailed 1-12 to 0-12. Johnny Barr got on to a long ball broken in the square and hand passed it to me. I was surrounded by Down men, hauled to the ground, and referee Tommy Sugrue awarded a penalty. Some disputed this afterwards because the camera angle doesn't really capture the illegal challenge. But I *was* fouled, no question. Charlie hit the penalty at a good height for Down keeper Niall Collins and, while the ball was parried, Down captain DJ Kane managed to prevent both Charlie and sub Johnny Barr from connecting with the rebound. My abiding memory of this incident was James McCartan jumping into Collins' arms. It was sickening.

I would never criticise Redmond for his penalty misses. He had the balls to stand up and take them, despite repeated, high-profile disappointments. Before the moment he struck that penalty, he had scored 4-29 of our total in the championship and he added another point before the end. Whatever about the odd over-elaboration or tendency to be a bit petulant, he really owed Dublin nothing.

We continued to own the ball for the remainder of the game, but only managed another point. Down's physical stature suited a rearguard action and they employed a primitive 'men-behind-the-ball' strategy with half-forward Ross Carr, in particular, doing a lot of sweeping in defence.

In the closing stages, Paul Clarke collided with Down midfielder Conor Deegan and I remember seeing the latter's hand go up in a frantic gesture to the sideline, a real bad sign. Lucky man though, I thought. He'll do his convalescing with an All-Ireland medal in his pocket.

The final whistle sounded on Dublin's fourth serious failure in as many years. I had now landed the hat-trick. We could have already eclipsed our illustrious forebears from the Seventies by this stage but, instead, we were ultimate failures. The decade of the Duds.

Reasons for our display weren't easily found. Despite the Curran gamble backfiring, no one could grasp anything tangible. We had ample time and opportunity to overcome our early mistakes; we panicked and just couldn't engineer scores. It might be a little churlish to say we left it behind us because the better team won, but it's hard not to lean that way when you consider our dominance in the closing stages. Did Down succeed despite choking at the conclusion of the game? Or were they ahead of the times – content to defend their slender lead? I remember skulking out of Croke Park thinking that it just wasn't meant to be.

Unlike 1992 and 1993, there was a nastier edge to the fallout. Everyone was irritable and scapegoats were sought by the different cliques on the panel. The following day, we were given to understand that Niall Guiden had attended a wedding on the Friday night before the game, which raised the hackles of more than one squad member. This was probably handy for everyone because it excused self-analysis, but it left a sour taste nonetheless. Then, that night, the mood darkened again when Johnny Barr, completely out of character, was arrested after a bizarre incident where he produced a replica gun on a bouncer who had thrown him out of a nightclub. Johnny was a great character and normally put the best side out, even in defeat.

This unsavoury incident isn't as remarkable as you might think. Volatility is a real problem in the wake of a traumatic defeat. A lot of young men aren't that well-equipped to deal with such a psychological downer, particularly because they have just shared a dressing room and a collective goal for over nine months, only to be cast adrift as individuals with nothing to show for their troubles. With so much inflammatory material around, it doesn't take much to ignite a situation or provoke a response.

Only three days earlier, I felt we were the most professional outfit Gaelic football had ever seen. Our preparations appeared flawless. We had intelligent, assertive management, huge talent in the squad, a tough core. Now people were feeling fucking sorry for us.

When that happens, you know you're in trouble.

Chapter 15

Rhapsody in Blue – Championship 1995

American Wake

In the wake of our defeat in 1994, I headed over to America to play in the New York championship; one of the few perks then available to players. For our trouble, we received sums of about $500 to $1,000 to play after receiving a 'weekend sanction' from Croke Park. This practice is now defunct, but it was really popular back in the Eighties and Nineties. The local players, some of whom would have their noses out of joint, referred to the travelling inter-county players as 'the Aer Lingus All Stars'.

I travelled on a number of occasions, playing for Leitrim and Kerry. I won three championship medals while I was there. Contrary to popular opinion, we actually took these games fairly seriously. I first played alongside Wicklow's Kevin O'Brien, already a veteran at this game, and our attitude was that if someone was paying good money to bring us out, then we wouldn't let them down. Not all players abided by this philosophy, seeing it as a free skite in the Big Apple rather than a professional commitment and, consequently, they were not invited back. My take was that there was plenty of time to enjoy yourself after the match.

The big New York games were littered with great stories. One hungover inter-county luminary was struggling to make any impact for Connemara Gaels on a swelteringly hot day in Gaelic Park when the coach lit on him at half-time over his poor display. 'Ah Jayzus,' he countered. 'How could I be expected to perform on that pitch? There isn't a fucking blade of grass on it.' 'Son,' replied the coach, 'I didn't bring you out here to graze.'

147

The first final I played in was a veritable who's who of Gaelic football at the time. The teams included Kevin O'Brien, Dublin's Pat Gilroy and Ciarán Walsh, Down's James McCartan, Paul Higgins and Brian Burns, Cork's Larry Tompkins and Niall Cahalane, among others. Like many of these trans-Atlantic clashes, it was an ill-tempered affair played on the dusty surface of Gaelic Park. Our Leitrim team defeated Donegal and I picked up an 'Most Valuable Player' award so my experience of the whole scene was pretty good. However, a lot of players had nasty experiences of the trip, particularly if they lost or failed to perform, as they were made feel pretty lousy in the aftermath.

In the following final in which the same two teams met again, Leitrim beat Donegal in the most bizarre circumstances. Donegal fielded a completely home-based outfit without any imported stars. Their approach seemed to be paying off as they were totally dominant and were leading by two points in the dying seconds of a brutal, low-scoring encounter. Then Gregory McCartan was awarded a 21-yard free but, before he could kick it, the ball was knocked from his hand by an opponent and the buzzer went to signal the end of the game. The crowd invaded the pitch, with the Donegal supporters sure their side had prevailed. However, the ref cleared the pitch after about five minutes so that the free could be taken. Donegal placed all fifteen players on the goal-line, but McCartan drop-kicked an absolute thumping shot through the thicket and into the back stanchion to win the game by a point. Now it was the turn of the Leitrim supporters and players to revel in the moment as the bewildered Donegal lads trooped off.

My last success in New York was for Kerry when I was invited to play for the county by Paddy Kearney from West Kerry. Paddy became a good friend of mine and we enjoyed many a good night in Queen's and Manhattan.

A 'Donkey' Off Our Backs

While Dublin's ability to claim the ultimate prize was still in doubt, our honesty on the field was never questioned. Where we perhaps failed the honesty test more than anywhere else was in the video room. Post-match video analysis, already the norm for most teams, consisted of an open forum where players were called to task for their on-field actions. In those days everyone was very defensive about their performances, something that's changed considerably in the recent years. Nowadays, I find players are a bit too willing to own up to their mistakes – a bit like an AA meeting – as if their honesty will somehow absolve them from their shortcomings. In 1995 a number of players were prepared to spoof their way through these sessions. Although we were exposed on screen, no one took responsibility for mistakes and we learned how to develop different excuses to suitably muddy the waters. Some were particularly adept at wriggling out of owning up to a gaffe. If Paul Bealin missed a catch in midfield, he'd point the finger at Brian Stynes, often concluding his defence with 'Isn't that right Stynesie?' The latter would gaze back, bemused. If Paddy Moran missed a tackle, he'd frequently claim that the referee had censured him moments previously – off screen, he would add – warning of an imminent booking. The half-backs, criticised for holding onto the ball too long, would counter that no forward was showing for the pass. Forwards, in turn, would complain that there was no point showing because the half-backs wouldn't deliver the ball anyway. On one occasion, the forwards suggested to the management that the half-backs should be allowed play with a ball of their own. However, Paul Curran delivered the final riposte when asserting that if the forwards were any good, he'd be happy to pass the ball!

At one such session, while we were preparing for the 1995 championship, Pat O'Neill addressed us afterwards about a video which had been compiled following Down's success the previous September. No one except Vinny Murphy had seen the tape, but O'Neill was keen to inform us of its content. Every so often during his account of what Down said and did he would look over to Vinny for confirmation: 'That was it Vinny, wasn't it?' Vinny would nod. O'Neill was fond, however, of mimicking the various regional accents of our opponents and he was particularly taken by the closing line in the All-Ireland champions' recording which simply said 'losers win nothing'. However, he delivered the line to us with a northern twang. 'Losers wan nawhin!' he exclaimed. At which point, Vinny shot up and disagreed: 'Dat's not what dey said, Pa'. Dey said "LEWSERS WIN NUTTIN!"'

The traumatic end to 1994 had the doomsayers out in force. Many, even our fans, felt the death knell had been sounded for this Dublin team. However, once the panel convened again for the league, we weren't long bonding again. If anything we were less cliquish than had hitherto been the case, with the

Northside gang frequently crossing the Liffey in a self-sacrificing, ecumenical gesture. Actually, we travelled south because of the hilarious *craic* in The Submarine Bar in Crumlin on a Monday night, where we were paraded around like Premiership stars before adjourning to the Spawell for a late one, a gang of groupies in tow.

Once we had reconvened, the management got to work on us with relative ease. After all, there was no need to map out the road ahead. Yet, for all our desire to complete what we all believed was unfinished business, the league wasn't taken seriously. It had failed in recent times to provide a platform for us to win the All-Ireland, so there was room to experiment. However, the league did provide an opportunity for Jason Sherlock, a minor in 1994, to mark his arrival on the senior stage, something he succeeded in doing, scoring a goal against Kerry down in Tralee. Though still juggling a UCD soccer career with his Gaelic football commitments, and only nineteen years old, his contribution the following summer would be profound.

Several things fell in to place for us in 1995. As well as Sherlock's arrival, the industrious Jim Gavin was back in the frame after missing the previous championship when his arm had been broken by Paddy Moran during a training session (he wasn't the first casualty of 'Puck' Moran's whole-hearted approach to games of backs and forwards). Paul Clarke continued his great form and I was prepared for centre-forward while, in defence, Keith Galvin quickly made a name for himself. In the absence of Jack Sheedy, who had badly damaged his knee, Paul Bealin and Brian Stynes forged a formidable midfield partnership. However, psychologically we were stronger than ever, which enabled Fran Ryder to exact even more from every individual, to raise the bar another fraction.

Here lay the key to our success.

Mind Games

The psychology of sport probably underpins most people's interest in it. We marvel at the physical and the aesthetic, but we are truly captivated by the psychological. It is in the unknown depths of the mind where battles are won and lost. Sport bears that out in all its cruel beauty. For four years, Dublin had fallen prostrate when faced with the moment of truth, and seemed to be mentally incapable of crossing the line. Observers had begun to accept that providence had abandoned the county footballers and that there would be no redemption.

Thankfully, we didn't accept this. Ten years later, I can only marvel at the resilience of the panel and our management. Our belief that we would once again achieve our ultimate goal was unshakeable as was our confidence in our own ability. Yet the demon of All-Ireland failure remained perched on our shoulders and only the gleaming sight of Sam Maguire could really rid us of the perennial darkness of defeat. That obsession was shared collectively.

We were the most consistent team in the country for years yet, because we repeatedly fell at the final hurdle, or close to it, we continued to raise more questions than we actually answered. Many of these questions were the age-old conundrums that exercise the minds of all sports fans. What gives a team a winning edge? How do perennial losers overcome their collective impediments? Why does tradition perpetuate success or condemn teams to regular failure? Why do racing certainties lose?

When a team achieves success, we often rather obliquely refer to the 'X' factor; the obscure final ingredient that tips the balance. Recent advances in sports science and, in particular, sports psychology, have helped GAA managers and players to understand this 'X' factor. Eureka! Unfortunately, it's not that simple. A greater understanding of the psychology of sport hasn't turned us into football alchemists overnight. What it reveals is an extensive list of qualities, attributes and desired strengths that are required to cut a winning edge. A checklist for success, if you like.

Pat O'Neill's task in 1995 was to reshuffle his deck of cards again and see could he find a winning hand. He needed an ace and, this time, fate would deal him one.

We were relegated from Division One of the national league in 1995 after drawing the final game of an ambivalent campaign against Derry in Croke Park in February. The game was something of a landmark. We were in the middle of pretty serious training, yet we managed to perform well in a tasty encounter between two sides with serious September designs. Derry actually went on to win the league, though lost out in Ulster later in the year to Tyrone.

It also marked my first proper appearance at centre-forward where I managed to score 1-1 off their All-Ireland winning captain, Henry Downey. This was despite training, without permission, with the Leinster hockey team that morning.

Keeping my double dealing under wraps, I had more or less nailed down a new role for myself on the half-forward line. It was liberating to play in an area where I wasn't as dependent on the service of others. I could win my own ball and look to create as well as take a score. I suppose most forwards will only ever feel really fulfilled when they score in a game though, and following my knee injury as an 18-year-old, I had conceded that I would never really become the high-scoring forward that my minor career might have promised. That said, playing on the '40' in 1995, I actually scored a lot more than I probably was expected to, matching the tallies I had accrued in previous years in the corner-forward berth.

My liberation wasn't just positional. I had shed my customary knee bandage and was moving more freely than at any other time since rupturing my knee ligaments for the second time two years previously. It's funny how you compartmentalise the highs and lows of the past, with the former receiving a much more prominent billing in the memory banks. I can remember the exact training regime that season, maybe because Fran Ryder was a stickler for routine. Having moved out to the relative privacy of Trinity College's sports grounds in Santry, our training regime was based on interval speed work. Following stretching and a warm-up, our session would begin with a brisk twelve-minute run. Then we would run 4 x 400m, 4 x 200m, 5 x 100m and 5 x 50m. Our times were all logged and would be posted on the dressing room wall at the following session, so it was impossible to swing the lead. Training would conclude with a match, which was usually an intense affair, particularly in the vicinity of Paddy Moran. Funny enough, we did little if any formal weights training, nor did we do a huge amount of strength exercises like press-ups, squats or sit-ups. Maybe it was accepted that we did that work ourselves or that our residual strength was adequate. Getting our heads right was probably of greater concern.

Jason Sherlock's Championship Debut – Dublin vs Louth

We travelled to Navan on 9 July to play Louth in our first outing of the 1995 Leinster campaign. Confidence and self-belief were high and, unlike the previous year, we hit the ground running this time. This was something of an achievement, given our tortuous and at times hair-raising bus journey through the well-oiled throng that lined the streets on the way up to Páirc Tailteann. There were no warm-up facilities of any kind at that time. We literally togged out and did whatever we could manage in the dressing room. Several players would try and do exercises to get themselves going. Paul Curran, for example, always did press-ups. I would go into the showers with a ball while some were content to strap themselves up and fiddle around with their laces. As we prepared in Navan, Pat O'Neill reminded us that the last time Louth defeated Dublin in the championship was back in 1973, when he himself was playing.

Despite conceding two goals to Louth, it was a pretty successful evening's work and we managed to defeat them 0-19 to 2-5. The game had a late throw-in for television purposes, so we had a run-out the previous evening in Parnell Park to familiarise ourselves with late starting time. Keith Galvin came in at corner-back for the injured Ciarán Walsh and franked his arrival by kicking a point after following his marker into midfield. I had lined out at right corner-forward, but traded places shortly after the throw-in with centre-forward Vinny Murphy. The move, which had been planned, worked out pretty well for me even though I had to contend with veteran centre-back Stephen Melia. I relished the constant involvement that such a pivotal role entailed and an early point helped settle me.

O'Neill, who always had a penchant for playing midfielders all over the park, had started Seán Cahill up front. However, after missing a couple of chances, the big garda was replaced after twenty minutes by Jason Sherlock. Jayo's impact was immediate. Less than sixty seconds after running on for his championship debut to rapturous applause, he had won a penalty. His speed of turn, and of thought, marked him apart immediately. Needless to say, he shipped a nice elbow from Gareth O'Neill before half-time, just to welcome him properly to championship football. Scarred by his high-profile misses, Charlie Redmond had ceded the role of penalty-taker, though Paul Clarke, his successor, fared no better, as his well-placed kick was saved by Niall O'Donnell. The more things change…

Buoyed by the miss, Louth came at us and goals either side of the break gave them a footing. Still, Clarke showed great resolve by continuing to perform after his miss while Redmond essentially won the game for us by scoring nine points. With Jim Gavin replacing Murphy late on, our final championship line-up was beginning to take shape.

I was really pleased with my own game at centre-forward, particularly early on when things were up for grabs, but why RTÉ television's *The Sunday Game* decided to name me man-of-the-match, considering Redmond's nine-point haul, I'll never really know. Anyway, I received the much-vaunted Festina wristwatch for my troubles, a gaudy trinket that I wouldn't even wear to the Seventies' night in the Spawell.

Giving it Socks – Dublin vs Laois

We were back in Navan for our next round on a sun-drenched 9 July. Nearly 30,000 fans packed into Páirc Tailteann, most of whom seemed to congregate around our bus again. This time I thought they'd overturn the bloody thing on the way into the ground. Significantly, Jason Sherlock was pencilled in from the start and, while Seán Cahill retained his place, Vinny Murphy was relegated to the bench.

Laois were well prepared for the challenge and should have gone a goal up after only fifteen seconds when Damien Delaney blazed wide in a one-on-one with John O'Leary. The chance at least signalled Laois's ambition and we had to endure a robust encounter. Jason Sherlock nearly hit the net in the first half after an excellent one-two with Mick Galvin. Galvin, already a veteran in the squad, was instrumental in bringing Jason along. They became good friends – Galvin was very aware of Jason's presence on the field and knew that speed was of the essence if our new rising star was to prosper.

Tied at 0-5 apiece at half-time, selector Jim Brogan moved me to left half-forward for the restart, as their centre-back Denis Lalor had kept me in check. The switch onto Eamon Delaney really opened up the game for me. Not only that, Paul Clarke excelled on the '40' with two quick points, so the management used the same interchange throughout the championship whenever either of us began to stagnate. With O'Leary acting as a sweeper and Paddy Moran and Keith Galvin dominating in defence, Laois lost their lustre somewhat and, when I grabbed the next point to put us 0-8 to 0-5 up, we started to turn the screw. The strange, almost spooky, thing about that point is that I had previously visualised taking such a score, almost exactly. The ref hopped a ball between two players and it broke to my man but, as he was about to collect, I nipped in on his blind side and drew it away from him into my own path. I soloed along the left wing under the stand and, after cutting inside, used Denis Lalor as leverage to swing the ball over the bar with my bad foot. Imagining a scenario in advance that actually transpires on the field of play is almost phenomenal. Many athletes recount similar tales. I remember jogging out after that score with the music from the X-files ringing in my ears. Later I would understand more about the concept of visualisation and how important it can be for success.

The real phenomenon that day arrived thirteen minutes from the end of the game, when the GAA's first real superstar exploded onto the scene. A probing ball from Jim Gavin was collected by Jason Sherlock who, after spinning away from George Doyle, hammered home a decisive goal with his stockinged foot. The goal, well documented in the GAA's annals, did more than make a name for Jayo. It generated a buzz in Dublin and, grudgingly, further afield. Sherlock won the game for Dublin, established himself as a senior player and had every kid in the country chasing him wherever he turned. How the association failed to formally capitalise on his popularity in the interim beggars belief. Keeping their heads deeply buried in the soil of the 1950s, the GAA's ruling fathers all but ignored his appeal. Not their sort of chap really. Down with that sort of thing. He'll disappear, they thought. Not so. A decade has passed since that landmark. He's been victimised on and off the field, spat at by a former senior Dublin official and under-21 selector, constantly written off and, the greatest joke of all, accused of being greedy just for being one of the few players to assert himself properly in the ever-increasing commercial world of the GAA. Sherlock is anything but greedy. He is a generous, helpful character who has done more to promote our games among children than anyone realises. He has survived, endured and, most significantly, improved. I was fortunate to have played with Jason throughout the last ten years for both club and county and can vouch for his exemplary attitude, his physical and moral courage and his principles. The only area where we didn't really see eye-to-eye was over the issue of playing through injury, but I'm still uncertain which of us was really right. It is a pity, though, that the game had no career to offer him. Fortune doesn't always favour the brave.

From a historical point of view, he made the difference in 1995. Walking into the dressing rooms in Navan that afternoon 1-13 to 0-9 as the victors over a strong Laois side, the sense of expectation was palpable. Despite struggling for periods during the game, no one had under-performed. Even the substitutes contributed handsomely, though Vinny Murphy's immediate prospects of making the starting line-up may have been improved had he rattled the net in the dying moments after being cleverly set up by Sherlock.

We sensed one of our future opponents had a hiding coming to them. Little did we know that the old enemy would be on the receiving end three weeks later.

Royal Jelly – Dublin vs Meath

History has preserved a nice snapshot of 30 July 1995 in my mind. Though we would eventually surrender the initiative to Meath again, at least my career included that blue-drenched celebration.

There was nothing unusual about the build-up to the game. There was still no special pre-match programme to follow, so I had my usual early-morning cycle, joined my father and headed to headquarters, which now boasted the magnificent new Cusack Stand. Though the new edifice lorded over Jones' Road, we were still stationed in the old dressing rooms under the Hogan, so I followed my own routine of togging out and heading straight to the shower area with a ball to go through my hand-passing drills. The pressure on the players was enormous and when we went thorough our warm-up on the pitch, it was noticeably difficult to breathe in the stifling heat. Yet, once the ball was introduced – and dutifully ignored as was the case for the opening minutes in most Meath-Dublin clashes – Charlie Redmond and Robbie O'Malley traded blows and Paddy Moran gave Colm O'Rourke the respect he felt the veteran Meath man deserved, shadowing him everywhere he went.

With the initial sorting out completed, we started to edge the first half, after trading early points. I kicked a sideline ball over for a point down at the Hill end of the Cusack, which settled me personally, but our whole forward unit –

which now included Jim Gavin from the start – was working really hard. Jason Sherlock was closely marked by Colm Coyle and it wasn't long before he managed to clock Sherlock and follow up with a few choice words. Thankfully, Jason scored the next point after being set up by Mick Galvin. We led 0-8 to 0-4 at half-time and the mood in the dressing room was decidedly upbeat without being foolhardy. We knew we were better but we also knew that being better counted for little against Meath.

The second, frantic thirty-five minutes were probably my most enjoyable in twenty years of football. Not only did everything fall into place for me and the whole team, but it did so against Meath, against Cormac Murphy. It wasn't a rout, far from it. Rather it was the manner in which we responded to adversity that was most pleasing. When Evan Kelly's goal levelled the match and Graham Geraghty added a point to put them 1-7 to 0-9 up, negating all our good early work, it seemed Meath had delivered their classic sucker punch. On this occasion, however, they showed their hand early in the second half and a selection of breathtaking scores from Paul Clarke and Charlie Redmond initially stalled Meath's momentum before the same duo effectively ended the contest.

Clarke tied the game with a fine score, while Redmond added a pointed free. At the other end of the pitch, Keith Barr and Paddy Moran tackled with an awesome ferocity. Redmond kicked an incredible score from play, a 50-yard point, with three men hanging out of him. Clarke added another and, shortly after that, a move that started with a great take in defence by Moran ended at the other end with a speculative shot from Jason Sherlock. The kick hung in the air outside the small rectangle at the Canal End and Clarke again, who had followed the kick all the way, met the ball on the meat with his fist and it crashed into Conor Martin's net. Most Dublin fans of recent vintage probably recall this goal as fondly as any, but I was situated directly in line with the kick, about forty yards out, and was sure it had gone over for a point. I didn't realise it was a goal until after the game when journalist Roy Curtis informed me. I've often lambasted team-mates for not being aware of the score or of the time remaining. I can't understand how I missed the goal. I'd love to think it was because I was in the 'zone', focused on the 'next ball'. But it was bizarre nonetheless.

After Trevor Giles and Paul Curran had added scores, I scored my third, after grabbing a yard on Graham Geraghty, probably one of the sweetest points I ever managed in Croke Park.

1-18 to 1-8: a scoreline to cherish. Unbeknownst to us, however, it was one that was going to have to sustain me and my county for longer than any of us could have imagined that beautiful evening. This was probably Dublin's most outstanding display during my career. It was one of those rare occasions where everyone performed to his ability and in many cases beyond it, and one replete with glorious moments: the kiss Jason landed on referee Pat Casserly's cheek after winning his free, Charlie handing the match ball to his young protégé Wayne McCarthy after the game, and Cork manager Billy Morgan's flippant appraisal on RTÉ of the threat that Jayo would pose against his side in the semi-final, words that would come back to haunt him.

Any Dublin player could be singled out for honourable mention, beginning with John O'Leary. Paddy Moran had a magnificent afternoon on Colm O'Rourke who, although playing in his last championship game for Meath, was still arguably their most dangerous forward. Paul Curran, man-of-the-match, drove us forward incessantly, while Clarke and Redmond's marksmanship was particularly memorable. From a personal point of view, I was reaching my physical peak and I found the freedom on the half-forward line exhilarating.

Feet of Clay – Dublin vs Cork

I'd love to be able to roll all the matches in 1995 off my tongue as one big positive tract. The semi-final against Cork broke the sequence for me. I was quiet; I didn't score and really didn't play well. Thankfully, Dublin won pretty comfortably, which gave me the chance to sort out the problems I encountered going into the game.

Firstly, I became obsessed with curtailing the influence of Cork's dynamic centre-back, Steven O'Brien. So obsessed, in fact, that half way through the first half I was no longer marking O'Brien, having been switched to the wing to get me properly involved. I spent the remainder in a duel with Brian Corcoran. During that opening quarter, we were seriously pressed by Cork who had stretched our defence and opened up a 0-5 to 0-2 lead. Then Jason Sherlock transformed our performance with another magical contribution. A clever and quick free kick from Keith Barr found Sherlock in front of full-back Mark

O'Connor on the Hogan Stand side, thirty yards from goal. He spun to face the Cork man and, when he shimmied, O'Connor slipped, allowing Sherlock to cut inside and angle a fantastic shot to the net past Kevin O'Dwyer.

Buoyed by our talisman, we took control and led 1-5 to 0-6 at half-time. Brian Stynes dominated midfield, assisted initially by Paul Bealin, but subsequently by Pat Gilroy, who deputised when Bealin left the field injured after half an hour. Paddy Moran delivered two big hits on Mark O'Sullivan and Colin Corkery, helping to curtail their respective influences.

Mick Galvin, however, grew in stature in the second half of the semi-final. He kicked four impressive points from play at vital stages, which kept Cork on the back foot. Allied to Charlie Redmond's steady hand, we had established sufficient leeway to withstand their late second-half rally.

A winning team always requires a variety of match-winners to step up to the plate throughout a successful campaign and the Cork match reflected this. My own display improved after the break, as I had a hand in a number of scores and tracked up and down the line. It wasn't enough to stop the gnawing sensation of unfinished business I felt leaving the field. Two days on the beer with the lads and a round of golf in Citywest was the usual antidote to any lingering doubts. It didn't work this time. I couldn't wait to regroup with Fran Ryder, to run myself into the ground and banish any demons from my head.

I had learned a valuable lesson: the only player I would worry about for the final was myself.

Deliverance – Dublin vs Tyrone

The build-up to an All-Ireland can be a suffocating experience and 1995 was a proper pain. Sherlock's explosion onto the scene had added to the already significant hype around town and the only hiding place came at training. Even then, the gaze was increasing with each session. Everyone around wanted a piece of us. Once again, real life became an irritant, something I struggled to tolerate, despite whatever brave face I put on.

I'm not sure if it was a need to feel professional and focused in our preparation that caused me to act like a killjoy, or whether it was simply arrogance, a feeling of invincibility and a belief that we shouldn't engage in the peripheral build-up to an All-Ireland. From my perspective, the pre-final carnival, so loved by fans and commentators, is a distraction; it can make you soft. Not all players would concur. However, after not reaching the final since, I regret that I perhaps didn't enjoy the build-up more: people stopping you in the street to wish you luck, giving you heartfelt, if irrelevant, advice; gruff well-wishers in the butcher's; bus drivers hanging out the window and barking Dublin slogans; the tame abuse from the driver of the Northern reg car. After four years of autumnal distraction, contemplating an August or September without any football, without any annoyance, was impossible in those promise-filled weeks. It would be seven years before I tasted it again and, with each passing season, I felt like a bigger chump for shying away from the well-wishers in 1995.

Personally, I would just try and avoid people. I would cross the road to avoid the situation where I would have to engage in a courteous conversation with someone. You'd be amazed how just talking about a game informally can add to the pressure. In my free time, I really didn't want to engage in any small talk about the All-Ireland final.

Another big chore was dealing with the media, or trying not to deal with the media. Players would always be conscious of doing interviews for fear that they would give ammunition to the opposition. We were also conscious, particularly in Dublin, that our pictures appearing in the paper accompanied by comments would be frowned upon by team-mates, management and people who knew their football. It might be irrational, but players are very superstitious about appearing in articles in the lead-up to big games; they're pretty convinced that if they are splashed across the pages, the inevitable result is a poor individual performance.

At the time, I craved the refuge of Santry. With kit-bag slung over my shoulder, I was no longer a churl. The modest dressing rooms at the Trinity College sports grounds were separated into several small compartments and each player sought the same personal space at every session. Same sneers, same quips, lads farting, moaning, slagging in whispered tones. Into 'Trapper' Dalton to get my thumbs strapped up, tell a few jokes. And out onto the pitch for some shooting practice before training started. Freedom.

A back injury to Dermot Deasy had hampered our whole championship to

Continued on p.177

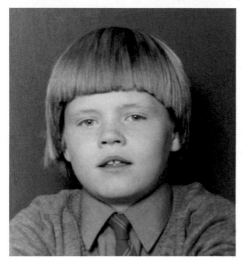

Above: School photograph of me in 1981, aged ten. Check out the bowl haircut! Apparently we were so poor that not only could we not afford the trip to the barbers, but the bowl that was used was obviously badly chipped!

Top Left: 'A plump little thing', sitting on my mother Anne's lap, with my grandparents from Donegal, Cassie and Frank Carr. Donegal would prove to be a haven for me.

Top Right: My First Communion day (1977) with my sister Aisling and baby cousin, Stephen Coleman, who made his way into the Dublin dressing room after the All-Ireland Final in 1995 to congratulate me. Thereafter, I would congratulate him on winning a medal while competing for the Irish soccer team in the Special Olympics 2003.

Receiving the 'Student of the Year' Award in St Vincent's CBS from by Br O'Connell, 1989. (The *Miami Vice* look was very much in fashion!)

Playing for Ireland against Wales in an under-18s International Home Countries Tournament in Coventry (1989). I scored a goal that day and we went on to beat England in the final, a proud moment in my sporting career.

Closing in on Meath's Cormac Murphy during the Leinster SFC semi-final, 4 July 1993.

Trying to get through Kildare's John Crofton and Sos Dowling. Leinster final, 26 July 1992.

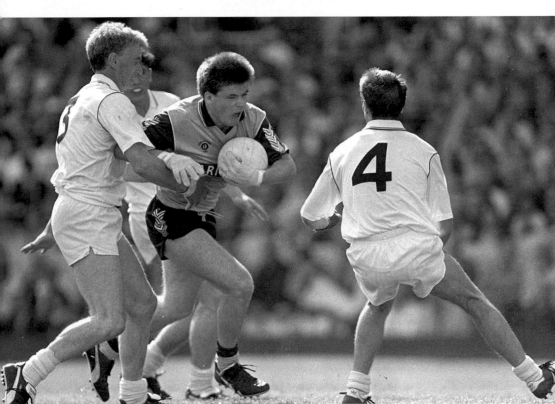

Courtesy of Sportsfile

Courtesy of Sportsfile

Giving Tyrone's Seamus McCallan the hand off during the All-Ireland final, 17 September 1995.

Jason Sherlock, Jim Gavin and myself exhibiting the Sam Maguire in December 1995. We certainly 'wintered well' that year.

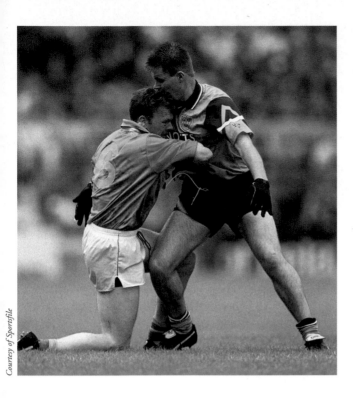

Trying to keep Meath's Enda McManus pinned down during the Leinster final, 28 July 1996.

Courtesy of Sportsfile

Referee Mick Curley sends me off during a Leinster SFC replay against Kildare, the same day the *Sunday World* plastered my name on their front page, 21 June 1997.

Courtesy of Sportsfile

The Na Fianna Team before the 1999 Leinster Club Final:

Back row, left to right:
Stephen Gray, Brendan Quinn,
Aaron Shearer, Mark Foley,
Ian Foley, Sean Forde,
Karl Donnelly, Mick Galvin.

Front row, left to right:
Pat McCarthy, Des Macken,
myself, Senan Connell,
Tommo Lynch,
Stephen McGlinchey,
Kieran McGeeney.

In action against Peadar Andrews of St Brigid's during the Dublin SFC final, my first county title success.
16 October 1999.

Courtesy of Sportsfile

With my son Frankie and my father Seán in the Na Fianna dressing room after beating Sarsfields of Kildare in the Leinster Club Final 1999 in Navan. (Frankie went missing shortly after that photograph was taken, which put an end to celebrations for about fifteen minutes. He was found in a corner of the opposition's dressing room.)

Courtesy of Sportsfile

Celebrating our Dublin SFC success over Crokes with Mick Galvin and Kieran McGeeney, 14 October 2000.

Courtesy of Sportsfile

Leading the team during the parade
against Kildare. Leinster final,
30 July 2000.

Courtesy of Sportsfile

Battling it out with Kerry's Mike McCarthy in the All-Ireland quarter-final at Thurles, 4 August 2004.

Courtesy of Sportsfile

Courtesy of Sportsfile

Top: Leading the lads out for our All-Ireland quarter-final against Kerry in Thurles, 4 August 2001.

Above: Standing by Tommy Carr and his selectors, John O'Leary, Richie Crean and Dom Twomey, after they were sacked. 2 October 2001.

Courtesy of Sportsfile

Playing Donegal in the championship ten
years after our final defeat in 1992.
Raymond Sweeney and Kevin Cassidy
make life difficult. 17 August 2002.

Courtesy of Sportsfile

You know when you've been in a game with Armagh as Enda McNulty's tackle shows, 5 July 2003. Enda is now a club-mate of mine in Na Fianna.

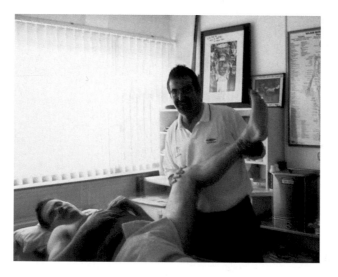

Alan Kelly, or 'The Great AK' as he is known in the trade, puts me through my paces in rehab.

After tearing my cruciate against Roscommon, 1 August 2004

Courtesy of Sportsfile

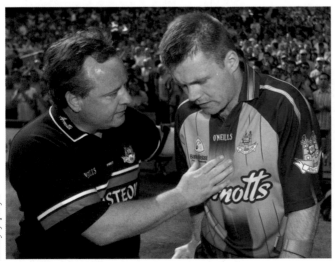

Tommy Lyons consoles me after the Roscommon game, 1 August 2004.

Courtesy of Sportsfile

Courtesy of Sportsfile

Courtesy of Sportsfile

Above: Preparing the speech for the GPA's annual general meeting.

Top Right: Mam and Dad spruce up for the GPA Gala Night 2003.

Top Left: With GAA top brass, Liam Mulvihill and Seán Kelly, on the playing rules task force in 2004.

Courtesy of Sportsfile

Armagh's Enda McNulty, Monaghan's Dermot McArdle and myself
with budding young players Lauren McConville from Armagh,
my son Frankie, and Steven Traynor (*far left*) from Dublin, at an
announcement by the GPA and Club Energise to support the first
ever residential Gaelic Football Summer Camp. 1 June 2005.

My children, Frankie (8) and Emma (5) at the Na Fianna Mini-Leagues finals day 2005, where Frankie picked up a couple of medals.

date and the final was no exception. It wasn't looking good for Deasy and everyone knew it though few could foresee the spin-off his difficulties would have. Two weeks before the game, we were going through our interval runs out in Santry. One thousand metres, 800 metres, 400 metres, and so on. On the Tuesday night, Jason Sherlock, who had a pretty good handle on modern training techniques from his experience with UCD in the League of Ireland, began to give out about such intense work in the lead up to the final. Then, in a 'A' vs 'B' game, Robbie Boyle gave Deasy a tough time, prompting Sherlock to suggest to Pat O'Neill that he switch the former onto the 'A' team. The response was curt. 'I'll pick the team,' said O'Neill. Sherlock, who was only really guilty of youthful exuberance, walked away after training, speaking to no one. He arrived out the next evening and maintained his silent protest. There was genuine fear in the camp that he would withdraw from the squad the week before the All-Ireland.

O'Leary, Keith Barr and Mick Galvin called to Jason's home later that night to confront him and let him get the whole experience off his chest. He did, and the final chapter in an incredible debut season could commence. The following night, our press night at St Vincent's club grounds descended into farce when a couple of hundred star-struck kids joined Jason in the warm-up lap before our light training session. We abandoned the session and faced the press.

Already without Deasy for the final, we received another injury scare in the run-up to the game when Charlie Redmond damaged a quad muscle that was hampering his kicking – not good news. While the injury wasn't bad enough to rule him out – he was still managing to strike the ball at training – Paul Clarke was put on standby duty for free-taking.

I worked extremely hard on my kicking following the Cork game, a couple of hours every day in St Brendan's. I practised so diligently that I had got myself to the point where I knew when the ball left my foot if it was going over the bar.

I woke shortly after dawn the day of the final. Lying on the bed as the September sunshine engulfed the room, I wondered what hand would be dealt this time, whether we would fall at the last hurdle again, if we would ever shed the tag of perennial bridesmaids. My thoughts turned to God, to fate, to destiny. Fear gripped me, so I got out of bed and hopped on the bike for twenty

Continued from p.160

minutes to shake off the negative feelings. By the time I returned, my head was a lot clearer, so I had breakfast and called over to my parents' house where my uncle Seamus and auntie Margaret had landed from Donegal for the game. Margaret called me aside and handed me a horseshoe she had taken from their pony at home. 'This'll bring you luck, Dessie.' Bizarre as it seems, I was happy to accept the token and slipped the horseshoe into the pocket of my gear bag.

My father was due to drive me to Croke Park as usual, but he had gone down to drop tickets into Christy Kearns, owner of Delaney's pub in North King Street, beforehand. He was then due to collect me but, when he came back up the road, he realised he couldn't get through Grangegorman. An enormous set from the film *Michael Collins* had been constructed in the area and the crew was having an open day, so there were thousands of people milling around taking pictures and looking for Liam Neeson. With no mobile phone, Seán had to return to Delaney's and use the public phone to let me know he was stuck. My old 'PMT' took a bit of turn for the worse, as time was pushing on, but I didn't panic as I always liked to arrive as late as possible to avoid hanging around in the dressing room. I grabbed my bike and cycled down to Delaney's past the bombed-out wooden GPO, through the hoards of film fanatics. I locked the bike in the hallway of the pub, where it remained for months afterwards.

The dressing room was pretty subdued when I entered. Throwing my gear bag onto the ground by the bench, I heard the metal of the horseshoe ring off the floor, which brought a smile to my face. I told no one, but after togging out, I had a little look into the pocket of the bag. After all the meticulous build-up, I was now peering at my lucky charm.

The tactical plan for the final against Tyrone was pretty simple: cut off the supply to Peter Canavan. Canavan's rare talent, an ability to create and take a score out of almost any situation, was already the stuff of legend. Ciarán Walsh had the unenviable job of marking him, as Deasy had been ruled out with injury, yet the real task was to deny Canavan any decent possession. To an extent we achieved that. Granted, when he did get the ball, we pretty much fouled the shit out of him, which wasn't planned, but our instinct was to stop him at every opportunity. Unfortunately for us and the Dublin fans, already reduced to nervous wrecks from four years of near misses, we couldn't stop him firing over free kicks from everywhere, out of his hand, off the deck, left, right, long-range, short-range – everywhere!

With No. 12 on my back, I started at centre-forward on Séamus McCallan. Before we could settle, Tyrone had three points on the board. We panicked from the start until Keith Barr drove a free kick over the bar from over seventy yards away, an incredible kick. As the ball disappeared into the Canal End, we exhaled and took control of the game; even the injured Charlie managed to put a free over the bar. Everything went sweetly for me. After we'd levelled the game at three points apiece, McCallan went down injured. Spotting the opportunity to find space, I wandered out into the corner and Barr stuck a quick free right onto my chest. Unmarked, I turned and slipped it over the bar. Settled, I added two more in the first half, one from just inside the sideline under the Hogan Stand. The remarkable thing about the first half from a Dublin perspective is that four different free-takers scored: first Barr, then Charlie Redmond, then me and, finally, Paul Clarke.

Our late goal in the first half was to prove the vital score of the game, however. Essentially we got it because of Jason Sherlock's quick reaction and his bravery. He chased a long ball into the square but had to go one-on-one with Finbarr McConnell, a man twice his size, to get his foot to it. Charlie followed up and pulled on the lose ball into the empty goal. I came in behind and actually called to leave it. One way or another, the ball was going to end up in the back of the net.

Leading by five points at half-time fooled no one in our dressing room and our caution was well-founded because Tyrone clawed their way back early in the second half with three points in a row from Canavan. It was a one-man show: Canavan would win the ball, we'd foul him, and he'd stick the free over the bar. I scored my fourth point to stem the flow before the game took a bizarre twist when Redmond was sent off for an attempted headbutt, but he didn't seem to realise his punishment and played on. He had to be summoned by referee Paddy Russell and sent off again for a second time. Paul Clarke restored our three-point advantage, 1-10 to 0-10, with a monstrous point from play. It was to be our last score, and what followed was a nerve-racking climax as we tried to hang on to our slender lead as Canavan continued to narrow it. I had received a heavy blow to the ribs and was struggling to breathe properly.

Our sideline team didn't realise I was injured but, ironically, while standing under the Hogan Stand in the closing stages, Redmond suggested to O'Neill that he should take me off to waste some time, given that I was standing at the furthest point from our dugout under the Cusack.

So I had to endure the frantic finale from the line. It was chaotic. After all the intelligent preparation of our management team, we seemed destined to suffer the death of a thousand cuts. John O'Leary had to make an acrobatic leap to prevent a goal. It nearly killed us to watch. All the players were standing on the line, issuing contradictory advice. 'Drop back, get men behind the ball.' 'Don't drop back, keep our shape.' 'For fuck sake, foul him.' 'Don't fucking foul him.'

Then Canavan played a ball to Seán McLaughlin who fired over the equaliser, or so we thought. 'BOLLLLOXXX!' This time there were no contradictions on the line. Mick Galvin noticed that Paddy Russell was signalling a free out. I was too nervous to respond, either way. O'Neill was gaunt. None of us could see that Canavan had been punished for handling the ball on the ground. Later inspection showed just how close a call it had been. The only mitigating factor was the fact that Russell blew his whistle immediately, before McLaughlin struck his point. Still, we were blessed.

When the final whistle blew, Galvin and I embraced. Five years after I'd first stepped into the Dublin dressing room, I had won an All-Ireland. For Mick it was nearly a decade. We didn't need to speak.

As I battled through the milling crowd, my father battled his way over to me, his face stained with tears. Always by my side, it was only proper we shared this moment. He had my young cousin Stephen along with him, so I carried him back to the dressing room with me after John O'Leary and Paul Curran lifted the Sam Maguire together. While I was standing on the steps of the Hogan Stand, boxer Steve Collins leaned over and grabbed my arm, reminding me that we were Cabra men and proud of it!

The dressing room was strangely quiet considering. Relief was the palpable emotion, the journey to this point had been long and painful; the shouting could happen later. There were also many missing faces – Tommy Carr, Eamon Heery, Dave Foran, Jack Sheedy, Mick Kennedy.

I dressed and met Seán outside who dropped me up to the flat; I had other business to attend to. There I met Noreen and produced the ring just as I had promised and asked her to marry me. She agreed. I changed into my official Dublin suit and tie and we headed over to Hanlon's pub for a quick drink with the lads before slipping off to Delaney's, where my family and relations had gathered. For the Donegal crew, it was like a second All-Ireland.

Jurys Hotel in Ballsbridge hosted the reception and the remainder of the night has evaporated into a smiling, drunken blur, the only fleeting picture remaining was of Páidí Ó Sé and Pat O'Neill arguing at around two o'clock in the morning and Bertie Ahern, then Minister for Finance, intervening. It was surreal.

The GAA's official lunch in the Burlington on the Monday was as much of a nuisance as it had been on the two occasions when I had attended as a loser. John O'Leary gave a painful rendition of 'Dublin Can Be Heaven', tolerated only because of the various cures being consumed and the laughter at Barr's post-match comment to an RTÉ interviewer, where he said the experience of winning Sam after all our near misses was like a 'donkey off our backs'. It was a classic 'Keithism' and a lot closer to the truth than the clichéd simile.

We were then guests at a civic reception in the Bank of Ireland and College Green before being introduced on a platform to the 20,000 who had gathered to celebrate. I kept my head down as Vinny Murphy stirred the fans. Then it was on to an open-topped bus for a parade down O'Connell Street. Less embarrassing circumstances than 1992.

When we ran out of crowd, however, the bus went up around Parnell Square before turning down Gardiner Street to drop us back to the cars. While we were stopped at a set of lights, the only bystander was a young kid on his BMX bike. As the street was empty, he looked up, bemused, at the shirt-and-tie festooned gang on board. After cycling away he pulled the brakes and returned to the bus, which was still stalled at the lights. Looking up at us, he shouted: 'Yiz fuckin' gobshites!'

Chapter 16

Fading Light – 1995–1998

The annual GOAL charity match between Dublin and an All-Star selection the Wednesday after our All-Ireland victory was hilarious. Played in front of empty stands and a packed Hill 16, Mícheál Ó Muircheartaigh announced that the backs would trade places with the forwards, which meant Jason Sherlock found himself marking Peter Canavan.

If it was a ludicrous carry-on to start with, but it became high farce when Sherlock's fan club of over a thousand kids breached the fences in Croke Park and started chasing him around the pitch. The game had to be abandoned, much to the annoyance of organiser, GOAL chief John O'Shea. We tried to placate him, saying that it was only a bit of *craic*, but he was convinced it diminished the whole event. The night concluded with a smashing session in The Baggot Inn, where the Dublin City Ramblers entertained a jubilant throng.

After several weeks of parading the Sam Maguire Cup around Dublin, it was something of a relief, physically, when we eventually returned to training for the national league in October. I enjoyed the *craic* immensely, but I became tired of listening to some of the lads enthusing about how it didn't matter if we never won another game, an attitude which would come back to haunt us all over the following few years.

I was named as an All Star for my efforts in 1995, a plaudit I was honoured to receive. Despite the annual whinge associated with these awards, their importance for players has never diminished. It capped a fantastic season for me. Unfortunately, it was an All-Star year without the reward of a nice trip to Hong Kong or Paris, which would have been an added bonus.

Our opening Division-Two game was against Leitrim in Croke Park. It should have been a celebration, a chance to parade the All-Ireland champions in front of their home crowd. Instead, the game was overshadowed by the shocking news that Pat O'Neill and his management team had decided to step down en masse.

O'Neill approached most of us personally to inform us, thanked us, and that was that. A lot of speculation surrounded the management decision, much of it alluding to what we perceived as the strained relationship between the sideline team and John Bailey.

However, O'Neill revealed to me recently that he had made his mind up to go the year before and that problems with the county board weren't an issue in the end. He had spent five years with the Dublin team, first as a selector with Cullen and subsequently as manager. He had a busy medical practice to attend to and was lecturing. He simply could not afford the time any longer.

The management team's differences of opinion with Bailey dated back to 1993. At that time, the chairman decided to establish a committee to oversee the Dublin football management team – to manage the managers, so to speak. The committee, headed by board-official Gerry Brady, was formed, and met with Pat O'Neill and his selectors. Much to the new body's embarrassment, some of the selectors reared up on the committee. Bobby Doyle, Brogan, Ryder and O'Neill put an end to it there and then. One of the officials on the short-lived committee was so mortified that he let Bailey know, in no uncertain terms, what he thought of this embarrassing fiasco. O'Neill and his three selectors were men of the utmost integrity and ability. Why on earth did the chairman feel it necessary to police this group? People can make up their own minds about the manner in which John Bailey has handled Dublin county teams' affairs during his long tenure as chairman. In my opinion, he interfered unnecessarily.

The relationship between Bailey and O'Neill obviously worsened following the decision to play the club games prior to the 1994 All-Ireland final, despite the assurances given to the manager that they would be postponed.

Against this backdrop, many felt that O'Neill's departure had been hastened, but this wasn't true, although he did admit that he felt Bailey was more than satisfied to see the back of him.

I regret that I wasn't part of any concerted effort by the players to get him to stay. O'Neill claims that it wouldn't have made any difference, but it was remiss of us, as a panel, that we didn't pull together and try to change his mind. There were a number of individual efforts made. Keith Barr made an emotional plea to O'Neill to remain. Then John O'Leary and Charlie Redmond approached Fran Ryder and asked him would he consider putting himself forward as manager to maintain consistency. Sadly, he declined, though O'Neill was pretty sure that he had left the door open for his trainer to replace him as manager. Jim Brogan would probably have stayed as well, but Bobby Doyle was keen to step down.

However, what probably led to the group's unanimous decision according to O'Neill was his contention that it was very much a management team and that he was merely a front for the group. They had an excellent working relationship so, in solidarity, they all went together.

By the time we lined out in our second league game, we had no manager. Surfing the crest of our celebratory wave, few of us really considered what lay ahead or, more importantly, what lay behind. We had just lost a brilliant management team, one that couldn't be faulted for our propensity as a team to press the self-destruct button.

Tommy Lyons, who had steered Kilmacud Crokes to an All-Ireland club victory earlier in 1995, was the favourite to succeed O'Neill. He seemed the logical successor but, as with most managerial appointments in Dublin, the process took a twist and, later that year, Mickey Whelan, one of the Dublin stars of the Fifties and Sixties, was appointed to the job.

The first indication that Whelan's tenure might not be a smooth ride arose when the addition of selectors was delayed. I'm not sure if there was reluctance on the part of potential candidates, but it was quite some time before Lorcan Redmond and Christy Kane were named as Whelan's assistants.

I liked Whelan. He was brash and quite arrogant, but his class as a player could be surmised from his outlook on football. He was an excellent coach, probably ahead of his time in employing some of the training techniques used by the All Blacks rugby team. His football drills were immediately appealing and I found him quite an engaging character.

However, his man-managing style was a lot softer than O'Neill's. He took players under his wing, was very approachable, particularly to youngsters. This largesse was exploited by some of the established footballers. They took liberties under Whelan that they wouldn't have done with O'Neill. I remember one incident where three senior members of the panel missed a training session because they were having a few pints after a round of golf. They phoned Mickey to say they were involved in a prize-giving ceremony and he accepted it. It was indicative of a malaise that set in after winning an All-Ireland.

On occasion, the new manager spoke his mind a little too bluntly, particularly at the outset when he told the panel that we had won an All-Ireland with one of the worst full-back lines he'd ever seen. I must stress, however, that Mickey only made one or two *faux pas* in this regard. He did, at times, air his opinions about footballers in the dressing room, which may have left him little room for manoeuvre, but they were isolated incidents. Players used these utterances as an excuse to blame Mickey when things went wrong.

He was probably on a hiding to nothing. O'Neill's tortuous journey to All-Ireland success was based on an exhaustive process of finding the right balance, learning the individual characteristics of each player, and managing them accordingly. Mickey Whelan now had to find that stuff out for himself.

I'll be honest; Lorcan Redmond and Christy Kane were extremely likeable characters. Lorcan had been part of an All-Ireland winning set-up in the past and went on to take charge of the Dublin under-21s. Yet they were old school. We had just emerged from a period of disciplined, energetic management. Jim Brogan, Bobby Doyle and Fran Ryder had all embraced modern managerial techniques, had a very hands-on approach, and tried to be as professional as possible. Their working relationship with O'Neill was very efficient. Lorcan and Christy didn't provide a foil to Mickey in the same way. The management team didn't possess the same authority as the previous group.

Like most new managers, Whelan was keen to put his own stamp on the team, but he didn't do himself a lot of favours by carrying out swinging changes to what was considered a successful formula. After openly criticising the full-back line, he dropped Ciarán Walsh and Keith Galvin while, up front, Paul Clarke – a key member of the 1995 set-up – was marginalised. Sherlock's role was also diminished and we lost Vinny Murphy and Mick Galvin altogether: the former moved to Kerry while Galvin retired, albeit temporarily.

Whelan brought former Dublin players Joe McNally, Niall Guiden and Eamon Heery back in to the squad. There were reservations about the return of

McNally and Guiden, largely to do with their commitment to training, which were expressed by our captain, John O'Leary, to Whelan. However, most of us were pleased to have Heery back in the fold. As a fellow clubman of Whelan's, Heery became the manager's staunch ally, defending him when things started to go wrong later in the season. Big Joe McNally was undoubtedly still one of the best forwards in the club game in Dublin but, knowing what we went through under O'Neill to win an All-Ireland, most of us doubted that he would last the pace. I was particularly uneasy about Guiden's return. Because we had been told that Guiden had attended a wedding on the Friday night before the 1994 All-Ireland, most of us believed that he had crossed the line and shouldn't have been given a second chance. As it transpired, we lost both Guiden and McNally to injury prior to the Leinster final.

A smooth passage through Division Two of the national league was expected – we had been relegated in 1995 – but it didn't help Whelan's bedding-in period when we performed fitfully throughout the campaign and failed to gain promotion at the end of it.

Amidst the upheaval, the relationship between the new manager and our captain deteriorated. Whelan may have seen O'Leary as the strongest link with the previous regime and an easy target to establish his authority; a kind of 'if I have a go at the captain, then the rest of the lads will listen' way of thinking. Or maybe it was simply a personality clash, we didn't really know. As the championship season commenced, O'Leary raised concerns about the shape and attitude of the panel. He didn't feel we were as fit as we should have been and believed some of the lads were cutting corners, literally, in their training. As captain he felt obliged to inform Whelan of his views. He was right too.

Things had become sloppy, lads were crying off too easily, holding back at training. Mickey didn't accept O'Leary's assessment. He claimed that our interval training times compared favourably with those in 1995 (we later learned Whelan had visited training sessions in Santry and copied down our statistics and times from the notice board, obviously in the belief that he would manage Dublin in the near future). The strain between the pair was palpable. The further Mickey drifted from the '1995' ethos that year, the greater the strain became.

O'Leary always led by example. He was a dedicated trainer and arguably one of the finest keepers that ever played. He was also a very committed captain and, as I would learn some years later, he understood the importance of a good, frank relationship between the manager and his skipper.

Although the difficulties between the two have been well documented, there was a reality that none of us really grasped at the time, namely that Dublin were in decline. I never felt Mickey Whelan had enough support to reverse the slide. Lorcan Redmond and Christy Kane, who were decent enough to commit their time to the job when a lot of football people in Dublin weren't tripping over one another to get involved, were unable to stop the rot. Lorcan had won his All-Irelands as a selector under Heffo twenty years earlier.

Mickey needed more hands-on help, men to whom he could delegate the job of ensuring that every player remained totally committed to his goal. That didn't happen. Whelan may have had the loudest natural whistle I've ever heard, but unfortunately it was falling on deaf ears.

We defeated Westmeath comfortably in Navan in our Leinster quarter-final, an occasion best remembered for the furore that accompanied Kevin Heffernan's arrival on our bus to Páirc Tailteann. His presence sparked rumours that he was acting as an advisor to Whelan. Heffo was on the bus again when we returned to the same venue to play Louth in the semi-final, a match we very nearly – and possibly should have – lost. The sloppiness of our preparation was exposed and only for McNally's vital goal in the closing stages, the All-Ireland champions could have made an embarrassing exit.

But McNally's goal and a flattering four-point win masked our precarious state. The Louth game indicated that there was a malaise within the camp. Whelan trusted our experience to sort it out. We were, after all, All-Ireland champions. This was a misplaced trust.

Things came to a head in the run up to the Meath match. After training, O'Leary, Barr and I had arranged a meeting, orchestrated in such a way as to allow the captain to take the players to task over their attitude. We informed Mickey and he felt it was a good idea. John delivered some stern words at the meeting. As I remember it, Whelan shocked us by turning on our captain and accusing him, unfairly, of being part of the problem. He also had a go at O'Leary, bizarrely, over his performance in Navan. The whole idea, which was well intentioned, backfired as a result.

Personally, I was also concerned about the manager's plans to move me from centre-forward back into the corner. I was unhappy about the move, yet I understood his motives. Sherlock was back at full-forward after appearing as a sub in the first two games in Leinster and, with Charlie in the other corner, he wanted a good ball-winner in that line. He explained this to me and I reluctantly accepted it.

Our new full-back, Davy Martin, was dropped going into the game and replaced by Dermot Deasy. As Deasy was a good friend of mine, I was pleased, but the move highlighted the difficulties for Whelan. He was trying to discover his own formula and time had essentially run out for him. As Guiden was injured, he introduced rookie Ciarán Whelan to wing-forward for the game in what was to be a fairly perceptive selection on the manager's part.

Mickey was as quirky as they came. The night he announced the team for the Leinster final, he informed the panel that only the starting fifteen and selected subs would be required in the run-up to the game as he didn't want any 'distractions'. It was unheard of at the time to ditch panel members, particularly as the emphasis had always been on the 'squad effort'. It meant no place in the subs for Ciarán Walsh and Paul Clarke and it meant we didn't have the proper numbers for our short training game before the final. Charlie Redmond's young teenage protégé, Wayne McCarthy, had to go in goals, while our team doctor, Noel McCaffrey, also had to line out. During that kick around, Mickey Whelan actually left the field to take a trip around the pitch in the county secretary John Costello's new car. Much was made of this incident subsequently, but to be honest I took no notice of it.

The 1996 Leinster final marks a turning point in the history of this Dublin team. In a typically bruising encounter, we forged ahead by two points in the closing stages when Heery, back in his familiar role at left half-back, kicked a smashing point. However, Meath's hunger, sharpened by their collapse the year before, gave them a vital edge in the last few minutes and they kicked the final four points in the game. For players like Darren Fay, Trevor Giles and Graham Geraghty, it was the step-up they needed. We had allowed their passage to the top. When our hunger was tested, we failed. We had our chances but, in truth, our will to win had weakened; damaged irreparably by our messy preparation.

Christy Kane's post-match comment in the dressing room afterwards that 'at least we can hit the little white ball tomorrow', has entered the folklore of the period as a kind of epitaph for the death of a Dublin team. It's a bit harsh. No one complained when Christy was organising our post-match golf on all other occasions. His innocent remark, reflecting the belief that life must go on despite the heartache of defeat, was only delivered to try and ease our pain.

I don't blame Mickey Whelan directly for our failure in 1996 as I think it was impossible for him to stop the rot. True, in that first year he may not have always helped his own cause. His clash with O'Leary was certainly damaging and there simply wasn't enough attention to the minute details that make the difference. But a lot of the slackness in our approach was our own fault. Whelan was handed a poisoned chalice. Losing an edge as a player is often impossible to detect until tested on match day. While we tried to address it before the Meath game, it was already too late.

Whelan trusted us – too much so – as mature All-Ireland winners, to rectify any problems. O'Leary felt it was the manager's responsibility to sort this out. Yet, we were in a position to go and win the Leinster final, two points up with twelve minutes left. Should a manager be blamed for our failure to hold on for victory? I didn't hear too many players, who had been swanning around town the previous winter talking about retiring happy with their All-Ireland medal in their arse pocket, blaming themselves when Meath kicked the last four points on that rain-soaked July afternoon.

Mickey Whelan's treatment of John O'Leary, however, was wrong. The manager did what most managers do: he came in, attempted to put his own stamp on the team, put his own beliefs into practice. Perhaps he should have appointed a new captain from the outset as it would have avoided a lot of the trouble in the camp. Only when I later became captain under Tommy Carr did I fully appreciate how frustrating it must have been for O'Leary to be dressed down in front of his team-mates.

There was a clear-the-air meeting of the panel later that year to assess our failure, which was positive enough. Everyone accepted their portion of blame and agreed to go at the forthcoming season with renewed vigour. O'Leary informed us that he had met Mickey Whelan prior to our gathering to make his own personal opinions known to the manager directly. This appeared peculiar to me because surely that was the idea of the team meeting. How and ever, the upshot of the private meeting was another row when a story a week later in the *Evening Herald* suggested that only O'Leary's stated support for Mickey Whelan had prevented a full meeting of the county board from sacking the manager.

O'Leary hit the roof. He had done no such thing. O'Leary had met Whelan privately before the squad meeting for a frank exchange of views and had phoned John Bailey to keep him abreast of his discussions. The captain contends that he informed Bailey that his preference, when asked, was for the management team to step down.

However, in the *Evening Herald* article, Bailey had a different version of events, claiming that the goalkeeper had phoned him to say that Whelan would be acceptable again to the players. This was the final straw for O'Leary who stood down as captain and agreed to share the goalkeeping duties during the league with his understudy Davy Byrne. Keith Barr was handed the skipper's role for 1997.

In management you certainly don't get much of a second chance to make a good first impression, so when the squad's attitude improved during Whelan's second year at the helm, it was probably already too late. Meath had gone on to win the All-Ireland in 1996 and that changed the landscape for Dublin. For nearly five years, we had held the advantage, but had surrendered it to a team of emerging talent.

Mickey tried his best to professionalise the set-up. He took us away on training weekends, one of which was to the Slieve Russell Hotel in Cavan, a trip that turned into a bit of a soap opera when Charlie Redmond stormed out. Redmond, whose in-laws hail from the area, was embarrassed after we had struggled to defeat local club side Belturbet. We hadn't a full-strength team for the game, as a lot of our players hadn't yet arrived in Cavan, so even one of our sub keepers, Adrian Henchy from Na Fianna, a good friend of mine, had to play outfield.

No one else minded. After all, the game was irrelevant – we were on a training weekend, as much an exercise in bonding as anything else. Charlie Redmond thought it was a shambles and he failed to turn up for training the next day and Mickey informed us that that he had retired. For all his prowess, there was no outcry in the dressing room. Perhaps we knew what the outcome would be. Later that evening, he staged a dramatic return with his father-in-law, bringing the curtain down on the weekend's sideshow.

After all the brouhaha and the dismantling of the 1995 team, Mickey acquiesced and reintroduced Paul Clarke and Ciarán Walsh to the starting line-up for our 1997 Leinster championship opener against Meath. Mick Galvin also returned to full-forward. The only newcomers were Ian Robertson and Paddy Christie.

It was another painful loss to Meath. Having trailed by nine points, we forged a terrific goal, which Keith Barr fired into the net to close the gap to three points. But we'd shot our bolt and we couldn't break them down in an interminable second half. The twist in the tale came at the death, as so often happens with Meath-Dublin games, when Paul Bealin crashed a last-minute penalty off the crossbar when a goal would have tied the game. In the dressing room afterwards, Paul Curran lashed Bealin out of it for not keeping his kick low. It was a tense aftermath. Players fucked one another out of it and the fallout from 1996 was heaped on yet another loss to Meath.

It essentially ended the Mickey Whelan era. He struggled on during the league, but stood down as the pressure was mounting on the county board to sack him. It was a frustrating couple of years for me personally. I was at my peak as a footballer, I had remained largely injury-free, something which was about to change dramatically. However, I don't harbour any grudges against Mickey Whelan. I enjoyed a good relationship with him during his tenure and he showed me great respect. Unfortunately, he was not a stickler for detail, he was loose in some departments and, once you give players an inch, they're happy to steal a yard. With a tighter team around him and with greater discipline, it could have been a lot different.

Unfortunately, his legacy is tarnished not just by his failure, but also by his treatment of O'Leary. But Whelan's legacy is our legacy, and all the players who played under him must share the responsibility for our demise.

Before the end of the league in 1998, Tommy Carr replaced Whelan as Dublin manager. O'Leary, who had retired after our 1997 defeat to Meath, was a candidate for the manager's job and it would have been interesting to see how he and John Bailey would have got on, given their recent history.

However, he didn't get the job and he had to be content with a role as a selector under Carr.

Six years after Mickey's departure, Na Fianna were preparing for a club championship game in Parnell Park. Our manager Mick Galvin was setting out cones for our structured warm-up, when Mickey Whelan strolled by after being involved in a previous game with St Vincent's. Looking over at myself and Galvin, he quipped: 'Jayzus lads, yiz laughed at me when I was trying to do that with ye!' And, you know, he had a point.

SECTION 3

SECTION 5

Chapter 17

Na Fianna

June 1984

The balmy June evening spread out before us as we packed into the van to drive to St Anne's Park in Raheny; Jim McKeever, as always, at the wheel. We'd been invited to take part in an under-13 football blitz. Things were a bit all over the shop at underage level in Na Fianna.

It was a happy place, but we were struggling with helpers, jerseys and for numbers. So it was no real surprise to the gang of exuberant kids to discover, when our depleted troupe arrived at the park, that we'd have to take part in a series of games over a whole day rather than the single match we thought we were heading to play. Our manager hadn't been told about the competition, which says something about the juvenile set-up at that time.

The smell is everywhere, grass and leather, the smell of summer, an association with happiness and excitement that is soldered into the memory banks of every footballer. We played our games with our small gang. In between games, rather than resting, we played soccer. It seemed like forever; we wanted it to be forever.

In 1984, times were tough – belt-tightening tough – an era long before soccer moms, jeeps and isotonic drinks. There was only Jim, always Jim, who could see his yellow-and-blue clad charges were exhausting themselves during their unexpected marathon. He nipped off to the shop and came back with a couple of bottles of 7-Up and a bunch of bananas, while the other teams wolfed into their packed lunches.

Eventually, we were beaten in the quarter-final of the blitz. We tramped off, past the bench adorned with the elusive trophies, the glistening plastic statuettes of the ideal footballer – mounted on a square of white marble, clutching an O'Neill's ball to his chest – the same man who was on the back of the standard-issue Christian Brother copybooks. He must have been some footballer.

It was a relief for Jim, much as he would have loved to see us win something. I sat with my red, salt-streaked face buried in my hands, my chlorophyll-stained knees aching from the parched ground. I had run myself into a standstill, five joyous hours of perpetual motion, punctuated by a momentary pause for a couple of slugs of 7-Up.

Wearily, we alighted from the van back in Mobhi Road. The place was empty. I fumbled with my plastic lock and hauled myself onto the bicycle. I wobbled towards the gate, where I fell off, completely spent. I lay on the grass behind the goalposts, dozing for half an hour, unable to move.

Eventually, the evening chill roused me and I remounted my bike and summoned up enough energy to make it up the hill to the chipper in Glasnevin where I devoured a vinegar-drenched single of chips, sending life coursing back through my young body.

1980–1997

Like any GAA man, it's hard not to get dewy-eyed when it comes to talking about your club. I am no different. I was smitten by Mobhi Road when I first laid eyes on it as a child in first class in St Vincent's school. My father had taken me up to the club to watch Kildare play Kerry in an inter-county sevens tournament and I was struck by the grandeur of the clubhouse, the expanse of the pitch and the cockiness of the kid in a Kilkenny jersey swinging his hurl beside me. As happens in clubs, the budding young Cat, Eamon Rainsfort, later became one of my closest friends.

When I first joined the under-10 football and hurling teams, Saturdays were a real treat. Seán and I would head up for our morning game before heading to his hockey match in the afternoon.

It was one big community, from school to club, a constant sense of anticipation, of excitement about impending matches. Roles were reversed back in the Seventies. Players were fed to the clubs by the schools, where idealistic teachers cultivated and developed an interest in Gaelic games.

Na Fianna was a perfect example. It's incredible when you consider that the men who coached us during the school week, in my case teachers like Jim McKeever and Fiachra Leahy, were present again in Mobhi Road on a Saturday morning.

It breaks my heart in today's commodity-driven society to think how respect for teachers has changed. We now want them to be automatons, there purely to ensure our kids accumulate sufficient points. The diminished role that teachers now play in sport has had a profound effect on society in general. Time is now money, so we can't blame the teachers. We should be looking at ways to compensate them and encourage them to get involved in after-school coaching and sports activities. For decades, successive governments and the GAA took the invaluable voluntary input made by teachers for granted. I hope that, in times to come, with drugs, obesity and a raft of social problems on our doorsteps, we don't rue not having done enough to keep teachers involved in sport.

While childhood days at the club were profoundly rewarding, we never actually won anything. We were always a bit short and the closest we came was at under-16 level, when we lost a championship final to our bitter rivals, Ballymun Kickhams (Na Fianna was formed in 1955 following a split in Kickhams). I was twenty-eight years old before I managed to break that unfortunate sequence.

Romance aside, it was a struggle for the few individuals to keep the show on the road. The support structure for kids was poor and wasn't particularly well organised at county board level.

The irony of my romantic attachment to Na Fianna is that, while the organisation at underage level struggled for a period, I broke ranks, rather precociously, and went and played soccer with the neighbouring and well-organised Home Farm.

The move may have become something more permanent had I really prospered at the soccer club. I didn't, so there was nothing to really negate the feelings of guilt I had for giving Na Fianna the cold shoulder, which I felt all the more so because Home Farm's pitch was right next to the GAA club.

In fact, I remember cycling up Mobhi Road to a soccer game and meeting the Na Fianna van, driven by Jimmy Gray, one of Na Fianna's most illustrious members. He blew the horn and waved frantically at me – I've little doubt I was needed to make up numbers. I kept my head down and ploughed on to the soccer game, but the experience helped to weaken my resolve and I eventually returned to Gaelic.

As a teenager, my enthusiasm for hurling and football grew and, the older I got, the more important Na Fianna became, particularly when the senior ranks appeared on the horizon. I made my debut for the senior footballers when I was just sixteen years old, on a team backboned by players like brothers John and Pillar Caffrey, Larry Norton, Clive O'Reilly, John Quinn, Tom Gray and Pat Smith.

I sat on the bench for my first championship outing against Cuala, itching for a run and, though I was still a scrawny minor, I felt I could have done something had I played. I had a lot to learn.

The following summer when I eventually made my senior championship debut as a 17-year-old against Ballymun Kickhams, I had played against the wishes of my teachers, as the fixture was slap bang in the middle of my Leaving Cert.

Our normal free-taker, Tom Gray, was injured and I spent the free time I didn't have during the week of the game practising placed kicks from all distances. Keen? Instead of lying awake worrying about *King Lear*, I was picturing myself on a different stage, proving that I had come of age, firing over the winning point against Kickhams in Parnell Park.

But in a case of life imitating art, or imitating Shakespeare to be exact, my fate was sealed from the off. 'As flies to wanton boys, are we to the gods. They kill us for their sport.' (*King Lear*). From the throw-in, John Caffrey won the ball and played a 30-yard ball right in front of me. I grabbed it, fumbled it, gathered it again and, while I was turning, got absolutely cleaved in a tackle. I broke my collarbone and cried like a baby as I was carried to the dugout.

I completed my exams with my left arm in a sling, much to the chagrin of my mother. Kickhams hammered us to boot.

Sadly, only two of my Na Fianna underage team, Ian Foley and I, went on to play senior football for the club – a pretty stark drop-off. In time, it would make it easier for me to push for change.

For years, senior football was a constant battle for survival for the club. On several occasions we were lucky to hang on to our status, avoiding relegation by the skin of our teeth, perhaps even to intermediate level. In fact we survived on one occasion because of a change in the league structures.

However, I was happy with my burgeoning career, firstly with the Dublin minors and then, after making the step up to under-21 level in both hurling and football and later to the senior football team. I became more pivotal to Na Fianna in both football and hurling as my experience grew at inter-county level, though the annual pattern was the same: one or two championship outings followed by a dog-fight to avoid the drop in the league.

Between 1992 and 1996, while Dublin was competing for top honours, the club drifted into the background somewhat, but when the county-team graph started to dip, it brought Na Fianna back into focus. I was at my peak, so it's probably no surprise that I started to get restless about our lack of success on Mobhi Road.

I toyed with the controversial idea of bringing in a few new faces to see could we inject some impetus into the senior football team. My former teacher, John Horan, an astonishingly faithful servant of Na Fianna over a protracted period, eventually stepped down as manager in 1997, providing the opportunity to bring in a new management team and a few players.

To many in the game, this may appear like sacrilege. I never saw it like that. I was ambitious, I wanted to win something with Na Fianna and my inter-county experience had taught me that the more professional your set-up, the greater your prospects.

My plan was to put together, firstly, a high-profile management team with a paid trainer. I approached the club chairman at the time, Paul Smith, for his official approval. He was open-minded and supportive; I wasn't the only one sick of our position in Dublin.

The first man approached for help was Pat Coffey from Tipperary, a passionate club man who had won a football championship with Na Fianna in 1979. He had spent a period managing the senior hurlers, during which time we became close friends. I told him I was hoping to put a new professional-type management team together, fronted maybe by someone from outside the club. The second step, I explained, was to bring in a few 'outside' players.

I reiterated that I wasn't trying to be disrespectful. I wasn't too concerned about the rhetoric and dogma that surrounds club traditions, particularly in parts of Dublin. Na Fianna had a very small catchment area in Glasnevin with an ageing population. My plan was based on ambition. Some might not like it, but I knew only too well how winning would change everyone's perspective.

As I was still pretty close to the Dublin 1995 management team, they were my first targets, but none of them could commit. Then I looked to my former team-mates and was delighted when Dermot Deasy agreed to train the team.

With time restraints, he couldn't commit to the role of manager, but it was still a big step for us. It was the first time in Na Fianna's history that a trainer was paid for his twice-weekly session, even if it was a paltry sum. The deal with the committee at the time was that we would raise the small amount of money ourselves.

However, I still needed a front man and, while I couldn't tempt any of the 1995 management team to come on board, I approached Tom Moriarity, our former sports psychologist with Dublin under Pat O'Neill, who had been involved for a period with the Civil Service GAA club.

It seemed like a novel move, having a fashionable psychologist on the line. He agreed. John Caffrey also joined up as co-manager to ensure we had a solid club link, while businessman Brendan O'Malley was the final piece of the jigsaw. O'Malley had little experience in football management, but he was a dynamic operator and would use his extensive contacts to provide a solid support structure for the players: doctors, dentists, training facilities. Brendan was able to organise them all, enhancing the whole set-up in the process.

As a number of the old guard had recently retired from the senior panel, it wasn't that much of an upheaval when we brought in a few country lads who I'd come to know through St Brendan's. Seán Forde, Tony Langan and Willie Evans were the first newcomers, followed shortly by Adrian Henchy, a hockey player and soccer goalkeeper who was persuaded to mind the nets for us and who would later join me on the Dublin panel.

We drew with Ballyboden in the first round of the championship. It was a significant result. Ballyboden were one of the favourites for the crown and, in my experience, we were generally fodder for the big guns, so at least we had established something. We lost the replay, but we had kick-started a period of change.

For me, Na Fianna would never be the same again.

Chapter 18

Out Of The Shadows – 1997–2005

Club conservatives will argue that once you start to bring 'outsiders' into the senior set-up, you can't stop; the drive for success becomes a constant search for better players. They may have a point, though I think it's laboured.

It is true that, after 1997, Dublin veteran Mick Galvin and Senan Connell, both from St Oliver Plunkett's, transferred to Na Fianna (though the latter ended up suspended for a year after making an error in processing his transfer form). Still, Galvin's move, and Connell's impending one, caused quite a stir around town. Plunkett's had been relegated to intermediate, and there were accusations of the boys jumping a sinking ship. This was grossly unfair. Why should personal ambition be frowned upon?

I didn't care what people thought, not in this regard. I had already consumed enough of the clichéd, gushing nonsense from bar-stool stalwarts and enlightened columnists to know that neither of these rare geniuses will be there to help you get a team together, or to work really hard to get the team right.

It would have been great had I grown up with a string of players who had played on the same team and aspired to become county senior champions together. But this is Dublin and, as I've already said, only two of my underage team reached senior level and this sort of a drop-off is not uncommon in the city.

Galvin was an enormous addition to Na Fianna. Not only did his cultured football skills help transform our whole style of play, but his influence on the other players, on and off the field, was profound. Mick had helped me enormously when I first broke into the Dublin team and I'll always be indebted to him for that. And to think we nearly didn't get him at all. I had asked him would he be interested in coming on board before I went on holidays. While I was away, I decided to phone Mick because the transfer deadline was looming. He told me that no one had been in contact with him about it.

Pat Coffey was dispatched immediately and, after a few gin and tonics in the Halfway House on the Navan Road, Mick managed to complete the form and get it to the county board hours before the deadline expired.

Another change in 1998 saw John Caffrey's younger brother, Pillar Caffrey, come in as trainer to replace Dermot Deasy and, soon afterwards, Tom Moriarity left. Pillar was a Na Fianna stalwart, a talented and uncompromising defender who had also played for a period with Dublin and had considerable coaching experience.

Maximising on the impetus instilled largely by Galvin's addition, we reached the county final in 1998, playing some of the best football I'd ever enjoyed with the club. Paradoxically, many of our life-long clubmen, like Tommo Lynch and Stephen McGlinchey, became even better players in a side now strong enough to express itself properly at the top level. The positive vibes coming from the club encouraged Karl Donnelly to return to Na Fianna after giving up Gaelic football to concentrate on his basketball career. Karl added a breath of fresh air on and off the pitch.

Like any newcomers to the final stage, we froze a bit on the big day, eventually succumbing to Kilmacud Crokes' greater experience and a late goal, but the occasion was memorable. If bringing some outside players into the club and appointing an ambitious management team was so wrong, how come it lifted the whole club, the whole community around Glasnevin and Phibsborough? I didn't need any further vindication. For the first time in my twenty years with Na Fianna, I'd witnessed the sheer ebullience that reaching a county final can bring.

In the aftermath of our 1998 defeat to Crokes, I was drowning my sorrows with a gang of team-mates in Copper Face Jacks nightclub when I ran into a couple of Armagh players, Kieran McGeeney and Diarmuid Marsden. Both were part of Ireland's international rules panel, but had been excused from the playing squad for the day by the then manager Colm O'Rourke.

We nodded respectfully but, for the life of me, I couldn't remember McGeeney's name. I knew his face well and I knew he was a serious player. We had marked each other previously, but at that time he didn't have the significant profile outside of his own province that he has now. My memory blanked. Then McGeeney approached me and, mercifully, just as he extended his hand, his name popped into my head. We got chatting about our county-final defeat and the influence former Down footballer Conor Deegan had exerted on the game.

Deegan was a powerful, uncompromising player, the kind of full-back you'd love to see anchor your team, but as an old sparring partner of McGeeney's and a new one of mine, our shared opinion was less than flattering (you know how intense club rivalry is). McGeeney spoke of how he'd love another crack at Deegan, which led us to talking about playing in Dublin. As he was now working in the city, he had been considering a move to a Dublin club and had already been contacted by St Vincent's.

Having at least signalled our ambition by reaching the county final, I suggested, very politely, that he might consider coming up to Mobhi Road for a look and gave him my phone number.

A couple of weeks later, McGeeney rang and said that he and his Armagh colleague, Des Mackin, would be interested in talking to the club. So Pillar, Galvin and I met the two of them and took them on board.

After word got around of our new transfers, it was quickly followed by rumours that Na Fianna were now involved in cheque-book recruitment; that we were paying players to join the club. I'm only too happy that I now have the opportunity to put it on the record that Na Fianna never paid a penny to any player. In this whole account of my life and career, my approach has been to be honest and forthright. I have no reason at this juncture to change tack. Na Fianna do *not* pay their players and it irks me greatly to hear the begrudging sneers around the city and further afield. It annoys me still further when some of our professional commentators on the game, men who have essentially earned their livelihoods commenting on the efforts of footballers and hurlers, also engage in this backbiting nonsense. These players reside in Dublin; it is their home. Are we really suggesting that they should not be allowed play football for clubs in Dublin?

Na Fianna were fortunate that, through informal contacts and chance, these players actually came to join us. They became part of Na Fianna, not just the senior team. They helped and encouraged kids. Players like Seán Forde and Adrian Henchy, two of our earliest recruits, are now in team management at the club. Solid, long-standing friendships have been formed. The whole experience has been immensely positive and I don't know what club would have done it any differently.

McGeeney was tempted to join the club by our ambition, by the structures we now had in place under our management, not by money. If other teams went down that road, that's their business. We paid expenses to our trainers, that is the accepted reality of running a team today, but the only potential reward on the table for McGeeney, Mackin and others was the chance of a Dublin senior-championship medal.

It's difficult to overstate what McGeeney brought to Na Fianna. Besides his obvious prowess on the field, he provided a massive boost to me personally, particularly in the dressing room and on the training ground. For years, my club-mates had to listen to me constantly droning on about raising standards, about the importance of greater sacrifice, of greater application, of discipline. At times, I wouldn't have been the most popular for it; I never shied from telling a lad to his face that he wasn't focused, that he was an underachiever. Now, there was someone even more zealous than me, a man who believed in realising his ambition.

The net effect on the rest of the players was a change in mindset, a change that ultimately provided the missing link that transformed us from a good side into one capable of landing three county championship titles on the trot.

In October 1999, I was twenty-eight years old. For well over a decade, I had made the annual pilgrimage to Croke Park and Parnell Park to watch the elite clubs of Dublin lift the county title and dreamed of the experience, dreamed of the vindication and liberation such a success would bring. Then it happened. Na Fianna, no longer a soft touch, no longer just the affable club on Mobhi Road, now anchored by the steeliest pivotal footballer in Gaelic football, with its life-long clubmen no longer prepared to accept mediocrity, Na Fianna defeated St Brigid's in the county final.

I'd longed for this day, feared that I might have missed my chance when Crokes had beaten us twelve months previously. When the final whistle sounded against Brigid's and we were embraced by the familiar faces that had surrounded us since childhood, the sensation was incredibly fulfilling. If we'd committed a sin in some people's eyes by bringing outside players onto the senior team, then justification was all around; in the hundreds of children who lined the driveway into the Mobhi Road clubhouse; in the tears of men who had spent half their lives driving vans, babysitting, cajoling, chastising, pleading, nursing; in the committee rooms where men and women now felt a renewed sense of worth in their arduous toil; in the mothers who held their yellow-and-blue draped kids up for the affirming hug from their dads, from Jason Sherlock, from Mick Galvin, from Brendan Quinn, from Ian Foley and, thankfully, from myself.

The satisfaction of celebrating with your own is hard to match. Great supporters of Na Fianna, men like Jim Birch, and me personally and my family, hosted great nights where the hospitality was confined by neither time nor money.

For Mick, Jason, Senan and me, it was an extra-special moment, having soldiered together in the blue jersey, and now to be able to share this magical experience. Galvin and Connell, in particular, could now justify their transfer.

Players sensed the importance. We had tried to remain aloof and trained away from the club so as not to allow any interference in our mental preparation. But we could no longer stand alone; the outpouring of emotion from the community surrounding Na Fianna was too great. It's a clichéd view, but it was different from winning an All-Ireland with Dublin; there was a sense of a family celebration. We went home to Glasnevin, together, with the cup.

Marvellous times. And they got better. Buoyed by our county success, our journey through Leinster was a defiant march. Our football was a confident expression of our ability and it culminated in a Leinster final victory over Sarsfields on a raw December afternoon.

Having ground out an All-Ireland semi-final victory over Crossmolina in a sodden Pearse Park in Longford, our remarkable season ended in Croke Park on St Patrick's Day 2000 where, sadly, we were outplayed by an experienced Crossmaglen.

We froze.

Suddenly the stage seemed unnaturally large. McGeeney and Mackin were up against life-long rivals from south Armagh. I believe that if the game had not been in Croke Park, if the focus had been less intense, the free-flowing, expansive football we had played throughout the season could have come to the fore.

In truth it didn't really tarnish the glow of achievement. It was just a discordant cadence, another niggling regret to be packaged away, a timely reminder that romance and sport are uneasy bedfellows.

Our second county-championship success later that year was achieved in less flamboyant fashion as is often the case for experienced sides. We had learned how to grind out results efficiently and the most satisfying aspect was defeating Kilmacud Crokes in the final, our yardstick of success for such a long time. Revenge was a fleeting emotion, however, as our Leinster campaign ended with a jolt in the Leinster final when O'Hanrahan's of Carlow out-slugged us on an apocalyptic winter's day in Portlaoise: one of those winter experiences where morning went straight into night, bypassing any semblance of daytime and where the rain blew horizontally. We didn't perform. It was a day for fortified hearts and some of our old weaknesses were exposed.

The consensus over the winter was that we were a tired outfit, so long on the road, and that perhaps we would be rejuvenated by change. Pillar Caffrey left in 2001, later to become a selector and then manager of Dublin. He was succeeded in the club initially by Mick Bohan from Clontarf. After injury subsequently brought the curtain down on Mick Galvin's playing career, Mick became our new manager, with Bohan as trainer.

In Dublin, we were surviving on the brink, no longer dispatching our now many rivals quite so easily. Still, we had enough arrows in our quiver to kill them off and lift a third county title, beating Brigid's comprehensively in the final.

Strongly fancied for a return to Croke Park in March, our Leinster championship campaign seemed to confirm our status as favourites until we could manage only a draw against Sarsfields of Kildare in Navan. In the replay, we took control and eventually ran out nine-point winners until an unfortunate oversight came to light minutes after the final whistle. We had mistakenly played a sixth substitute, even though it was in the dying stages of a comfortable victory. The error was to have serious repercussions for our season.

Sarsfields had the grace to offer us a refixture and the Leinster Council sportingly sanctioned it to be played at Newbridge, but the drama didn't end there. Sarsfields could have won the rematch, having led by five points at one stage, but we fought back and grabbed an equaliser at the death to send the game to extra time where we eventually pulled away. The efforts exacted a heavy toll on Na Fianna. However, we weren't alone. Our Leinster final opponents, Wicklow champions Rathnew, had played out their own epic drama with Dunshaughlin.

To be honest, I was never a big fan of Rathnew and how they played. We had been involved in a fairly briary clash a couple of years previously down in Aughrim and they were fired up to take on the 'Dublin giants'. Despite their argumentative approach, we got a good foothold in the final in Newbridge and were content enough heading into the second half. I warned our players not to get sucked in and not to retaliate to any intimidation after the break.

Within minutes of the restart, barely having finished warning my team-mates, I received my own marching orders.

With the ball under my arm, I was tackled and I overplayed the ball. Referee Mick Monahan blew me up for over-carrying. Reluctant to give the ball to my opponent for a quick free, a grapple ensued and I swung out with my forearm. I thought it was an innocuous action but, nonetheless, Rathnew's Barry Mernagh collapsed to the ground clutching his face. The linesman consulted with the ref and I was sent off. I'm not excusing my actions; I shouldn't have risked putting myself and my team in that position. I had already scored 5-29 that season and was in good form, so I left Na Fianna exposed for the remainder of the game. From a commanding position, we crumbled, allowing Rathnew to come back and draw the match.

I was suspended for the replay, which took place two days before Christmas. The sides finished level again but, in extra-time, Rathnew's confidence and ruthless application of their game plan exposed our leg-weary efforts. Not even McGeeney's fortitude could counter our collapse. As Na Fianna players lashed out in frustration, we appeared as the aggressors in a niggling, ill-tempered game. It was a depressing experience, one that evoked some of my own inner demons because, after the game, all I wanted to do was go toe-to-toe with any one of their complement who was up for it. It was one of the most frustrating afternoons I'd ever spent on the line. If many of our rivals inside and outside the county rejoiced in our loss to Rathnew, then they must have been ecstatic the following summer when we repeated our six-sub cock-up.

In the Dublin quarter-final against Raheny, in a mix-up over the new-blood substitute ruling, we once again threw on a sixth replacement in the dying seconds of the game. This time there was no reprieve. Raheny stayed silent, something which we're not likely to forget on Mobhi Road, and the Dublin county board duly kicked us out of the competition.

We decided not to give up without a fight. While we had broken the rules, we had won the game comfortably and felt that, as far as sportsmanship was concerned, we hadn't essentially done anything wrong. We sought, and won, a high-court injunction to stop the county semi-final going ahead, although in the end the judge ruled against Na Fianna, duly ending our season.

We certainly didn't make any new friends out of the whole experience though, personally, I didn't really care about that. What was important is that the Na Fianna committee backed us, and though it was a difficult decision for everyone, the club remained united behind the senior team. That mattered.

In the aftermath of the whole debacle, Mick Galvin offered his resignation as manager, which, thankfully, wasn't accepted, but the episode seemed to somewhat hasten our decline as a team.

Armagh's success has also had a knock-on effect on Na Fianna because of the unavailability of their players on occasions. It's a hazard we've had to accept; if you play men from other counties, then their priorities will be compromised. We have also had to contend with retirement and the fact that the panel has entered a period of transition. Still, we exited the championship in 2003 and 2004 by the narrowest of margins, suggesting that there is a resilient foundation on which to rebuild our ambitions.

Personally, my own recent experiences with Na Fianna have mirrored my injury-blighted inter-county career. In fact, after rupturing the cruciate ligament in my left knee against Roscommon in August 2004, I suffered a re-occurrence of the injury when playing for the club in a play-off game against St Vincent's later in the year, undoing several months of rehab in the process. The damage was serious and required cruciate reconstruction surgery.

Still, the pilot light that flickers inside gives me hope that, maybe, just maybe, I could reignite my ambition and end my days as a county champion, perhaps even contributing in some small way to the success.

As someone whose ambition might have initially been out of sync with a lot of my club team-mates, I think eventually most of the sceptics at least understand where I was coming from, what the ultimate goal was. Success perhaps eased some of the misgivings they may have had about me, about the demands which I frequently placed on them.

Nonetheless, I have forged some great friendships through Na Fianna, some from the old days and many from the recent past. It's testimony to what we did in the club that the life-long Na Fianna men and the 'blow-ins' became undistinguishable from each other. The McGeeneys, Mackin, Clancy, Colleran, O'Neill, Ledwith, the McNultys: no matter where football takes them, they have established enduring relationships with people in Mobhi Road. There were a lot of Na Fianna men, some of whom were in the front line of our successful journey, others who I'd played with during the leaner days, and some who belong to both eras. Many lads may have felt in the past that they were forgotten when success knocked on our door. One or two I wouldn't have seen eye to eye with at all times but, nonetheless, I won't forget men like Donal Keegan, Gerry and Stephen Gray, Leo Fay, Ian and Mark Foley, John O'Neill, Pat McCarthy and Brendan Quinn. All part of my life with the club.

Seán Forde, now a selector on the senior team, has remained a close ally and valued friend. We have shared a lot of serious and funny moments together since he first landed in Mobhi Road, none more so than when he suggested a novel fundraising idea for the senior team. Pat Coffey and I had managed to scrape nearly £300 together for a senior-team kitty back in 1997 and Forde, not averse to throwing a few bob on a horse from time to time, suggested we wager £150 each way at odds of 6/1 on a Michael Hourigan-trained horse named Father Andy – supposedly the next Doran's Pride – which was running at Leopardstown. The horse was a sure thing in his estimation.

So, after playing St Mary's in a league game that morning, we headed out to the track in Leopardstown, convinced that we would have a new stock of medical supplies and training bibs on the strength of our trip. Unfortunately, Father Andy never blessed us with his presence as the leaders crossed the line, and was probably still running as we adjourned to the bar for a pint.

Coffey and I looked at one another, a glance that confirmed just how idiotic we felt at that juncture. Mugs! It wasn't long before our ire was directed at our punting guru. Fordie had to endure a few very sour pusses for the remainder of the evening and has never been allowed forget his investment advice.

Not unlike my experiences with Dublin, the trips away with Na Fianna resonate in the memory. Having enjoyed a sustained period of success, we managed to raise a substantial sum of money to take the Na Fianna panel away to Lanzarote for a holiday. I shared an apartment with Karl Donnelly, Adrian Henchy and Des Mackin.

Our residence became known as 'the Villa' and ended up as the focal point of the week's entertainment not, as you might imagine, because of any debauchery, but because of the late-night, post-session discussions which were punctuated nightly by bouts of uncontrollable, convulsive laughter.

Such occasions, rare and wonderful in the life of a Gaelic footballer, create life-long bonds, a shared time of happiness that, hopefully, we will be able to recall again when our memories and yellow jerseys are dimming with age.

I will always be a Na Fianna man. Thankfully, a new chapter in my club life is beginning with my son Frankie's involvement with the under-8 football and hurling teams and, soon, Emma will start in the nursery. Standing on the line with the kids on a Saturday morning is pure pleasure. In time, it may become serious for Frankie and his team-mates but if it doesn't, the enjoyment will be no less diminished and I'm only too happy to help out in any way I can.

Sadly for many of our members, the demographic realities of life in Dublin no longer enable families to remain with their clubs and they have to plant roots elsewhere. The family bonds with Mobhi Road underpinned the club's existence: the Grays, Clerkins, Caffreys, Reillys, Ryans, Gilligans, McNultys, Brosnans. Strong-willed people sacrificed their social lives and their time in return for the satisfaction of being part of a community. I don't dwell on the romantic, but neither do I underestimate the contribution that everyone makes to a club like Na Fianna.

My drive to be successful seems austere, as does the degree of autonomy that the senior team has created for itself, yet I know how much handing over a championship medal to a long-serving club activist like Trish Gilligan meant to her as she lay on her sickbed. It was great to see the people who never participated on the field share in the club's success, helping in a small way to vindicate the hours spent organising lottos, making tea and sweeping out dressing rooms.

This year, 2005, marks the fiftieth anniversary of Na Fianna. It is a diverse community, serving its members in a variety of ways. For me, it now reflects an ambitions club, a winning set-up to be feared and respected in the capital and, hopefully, never again to be taken for granted. With a €2m clubhouse development underway, I know that my personal ambitions on the field are mirrored in the committee room. If I have helped in any way to establish those credentials, then I am happy. Am I satisfied? Well maybe one more autumnal visit to Parnell Park and a chance to share a podium with John Bailey would close the chapter on a remarkable period in my life. A happy ending.

SECTION 4

Chapter 19

The Head and the Heart

In the decade and a half I've spent with Dublin, Gaelic football and hurling have undergone a revolution. Sports science and psychology are now cornerstones of the ambitious teams' preparation, even at club level. I am particularly interested in both, if, for no other reason, they can help to prolong one's career! I thought it might be worthwhile to share my own experiences of preparing for an inter-county championship and chart the changes that have occurred since I first stepped into Gerry McCaul's dressing room in 1990.

I'm only too aware of how these practices are viewed by some people. I have a hard-core group of friends who are quick to remind me of how society in general seems preoccupied today with mumbo jumbo, gurus, quick-fixes, diets and jargon.

However, sports science is merely a body of evidence based on analysis. The scientists have looked at sport, examined the athletes, studied injuries and, based on their findings, have introduced new concepts and techniques and whittled away any bad practices from training. Sports science in Ireland is still in its infancy in many ways and there is a shortage of experts. However, slowly but surely its guiding principles are becoming the established norm, at least with the top counties.

Psychology was always with us. Much of the documented approaches available to coaches today contain practices that many players and managers from the past could readily identify with. Rather than dispensing with tradition, science merely helps us to understand it, and to shed any of the useless myths that surround it.

Modern practices don't guarantee success. The experts are not sports alchemists who can take a bunch of talentless players and win an All-Ireland.

The sports scientist assists players to become better athletes, to become more powerful, develop greater cardio-vascular capacity, and to improve their agility and speed. The sports psychologist assists players to prepare mentally for pressurised games. They can help the team or the individual to develop a resolve or to become mentally stronger.

The Head

Sports psychology in a team game is a difficult concept because a lot of the mental exercises can only be applied by the individual. It highlights the paradox of team games. Success can only be achieved by the collective, but motivation is an individual pursuit. A shared goal brings both the individual and the team together and, when this happens, it increases a team's chances of winning. But it isn't easy to achieve that, even now when most players are aware of the importance of getting their heads right.

My first experience with 'official' sports psychology came when Dublin manager Pat O'Neill introduced a psychologist to the set-up. Given our high-profile losses to Meath in 1991, Donegal in 1992 and to Derry in 1993, our mental toughness was questioned. Hardly surprising. Against both Meath and Derry, Dublin conceded winning positions. Questions were asked.

My own informal take on our collapses, particularly in 1993 in the All-Ireland semi-final against Derry when I was on the field is that, when the pressure came on, too many of the Dublin players resorted to trying too hard. We jettisoned the game plan, stopped taking the percentage option and tried to win the game individually. This resulted in lads taking shots for points from difficult positions, going for goals when they weren't on and taking points when a goal was really required. We were obsessed with trying to do the right thing as individuals rather than as a team and sticking to a disciplined game plan. In this naive approach lay our weakness.

Unfortunately, in the All-Ireland final against Down in 1994, this problem arose once more. Our emotionally charged meeting on the eve of the game, where we swore to one another that we would not lose, backfired completely when we gave a rudderless performance the following day.

The application of sports psychology helps us detail how a player must get himself right if he is to perform consistently and assist those around him. In

1993 against Derry, and in 1994 against Down, Dublin showed how psychological weaknesses can unhinge the most solid of game plans and nullify a player's obvious talent. Colloquially, we talked about 'losing our shape', lacking 'composure'. Others put it down to a shortage of talent – that we simply weren't good enough, but the evidence contradicts that view. What should be considered here, however, is that, for all the individual ingredients that go into the construction of a winning formula, there are extreme versions of the same ingredients that can turn positives into negatives. An example would be confidence and arrogance. Confidence is vital if a player is to realise his talent in any contest. Arrogance, on the other hand, can often blind a player, leaving him ill-equipped to deal with adversity or leading to complacency. A confident defender with huge self-belief, for example, might concede two early points but go on to snuff out his opponent and make a match-winning block in the last minute. An arrogant defender might not have visualised or even thought of this prospect, leaving him unable to cope with the early setback and possibly going to pieces subsequently.

In Dublin's case in the 1994 final against Down, there was no shortage of players in those tense last twenty minutes willing to take responsibility and show courage. However, they were probably exaggerated versions of responsibility and courage. You had control freaks wanting to dictate, stubbornly, how we played. What the sports psychologist preaches is, when the shit hits the fan, individuals remain disciplined, physically and mentally. How often do you see a player on a team in trouble make a stupid tackle, drag a fellow down rather than doing what he knows to be right, which is to apply the proper tackle that he has been taught and, indeed, one he has practised repeatedly for months or maybe even years? Why does a forward try an impossible shot for goal when points can still rescue a game and, conversely, why does a forward try for a point when it's patently clear that only working a goal can rescue a game?

Dublin had all the collective responsibilities covered in 1994. Our management had a workable plan, we were as fit as we needed to be, we shared an insatiable desire to succeed and we had the talent in our squad to win an All-Ireland. So why didn't we? Well, a cursory look at the individual characteristics that each player must possess on a winning team probably reveals the obvious answer, namely, that psychologically, Down had an edge on us.

So what does the list of characteristics contain? What does a player need to be successful? From my own experience of nearly twenty years, with Na Fianna and Dublin, my list is as follows: discipline, respect, confidence, courage, enthusiasm, perseverance, leadership, belief, responsibility, self-control, gratitude, tenacity, diligence, humility, poise, consistency, competitiveness, trust, loyalty, patience, initiative, intelligence, talent and maturity.

Now, when you consider that you need fifteen to twenty individuals, each with an accepted high level of talent to start with, to then possess or develop as many of the above characteristics as possible to make up a winning team, you can appreciate just how difficult it is to win an All-Ireland.

Where's the fun gone? you may ask. Well, the very people posing that question from the bar stool on a November night will be the ones roaring abuse at you from the stands in the last five minutes of a championship game, hammering you for dropping a crucial ball when their cherished county pride is at stake. Performance is now scrutinized in fine detail, not just by management, but by the media and the fans themselves. This in-depth analysis raises the stakes considerably for the players. They, in turn, have responded by professionalising their training, preparation and attitude.

Take 1995. Strengthening our mental resolve became a vital task for O'Neill and Dublin. Our psychologist Tom Moriarity gave some basic coaching in preparing ourselves mentally, but this approach was still regarded with suspicion by many of the players. It's really hard to know whether the Dublin management succeeded in improving our mental resolve or whether they just changed the line-up to include players who were naturally stronger, mentally.

Gerry McCaul, Paddy Cullen, Pat O'Neill, Mickey Whelan, Tommy Carr and Tommy Lyons – they all had their own homespun psychology, a lot of which fitted in with the more recent, formal approaches taken by management teams. Take Cullen, for example. Paddy was constantly trying to instil confidence in the squad, a belief that our superiority was pre-ordained. 'Lads, send these fellas home on their tractors, go out there and blow them away,' he'd say, making the shape of a gun with his hand. It sounds arrogant, but it was only when I spoke to some sports psychologists that I realised exactly what Paddy was doing. Tommy Carr used the expertise of Neil O'Brien during his term. Neil was a life coach who had gained experience from the corporate world, along with various different sports codes and, in particular, golf. Neill opened our eyes to techniques used in other sports and, personally, was of tremendous benefit.

I had my own way of preparing mentally in the early 1990s. For me, physical and mental strength went hand in hand. Only through practise and extra training did I feel I was mentally prepared. Taking to the bike on the morning of a big game was part of my approach. The simple physical act seemed to relieve the overwhelming stress that built up in the approach to a big game in Croke Park. In the weeks leading up to those matches, I was out in St Brendan's every single day, trying to kick balls over the bar, imagining myself in match situations. It was mental rehearsal, my way of getting my head right by instilling more confidence in myself.

With most county teams on a physical par, increasingly, it is the six inches between the ears that are becoming the deciding factor in the destination of the Sam Maguire. Armagh and Tyrone, in particular, have been pioneers in this regard.

Before the traditionalists spontaneously combust, it's important to state that I'm talking about inter-county players, men who should have already reached a high level of competence in their sport: able to kick with both feet; catch the ball over their heads; pick out a pass; take a score; tackle properly. Also, I'm not ignoring factors such as accident and luck. I know what it's like to face an empty goal from two yards and hit the crossbar!

I'm taking some liberties, but if we accept that the differences between, say, the top eight or nine teams in the country aren't as great as you'd imagine, then what gives a team a winning edge? Tyrone hammered Kerry in the All-Ireland semi-final in 2003, Mayo defeated Tyrone in the All-Ireland quarter-final in 2004, and Kerry hammered Mayo in the All-Ireland final in 2004. What gives?

Here's a technique that was shown to me recently and can be quite useful for all footballers. It's also quite revealing in regard to our attitudes to mental preparation.

Sit back, relax and close your eyes...

Mentally visualise your best performance ever, for school, club, college or county. Recall the sights and sounds, the feeling of this, your greatest performance. Picture that time, when you were invincible. This is your best day ever! Every decision you make is right, every pass you deliver is spot on, every move is timed to perfection, every tackle is properly timed, every sidestep leaves your opponent for dead. You are on top of your game. Feel it, sense it.

You are now playing in what has become known as 'the zone'. How good does this feel? Imagine you're watching a film of your performance; the camera is on you alone. You feel no fear and have no worries. You are in complete control. Every break of the ball is yours. In your mind's eye, you look around. You experience where you are – the venue, the position you're playing in and the jersey you are wearing. You are aware of the day, of the time, the month, the people you are with and those who are watching. What do you hear? Feel the atmosphere. Breathe in the air, feel the wind and smell the grass. Visualise! Enjoy! You are the man!

Now for the hard bit.

Let the above image fade slowly. Close it down. Now, in its place, recall your worst ever performance. Typically, it's on a big match day when you just failed to perform. Think of that particular game: where it was; for whom; who it was against. Your opponent is totally on top. Anything you try just doesn't work. You cannot get into the game. You cannot get your hands on the ball. When you do, you mess up. You drop, mishandle, deliver a bad pass and kick it wide.

Experience how you're feeling: exasperated, ineffective, tired and weak. You sense doom. No matter how hard you try, it just won't happen.

Now stop. Back to reality.

Be very honest and compare your own individual performance at your best with your worst. Examine the difference between those two performances.

Was it fitness? Strength? Talent/personal skill levels?

If the answer is yes to any of these three questions, then what percentage was that difference? Minimal, I'd venture.

Now ask yourself, was the difference mental? And, if so, just what was the percentage? Was there only a slight difference in your mental attitude or outlook or was it a more significant difference? 10 per cent? 20 per cent?

If you reckon that the difference between the two performances is greater than 50 per cent mental, then ask yourself, just how much time do you spend on your mental game, as an individual and as a team? Do you split your preparation on a 50-50 basis between the physical and the mental? If you spend six hours engaged in physical training per week, would you also spend six hours preparing mentally?

No, we don't. If the above exercise highlights the importance of the mental approach, then why do we ignore it so much? Tradition is the answer.

Realistically, it's not possible for amateur teams to prepare mentally seven days a week, so it has to be carried out by the individual player and not just in the dressing room or with a sports guru. It has to be done in the home, at work, in bed, at the gym or on the practice field. We have to buy into the importance of mental training, of toning up the muscle in our heads. Performing consistently, at a high level, is a mental thing. Top performers obsess about consistency.

Most counties don't commit enough time to this side of their game. Others may do it in an ad hoc way with no structured approach, leaving it up to the individual or manager. Armagh, however, have shown how it can be applied systematically to great effect. Were they a better team than Kerry in the 2002 final? Not according to the pundits but, then again, do the pundits give due credit to mental strength and mental preparation? The teams from the six counties over the years may have had an advantage in this regard. The quasi-religious zeal with which they achieved a group focus cannot be underestimated.

If the jargon and clinical nature of sports psychology is a little off-putting, get over it. It has always been with us. Now, people have documented it for us, made it accessible for all coaches to throw in a bit of what Mick O'Dwyer or Kevin Heffernan would have done naturally. I remember, following the 1999 All-Ireland final between Meath and Cork, Páidí Ó Sé remarked in his post-match comments that 'Meath won because they believed they'd win'.

It is difficult to measure the quality or quantity of the mental work players do. Some will be better than others but, unlike fitness testing, it's almost impossible to quantify. Yet it's hard to escape the fact that mental preparation is arguably more important than physical. I think the stigma traditionally attached to psychology is lifting and that more and more teams are searching in this area to improve their performances. Suffice to say that if mental preparation can become part of a player's every-day practise, then he is enabling himself to perform at his best by choice rather than by chance.

Like most of the self-help manuals and life-coaching bibles, sports psychology has its fair share of numbered guides to improvement, their 'three personal keys to success', if you like. Some, undoubtedly, state the obvious. However, in sport, repetition is everything. We wouldn't sneer at Maurice Fitzgerald for practising the same strike of a ball thirty times a day, nor do we question why, after thirty-six holes of golf, a top pro might head straight to the practise area. Repeating positive mental notes in your head can be just as important as physical practise, particularly when it comes to big-match day. Just consider how many great players have underperformed, repeatedly, on the big day.

Legendary Olympian Jesse Owens stunned the world of athletics and the Nazi regime in 1936 when he won four gold medals at the Berlin Olympics. What was even more extraordinary about his heroics was that they were achieved despite the fact that he had spent over two weeks travelling to the Games by boat and train from the USA. While onboard the passenger liner on the Atlantic, his training opportunities were minimal; they were non-existent once he hit dry land. However, he spent a great deal of his travelling time visualising his events. In his mind's eye, he saw himself hitting the tape first; he had a clear picture of how he would win. It was an incredible example of the power of mental preparation and positive thinking.

Just as in life itself, sportsmen and women are conditioned to believe a certain way. If we are conditioned to be negative about something then, more often than not, we will behave negatively in that regard. A good example of this is the idea of winning back-to-back All-Irelands. Most players now accept that it can't be done, or that it is unlikely to be done. Why?

In 1983, the Sydney to Melbourne ultra marathon, a gruelling 875km road run, was won by a little-known farmer from Victoria named Cliff Young. He was the laughing stock of the long-distance athletics world in Australia prior to the race because of his unorthodox 'shuffling' style and the fact that he wore boots and long trousers. Previous races had been won by athletes who, to a man, adopted the same method – eighteen hours' running and six hours' sleep.

It was the accepted formula for participating in such a demanding contest. However, along came Cliff, who had no idea how anyone ran such a race. His coach made the mistake of waking him at two o'clock in the morning on the first day of the run, three hours before the rest of the athletes. By the time the remainder of the field was on the road, Cliff had built up a huge lead, one he never surrendered. He continued the same practice every day. His ignorance of protocol was to prove the key to his success. All Cliff knew was that he had to get from Sydney to Melbourne as quickly as possible. He won the race by a huge margin. Staggeringly, he was also sixty-one years old.

He hadn't been conditioned to believe in the standard approach. Of course, as soon as he achieved his success, his method became the accepted one. Not only that, the athletes adopted the 'Young shuffle', which proved to expend less energy and was more aerodynamic.

So if a player kicks an average two points per game, what's to stop him kicking seven or eight? Technique? Not enough practise is the usual retort. But this is not necessarily true. Most inter-county players *do* practise their technique religiously, so why the small returns on the scoreboard? More than likely, the player has conditioned himself into believing that's his quota – 'I'm a two-point-a-game-man'.

What's stopping players winning back-to-back All-Irelands? Besides the obvious difficulties with amateurs giving intense professional commitment two years on the trot and the weakening of desire that comes with success, players have now conditioned themselves into believing that this feat cannot be accomplished. We should all take a leaf out of Cliff Young's book.

Another aspect of sports psychology which has opened my eyes in recent years is the idea of positive affirmation. I'll hold my hand up straight away because I could be highly critical of my team-mates (I may have been correct in my assessment, but completely wrong in my attempt to improve a player's focus). The GAA has a tradition of being desperately critical, bollocking players out of it, even from a young age. While training with the Na Fianna under-8 team recently, I decided to try out the positive approach, praising the kids at all times, regardless of success and failure. This wasn't my normal style. Usually, I would say to the lad, 'No, you didn't do it right, let's go back at try again.' Now I would say, 'That's a great attempt, but I bet you can do it even better.'

I was amazed at the results. Not only did more of the children do more of the drills correctly, but they enjoyed it a lot more. They were thrilled with themselves at the end of the session.

I don't think we really appreciate the power of positive language, even for adults. Some years back, I was asked to go out to a Dublin minor football squad session to talk to the lads. Afterwards, one of the players came over to me and told me a remarkable story, one that has stuck in my head. Having been selected for a Dublin trial, the player informed his club coach, who was thrilled at the news. The coach told him this was a great opportunity for him, that he was one of the club's best young players and that he firmly believed that he would make the Dublin panel. His parting advice was, 'Make sure you practise every day before the trial.' When the kid went home, however, his father treated the news rather differently. 'Son, don't get your hopes up too much,' he cautioned. 'There are an awful lot of good young players at those trials, don't be disappointed if you're not picked. And son, whatever you do, don't go kicking around for the week and injuring yourself before the trial.'

This raises the notion of optimism vs pessimism. The father's concern for his child's emotional well-being was perfectly understandable, but was it of any real benefit to him? Compare it to the positive outlook of the club coach. The player in question, by the way, went on not only to make the Dublin panel, but to make the first team as well.

Personally, I have huge time for the whole idea of goal-setting. I believe that there are advantages in setting targets, both individually and collectively. To do this, there are two concepts which are important: vision and visualisation. The vision for a player or indeed a team could be to win the Sam Maguire. This is considered heresy by some managers and players. The 'one-game-at-a-time' mantra doesn't, on the surface, seem to allow any room for such a lofty goal. Ultimately, we have to ask ourselves as players 'Why are we here?' If we accept that visualising a successful outcome is crucial, then practising this visualisation can be of great assistance.

Obviously there are different degrees of visualisation. Some players will be better at it than others. One player may be capable of picturing his team walking up the steps of the Hogan Stand or the county ground to collect the cup. Another may picture the euphoria at the final whistle and the embrace of a team-mate. Others may be able to set the scene for the game itself and visualise themselves overcoming their opponents in all manner of ways. They can possibly even see the finer details of their performance: a crucial block, an interception, a score from a free in the dying moments. Of course visualisation requires practise. Players need to replay this picture over and over again and to add detail to it continually to make the film in their mind's eye more comprehensive. The more this process is repeated, the greater the subconscious struggles to make the picture a reality. For example, if you're a 'two-point-a-game-man' and you practise regularly by visualising yourself kicking seven or eight, a conflict will develop in your head which your subconscious tries to rectify, replacing the old picture with the new one. Eventually, the seven or eight points will start to emerge as the regular vision in your mind. You'll be surprised how powerful this technique can be. Positive mental rehearsal can transform an average footballer into a damn good one. It's almost as if he convinces himself that he is better than he actually is, and improves his performance as a result.

In the lead-up to the 1995 All-Ireland final, I worked particularly hard on my mental preparation. I knew I was fit and skilful enough, so I visualised myself performing superbly on the day. I visualised my massive work rate, my inter-linking with other forwards and my running at opponents. Pat O'Neill had told me prior to the game not to forage too deeply, to push forward more, that the team needed more scores from me personally if we were to win the title.

I rehearsed this over and over again: shooting/scoring, shooting/scoring. The outcome was that I scored four points in the final, and this from an erstwhile 'two-point-a-game man'. This may sound a little implausible, but it has proven to be beneficial to a lot of athletes. However, I'm not naive enough to think this works without fail; some individuals may never be receptive to these techniques or sports psychology in general. Since 1995, I have used visualisation with mixed results. But because of the benefits in 1995, I have always recommended that players should attempt to use positive mental rehearsal in preparation for games.

Goal-setting is also vital. Back in the early 1990s, during our traumatic search for the ultimate prize, the Dublin squad regularly spoke about winning the All-Ireland and I don't think it was coincidence that we put ourselves in with a chance of achieving that aim nearly every year.

The absence of long-term goals for a struggling team only helps to keep the team exactly where they are. Every team, every athlete, needs that vision. Why else do they do it? I think it was unfortunate that, as Dublin weakened as a team in the latter part of the decade and subsequently, there was practically no communal discussion about our ultimate targets: no talk of winning Sam. I might be naive, but there are plenty of examples of how negative thoughts, or no thoughts at all, achieve negative results.

My advice is simple. Set goals for everything: for training, for matches, for your season. Set yourself a vision and see yourself achieving it.

The Heart

If the introduction of psychology to team preparation in recent years has been significant, the transformation of physical training has been extraordinary. Traditionally, training for Gaelic football teams was punitive. It wasn't acceptable just to train hard, you had to train hard for hours, suffering in the process. Fatigue and dehydration weren't even considered. No one reflected on the value of the training.

When I first started with Dublin, the traditional approach was still the norm. McCaul's training was cruel. He wasn't unique, that was the accepted method. Meath tortured themselves on the Hill of Tara, Down pounded up mountains, Dublin even dragged their veteran stars, such as Barney Rock and Kieran Duff, on energy-sapping long runs around Parnell Park. The simple philosophy of 'no pain, no gain' persisted.

However, the experts will now tell us that all these sessions did was blunt players' speed and diminish their power. With little or no emphasis on rest and recovery, it was hit-and-miss whether a footballer would be physically right on a big match day.

When Fran Ryder took over training under Paddy Cullen, he changed the format. His background in physical education meant he took a more scientific approach. He used a lot of interval training, 800m, 400m and 200m runs, which were all timed. This gave him the ability to assess our progress, or lack of it. Diet also became an important factor. At the time, the popular diet for athletes was a high carbohydrate-based programme. Hydration, rest and stretching all improved under Ryder.

There was no formal weight training, but the biggest advance under Ryder was the fact that there was continual assessment and individual monitoring with times and results posted on the walls of the dressing room.

Mickey Whelan's techniques were very interesting in that he tried to use the ball, even for physical work. He was probably ahead of his time. The modern-day scientists are now leaning towards an individualised training programme that continues away from the group session, leaving the collective training to concentrate more on skills, ball-work, tactics and strategy. But Mickey's programme hadn't enough individual assessment to ensure that each player was up to scratch.

Tommy Carr was the first Dublin manager to employ an outside fitness expert when he brought in Dr Liam Hennessy, director of fitness to the IRFU. Our training was radically changed to a format that is now pretty close to the norm, at least for the top teams. Hennessy stressed the importance of physical conditioning. Structured weight programmes during the winter months were introduced, followed by cardio-vascular work on the field both with and without the ball. Subsequently, I became very friendly with Liam and, with the knowledge that he and 'The Great AK' (Alan Kelly) have shared with me, my career has been prolonged significantly.

Another feature of Carr's training was the use of the gym for recovery sessions. This consisted of some work in the pool, or spinning (using the stationary bicycle to work the stiffness out of the legs).

When Tommy Lyons replaced Carr, he reverted to a more traditional set-up. He wasn't a big fan of weights, nor did he really value the gym. He may have had a point, though I'm not sure he was making it in the right context. Weights and gyms are only useful under expert guidance and this is the heart of the matter. There is a lack of expertise in Ireland and it is vital for any player embarking on a weights or a gym programme that he is assessed and monitored by an expert so that the schedule can be altered continually to suit the player. Lyons mixed a lot of the new and the old. He introduced a rugby kicking coach, yet was prepared to run us around Leopardstown race course a little more than twenty-four hours after a championship match. Some viewed it as a kind of punishment for a poor performance or even a purging session for any post-match drinking.

As I missed a lot of pre-season work with Lyons, I wasn't privy to some of his winter sessions, but in his last year in charge he acquiesced and adopted a weights programme plus regular gym sessions. Lyons also accepted the modern consensus as to how a team should prepare the week of the match and he emphasised the need for rest and recovery before a big game.

Managers today are still learning, but one common practice among the top teams is the inclusion of an outside fitness expert. Traditionalists may scoff, but this is hugely important for player welfare. Sports science is geared towards specific training for the sport in question. It's also about avoiding injury and promoting health protection. The irony, lost on critics of modern training, is that it can actually facilitate more ball-work, freeing up valuable time to practise skills and play matches. If a player is looking after his personal fitness, following the strict guidelines laid down for him, squad sessions can then be about improvement rather than simply getting fit.

Perhaps the most important development in recent years is the introduction of constant physical assessment, beginning with medical screening at the start of pre-season training. In the wake of Cormac McAnallen's tragic death, medical screening is now strongly advised and there is simply no excuse for county teams not to include it.

In Na Fianna, we are lucky to have the services of Will Heffernan available to us. Heffernan is an expert in physical training and has recently worked with the talented European 400m indoor champion, David Gillick. Will has been hugely beneficial to me personally, assisting enormously in my recovery after knee surgery and, while I might not be in the running for a 400m medal, his expertise has afforded me a place in the race. What experts like Will tell us is that we must constantly look after and monitor our health and training. To the naked eye, it's impossible to adequately assess a player's fitness. Professional rugby players now have their resting pulse checked every single day. Any signs of fatigue are dealt with accordingly. Training is constantly tailored towards the individual's well-being.

I shudder when I think back to my young days with Dublin where I often trained privately before joining the squad for another session and played hockey matches the morning before a Gaelic match in the afternoon. No wonder I'm a crock. It would be mildly funny if the same thing wasn't still going on today. In many different teams, young players are still facing the ridiculous physical demands of their Association.

The pioneers in sports science have been the Australians and, increasingly, their influence is being felt across the globe. Ireland is no exception. In Australia they have worked out that, for every one million people in their population, they win approximately three medals at every Olympics – much better statistics than the USA, Russia or Germany. Why? Simple. They have invested in sport – culturally, financially and educationally. We delude ourselves in Ireland; we tell ourselves 'we're a great sporting nation'. We're not. Much of our time is devoted to lip service. We can be suspicious of our top sports men and women; we are begrudging. Our ideals are mixed up and I often wonder if the GAA has been as much of a hindrance as a help to sport in general. By providing a sporting infrastructure for two games alone, has it not let successive governments off the hook for not providing municipal sports centres in every major town? Think of the saving in health costs if proper facilities for all sports were available everywhere in Ireland. And why have we now a proliferation of private, expensive gyms, many of which have been funded with the help of the exchequer?

If ever one wanted physical proof of this, there's a corner of Clontarf on Dublin's Northside which emphasises the gulf. Some years back, the Westwood gym was built, a magnificent private structure with state-of-the-art facilities. Less than a hundred yards away, there is a public running track which is in bad condition and under-resourced, often used by kids on motorbikes and scooters. With proper funding, this public amenity could be of huge benefit, particularly to a lot of the inner-city soccer clubs who use it. Its proximity to the private club reflects, in many ways, Ireland's attitude to sport – it's a business, not a right.

Good sports facilities should be available for everybody and for all codes of sport. In Australia they even assess children at a very young age to see what sports they would be best suited to. Recently, in some codes there, they have taken to DNA profiling of children to predict height, growth, speed, stamina and, in so doing, assessing suitability in various different sports. Granted this opens a whole different debate about the ethics of such procedures and whether it might be a step too far. Suffice to say, we have a long way to go in Ireland.

So, how do the elite GAA players prepare today? Well, let's look at a typical season for one of the top Gaelic football and hurling teams.

Training begins usually around November. Players are screened, weighed and assessed physically. Then the process of conditioning begins with approximately an eight-week weights programme, individually tailored to suit the strengths and weaknesses of each player. It is vital this is monitored by an expert. Failure to do so can be, at best, ineffective and, at worst, damaging to a player. A little knowledge is a dangerous thing and, thankfully, most top managers now defer to the experts to supervise their pre-season training.

A handy tip for all training is to introduce an element of competition to the proceedings. Pinning lists to the wall can help a player to concentrate on progress and improve the quality of training. It also helps managers to monitor exactly how effective their programmes are.

All manner of weights are used, though most experts agree that the most beneficial of all are squats, which help build up large leg muscles, vital for the power and speed required to play football at the top level. The emphasis is now on speed and power. For years, we apparently wasted our time working up the miles for no reason. In fact, the experts now tell us that our cardio-vascular fitness should ideally be little better than that of the ordinary punter on the street. It sounds crazy, but it is the result of years of analysing sports, monitoring athletes and determining what exactly is needed physically to play the game. Allied to the weight training, most players now include flexibility work (the big rubber ball you see in gyms) to improve their core strength and to strengthen stomach and pelvic muscles. Some now even do yoga – anything for the edge!

While this programme is underway, players are encouraged to follow detailed diets. A lot of fuel is required to feed the muscles, so the trend is now towards a high-protein intake to help this process. This, of course, is not at the expense of carbohydrates or fibre – it simply helps to compensate for the extra work. In the past, putting on weight was considered sacrilegious during pre-season training, but now this is exactly what players are encouraged to do, with the knowledge that when the cardio-vascular training and the ball-work begins, any excess fat will be shed quickly. The heavy lifting concludes the programme, although players are encouraged to continue some weights work throughout the season to maintain their strength.

With the current season structure, pre-season is followed quickly by the national league and it's up to the manager whether or not he wants to use the competition as part of a cardio-vascular training programme or whether he wants to try and win it. The latter would require starting pre-season earlier the previous year and spending a couple of months preparing for the league. It is a very difficult period for managers and players. The demands of clubs and colleges (which also crank up in the early spring) and the difficulties of trying to get individuals to stick to a detailed programme with an emphasis on rest and recovery, becomes a juggling act. I'd love to see the day where the county management (or at least one body) dictates the training programme so that clubs, underage county squads and colleges are working in tandem. It isn't the case at present. Injury and burnout are big risks for players whose commitments may be split three or four ways during the spring.

Out of the gym, the players now begin their cardio-vascular training on the field. However, the days of middle-distance runs, hill work and hours of sprinting are disappearing rapidly. The favoured approach now is the 'speed, agility and quickness' technique, known better by its acronym SAQ. This consists of players using ladders (like a light rope ladder) laid out on the ground, through which the player sprints. Another feature of training today is plyometrics, a nimble-footed approach that helps agility and balance. Resistance training is also *de rigueur*, whereby a belt (known as a 'viper belt') is tied to a player and he is forced to pull on the strain. When this belt comes off, you feel like Forrest Gump, sprinting along unrestrained. It is important to note that each of these components of training and conditioning assists in the development of a well-balanced athlete or player. To use only one or two of these elements is not getting the job done. All the time, the emphasis is on quality with an acceptance that by the time you show up at a training session in March or April, you are already fit.

Many of the techniques now employed by GAA teams are adapted from athletics (some via rugby). However, athletes are much more disciplined about training and there is a lot more we can learn from them. I regret not keeping a training diary when I was younger. This is an excellent way to maintain a consistent push towards your goal and can help your mental preparation as well.

The days of a dozen laps, a few sit-ups, press-ups and a game of backs and forwards are over and that's no bad thing. The benefits of modern training will, hopefully, be felt in time, when players, forced to cope with increasing demands on the field, will receive greater protection off it by following well-structured programmes formulated to avoid injury. It should also benefit the performance of a lot of moderate footballers who find it increasingly difficult just to go through the motions at training and will be persuaded to think about what they do and how they do it.

Unfortunately, the increasingly competitive search for a winning edge raises the spectre of drug-taking in Gaelic games. There is quite a lot of innuendo surrounding this issue. Some people are convinced the practice is already widespread, but there is little if any evidence to suggest this is the case. I have never witnessed the use of performance-enhancing drugs. However, the legitimate use of drugs (painkillers and legal dietary supplements) is often confused with illegal abuse.

As a footballer who has struggled with injury throughout my career, I have had to use painkilling injections on a number of occasions, often in far from ideal circumstances. On one such incident, I was playing a club championship game with a broken finger and, after receiving a shot into my hand, I suggested to the doctor that he apply the remainder of the syringe to my knee. He did. These ad hoc arrangements are commonplace in the GAA. Resilience, toughness, pride in jersey and place are held up as virtues in our games, so it's hardly surprising when a player decides to go the extra step to ensure he can contribute. I'm not sure the use of painkillers (cortisone, for example) is something that can ever be properly formalised, as the choice, so long as it's legal, will ultimately rest with the individual.

The use of supplements has become commonplace. These are substances that are used to boost recovery and build up muscle, but using them can be quite dangerous, as you can never be sure that they are not contaminated. There is a perception that the culture in the GAA is now one of players treading the thin line between legal and illegal use of drugs, but this is not true. However, vigilance is required to ensure that we don't drift down that road. Education, the facilitation of regular drug-testing and medical screening is hugely important in this regard. It's been a hard slog over the last few years to get everyone involved properly clued in to the dangers of drug-taking and to where the responsibility for the application of the law actually lies. Initially, the GAA was slow to accept responsibility for drug-testing, arguing that its playing members were club players and therefore exempt from regular testing. However, the authorities refused any derogation and it is now up to the Association to ensure that tests are carried out in accordance with international law. It is also the GAA's responsibility to ensure that its members are properly educated in regard to banned substances. Players and managers, for their part, have to ensure that the lines of communication are constantly open and that a player doesn't inadvertently fail a drugs test because of some innocent use of a cough mixture or supplement. Punishment is severe, regardless of the circumstances.

The Ball

Coaching in Gaelic football has become more interesting, with a real focus on assisting players to develop skills that have probably been taken for granted by previous generations.

Traditionalists lament the demise of the skills of high fielding, long kicking and long-distance point scoring. However, in a modern-day game, where space and time are at a premium, these elements are no longer seen as readily as before. Players are so quick and athletic that the speed of the game has increased exponentially. The footballer now has to make split-second decisions and execute them in the blink of an eye. It is a good deal easier to kick a point from forty metres, standing on your own in fifteen metres of space, than it is to attempting the same shot while racing at breakneck speed with an opponent up your arse!

Coaching and strategy, in the future, will concentrate greatly on drills or plays that will create space for the individual. More emphasis on two-footedness will assist in this endeavour. Good handling is critically important. In soccer we hear of the 'first touch'. Gaelic is no different to any other ball sport. If your first touch is clinical, it affords you greater time and space and allows you play with confidence and fluency.

Ball-handling drills should be introduced at every opportunity in training, even combined with running drills because, when fatigue sets in, concentration invariably drops and mistakes occur.

Training sessions should be more specific, with the individual tasks of backs and forwards separated. Blocking, tackling, passing or shooting drills need to be as realistic as possible and should be carried out at pace and as close to a match-like situation as possible. Forwards should be pressurised while shooting and defenders, likewise, when passing. Free-takers should practise free kicks while very fatigued (tongue hanging out after acute burst of activity, for instance!). Forwards need to know how to block and tackle, as the first line of defence starts up front. In training, matches introducing a three-point score for a block or dispossession can often focus the mind of a player. Also in training games, we should strive to make them as near to the real thing as possible: awarding frees for fouling, dismissing a player for repeated transgressions, keeping the score, making sure players are aware of same and what time is left on the clock. Players must communicate constantly and play with a great intensity. Replicate the 'big match' situation.

Strong competition within a squad is vital, not only for places on the team, but to ensure that training games can be won and lost. Players need to grow to hate losing and even become annoyed at the thoughts of defeat. The nature of the contest should be irrelevant: a benign seven-a-side training match should be treated the same as a competitive game.

Competition is healthy in other aspects of training also. Identifying success is important. Who is the most accurate point-taker? Who is the best passer? Who makes the most blocks? It also assists players in setting goals for themselves at training. It always angers me to see players come to training for the sake of it, merely to have their attendance noted. Every time a player togs out it should be viewed as an opportunity to improve some part of his game. Some players only like to practise what they are good at and comfortable with. The good players pay more attention to their weaknesses. Most of all, a player must have that hunger to improve, to succeed.

Winners and Losers

So, there are a number of critical factors that are keys to success in sport, and Gaelic games don't stand alone in this regard. Talent in a squad is a prerequisite, but it is not always the most talented squad that wins out. Motivation is absolutely vital. Players with a dream, with a vision, an aspiration to win are the cornerstones of a successful outfit. A good management team, with all the attendant qualities, underpins the successful squad: man-management skills, good tacticians, expertise in training and coaching, excellent leadership qualities, an ability to form an opinion on a player's ability or potential even in different positions, good discipline and organisational skills – all these components are necessary in the backroom team.

Managers and players must create a certain culture within a squad. It may be simplistic to call it a 'winning culture' but, as that's the ultimate aim, there is really no other way to describe it. This culture is created with all the elements outlined above coming into play, but perhaps the most important factor concerns the removal of the 'participation culture', where players are only along for the ride, happy just to be playing or involved in the social scene. This culture must be dismissed if a team is to be successful, if it is to win. And it must be removed from every single member of the squad – even one or two lads whose ambition is limited to 'ah, sure it's great to be here' can weaken a whole squad. Only when every link in the chain is strong can everyone pull together and realise their dreams and ambitions collectively.

Championships are won far away from the big stadium and the great crowds. They are won on the training ground. More importantly, they are won in the hearts of men who desperately desire it and in the minds of men who truly believe it.

SECTION 5

Here's to the crazy ones. The misfits. The rebels. The troublemakers. The round pegs in the square holes. The ones who see things differently. They are not fond of rules, and they have no respect for the status quo. You can quote them, disagree with them, glorify, or vilify them. But the only thing you can't do is ignore them because they change things, they push the human race forward. And while some may see them as the crazy ones, we see genius. Because the people who are crazy enough to think they can change the world, are the ones who do.

Apple Computers Inc

Chapter 20

The Gaelic Players' Association – 1999–2005

Letter to the Editor of *The Cork Sportsman* – 11 August 1908

Dear Sir,

I have been asked by your correspondent in the last issue of The Cork Sportsman *to give my reasons for four picked men not travelling to do battle for Cork against Limerick on Sunday last week.*

The principal objection in the way is the distance to Ennis. Imagine a man travelling 120 miles by rail to a match, which should be played thirty miles from the City of Cork. Starting from Dungourney at six o'clock in the morning, walking six miles to the railway station, going on to Cork, Mallow, Limerick, then into County Clare and playing a hard hour's game, starting from the latter place at half past six in the evening and arriving home at two, or perhaps three o'clock next morning. We have done it before and will be prepared to do it again if we are required by any of the hurling teams in Cork. Give me the name of the county board, Munster or general council man who will do it? Would they walk half a mile from the station to the playing ground without a car while the players have to rely always on shanks' mare? I have seen, to my disgust, the players draw the crowds, make the money and lose their sweat at many a hard hour's game, while those gentlemen at the head of affairs take charge of the bag and jump in their cars again before the match is over – off to their hotel to count the coin made by the rank and file.

They will scoff at the application from injured players for compensation. We have several instances of it. At the last two finals – the All-Ireland one at Dungarvan and the Railway Shield at Kilkenny – where the gates totalled £440, six applications came before the meeting of the central council on 2 August, and the certificates sent in the usual way – five from Kilkenny men and one from a Dungourney man in Cork. The

Dungourney certificate stated that this man was unable to work for five weeks. Alderman Nowlan, be it said to his credit, urged on the meeting the necessity to treat the men fairly and was ably supported by Mr Lalor, Kilkenny. In the face of this we find that the Cork representative – a gentleman by the name of Mr James Harrington – moved the reflection of all the applications and, in support of his motion, said that none of the players left the field, whilst the other Cork representatives said nothing. After a lengthy discussion, the six applicants were rewarded the handsome sum of £7. Who made all this money? Was it Mr Harrington might I ask? No. The men who risked life and limb are forgot, five of them get £1 each, the other £2. If I am rightly informed that man – put in that position by the Gaels of Cork – never caught a hurley in his hand, never felt the sting of the ash on his shinbones, does not know what it is to be laid up. When that man acts like this in the central council, what inducement is held out to players by the Munster council when he is chairman of that body?

When Mr Thomas Dooley represented Cork, he always did his best towards injured players, but was cast aside at the last convention. Kilkenny have threatened their withdrawal from the central council. Dungourney can do the same and what is the case with Kilkenny and Dungourney today will be the case with the other counties tomorrow. It is time for the Gaels of Ireland to wake up, take the bags from these gentlemen, show them the outside of the gates and have men of the type of Austin Stack, Maurice McCarthy, Dick Fitzgerald and Dan Frazer at the head of the Association in Munster. The governing body has been captured by non-players, and the players themselves – the men who pay the freight – seem to have no direct representation on it. As Dungourney were champions for 1907, and this year is yet unfinished, I think they were entitled to as many representatives as any club in Cork.

James Kelleher
Hon Sec, Dungourney Hurling Club

1999–2001

By the time I had served my first season as Dublin captain, I was already predisposed to the idea of a players' representative body. Myself, Jason Sherlock, Paul Curran and Jim Gavin had spoken about the idea of getting some kind of agent to organise boot and gear deals and look into the area of generating a few bob for the Dublin panel. There had been a few ad hoc approaches made to us, but as a number of players had existing informal deals with boot manufacturers, we couldn't achieve a consensus for everyone to wear the same pair of boots.

The upshot was that three of us received some gear out of the back of a car and around £3,000 between us to wear their products. While it was tacky, informal and a breach of the GAA's rules, similar activity was going on the length and breadth of the country. Though personal product endorsement and sponsorship were still forbidden under the GAA's amateur status, pressure was already mounting for a relaxation of the rules due to increasing commercial interest and player unrest. The multi-million pound capital investment in Croke Park also seemed to be changing attitudes, even if it was a subconscious influence. As the new millennium approached, it was already becoming obvious that something formal needed to be established.

For years, I had listened to players sitting on bar stools over the winter complaining about how they were treated. They didn't really buy into the traditional GAA line, certainly not the one that highlighted our ethereal rewards – honour, adulation, camaraderie, recognition – they wanted something more tangible. In times past, job opportunities could be assured for any decent county player, but the Celtic Tiger was already in full swing and the allure of employing a player whose primary commitment lay with playing football was already fading. The stakes were rising. The demand of the county set-up was becoming more severe. With payments to managers on the increase, the knock-on effect for the player was beginning to be felt as professional responsibilities were being passed on. What benefits were available were being offered to the successful counties. Many of the less successful squads were still operating in the Dark Ages.

No matter how many times they were told that they were just another part of the Association, many inter-county players knew they weren't. Who, after all, was filling the coffers of the GAA, allowing all the myth-makers to wax lyrical about how wonderful an organisation it was? Who was carrying the sponsors' logos on his chest, helping to fund the county boards? When it came to expenses, there was one rule for county officials, another for the players.

I was fed up with the resentment, fed up listening to players moaning and never lifting a hand to act. The money in the shoe, out of the backs of cars, the quiet arrangements where some players received products or even cash under the table, while most didn't even receive basic expenses, couldn't go on. Worse still was the failure by several counties to even consider proper facilities for their senior teams and the litany of abuse being dished out by officials: failure to pay mileage expenses, refusing to pay for physio bills, even failing to provide meals.

Then, in September 1999, Kieran McGeeney rang me to let me know that a new organisation called the Gaelic Players' Association was being formed in Belfast by Donal O'Neill, a former sports marketing employee with International Management Group, who had recently returned from working in Asia. O'Neill, who was from Newry and a member of the extended Down/Armagh football dynasty, came up with the idea of forming a players' body similar to the many representative groups around the world. After several meetings with prominent Ulster players, there appeared to be sufficient interest to move the concept forward. However, unlike other models, the Gaelic Players' Association, which was given its new title by Derry player Fergal McCusker, would represent amateur players. From the outset, O'Neill believed a players' group would transform the landscape.

McGeeney picked me up at St Brendan's Hospital after my shift on 15 September and we headed north for the launch of the GPA. On the road, we spoke about player-welfare issues, the first proper conversation I'd ever had on the subject. I was taken aback by Kieran's perspective. He'd obviously thought a lot about the whole subject and I found the conversation illuminating. I was excited, but little did I realise where that journey would take me.

The launch took place in the Wellington Park Hotel in Belfast and about twenty-five county players turned up. Only two of these were non-Ulster players: Ja Fallon from Galway and me. No one was sure what we were doing, less still where we were going, but Donal O'Neill used his experience well and fronted the whole press conference. There was a palpable excitement about the occasion as journalists outnumbered the players present. But, as if to indicate the difficulties that lay ahead, a couple of the players who showed up on the night subsequently never committed themselves to the GPA, including Derry's Joe Brolly. Still, there were a number of high-profile players prepared to lead the way: Peter Canavan, Paul McGrane, Fergal Logan, James McCartan, Benny Tierney, Dermot McCabe, Ciaran O'Neill, Anthony Tohill, Paul Brewster, Fergal McCusker, Ja Fallon and Kieran McGeeney. From the outset, we secured the services of Ciarán McArdle to look after the GPA's finances. Logan and McArdle were vital to setting up the proper transparent legal and financial structures of the organisation.

After the provisional launch, there was a lot of informal chat about what we might do next and we agreed that each of us would return to his respective panel and simply spread the word, ask players to join up and take it from there. We then launched the GPA nationally in Dublin's Jackson Court Hotel in December and the initial signatories were bolstered by the presence of players like Kildare's Glenn Ryan, Brian Lacey and Anthony Rainbow, Dublin's Jason Sherlock and Senan Connell, Laois's Mick Lawlor, and several players from other Leinster counties. Many other players also attended, and the GPA was given its first nudge forward.

There was a great buzz in Dublin that night. Players felt emboldened by the gathering and promised much. Before long, however, it became apparent that players were leaving everything to Donal O'Neill, who had already become the 'face' of the GPA. He was trying to get the fledgling organisation off the ground on his own and he discovered that I was one of the few new members prepared to do some of the initial donkey work. Even the most basic administration can be ball-breaking, which I found out from the start, especially when you're squeezing it in around family, work and football. I understood why players were reticent to throw themselves into that area.

Croke Park ridiculed the movement and GAA president Joe McDonagh's response was to use his loyalty to the Players' Advisory Group, which he had appointed, as a reason not to take us seriously. Also, he believed that progress was being made on the issue of player endorsements following the recommendations of the Amateur Status report in 1997. After Congress in April

2000, the GAA planned to appoint a 'central' agent to explore the possibilities and potential for product endorsement by their players and counties. Players simply didn't buy it. If they had, they certainly wouldn't have rowed in behind the GPA.

We wrote to GAA director general, Liam Mulvihill, requesting a meeting. He declined the invitation. My own belief in the potential of the GPA was seriously tested around this time. I was disillusioned by the apparent lack of support. Whatever about officials, an awful lot of players were suspicious. Snowed under with the paperwork needed to administer such an organisation, at one point I rather shamefully started avoiding Donal's calls and was seriously considering walking away in frustration. We had no staff, no structures, and no premises. It was a difficult sell, as we were pedalling an ideal. However, my disillusionment was short-lived as the GAA's defiant stand motivated me greatly. I felt that what we were doing was far too important to walk away without a fight, so I knuckled down again and, if anything, worked even harder.

Donal appeared on the *Late Late Show* with Jamesie O'Connor, which was a big boost for the GPA, although it very nearly didn't happen. A date had been agreed for their appearance and Donal had twenty players lined up to air their grievances on a wide range of topics. At the last minute, the item was pulled by the producers and Donal was furious. If they didn't rearrange an appearance, he threatened to go to the media to explain why he believed their slot was being cancelled. In the meantime, GAA PRO Danny Lynch criticised the *Late Late Show* and Pat Kenny for including the GPA on their bill, claiming it was a bid to be controversial and to boost ratings. The following week the item went ahead, with the GAA refusing to put forward a representative to debate the issues.

At any point during those shambolic early days, the GPA could have gone belly up. If it hadn't been for O'Neill's perseverance and his ability to put a positive spin on events, we would have been finished. But there was another key to our survival: official GAA's truculence. They could have killed us with kindness or, at least, subsumed us into their organisation with a series of flattering proposals. They didn't; essentially, they ignored us. In March 2000, we were thrown a lifeline, ironically by GAA president, Joe McDonagh.

Donal's first public demand was for a better mileage rate for players who were receiving as little as 12p per mile from the GAA, far less than county-board officials. In a lot of cases, boards were refusing to pay out any expenses. O'Neill realised that our demand was likely to receive widespread public support, but he didn't account for a lot of conservative voices in the media who rarely, if ever, took the GAA to task about anything they did. The GAA were also aware that O'Neill was busily trying to procure a deal on behalf of some of our members, trying to get the ball rolling on the whole issue of endorsements.

It provoked an offensive by McDonagh, who was just completing his tenure as president. He warned the GPA that the GAA would 'take serious issue with any group that will negotiate sponsorship at national level outside our organisation.' The GAA denied repeatedly that they were reacting to the GPA, but they were having difficulty convincing anyone. We believed we were provoking a response and McDonagh's threat was just what we needed.

However, in an attempt to cut off any GPA push towards product endorsement, McDonagh announced that inter-county players would be allowed to endorse products. There was a catch. Players would only be allowed retain 50 per cent of any earnings, as the rest had to be divided up between a players' fund, a welfare fund and the county board.

At that juncture, the sort of figures being spoken about for endorsement deals or player appearances were small, so any dilution of funds really meant it was hardly worthwhile.

McDonagh's intervention inspired us because we felt that we were putting pressure on the ruling body to act. We reacted to the GAA following their announcement, predicting that their restrictions on the endorsements would simply not work and we ploughed ahead with our own plans.

As the public face of the GPA, Donal was treated with great suspicion everywhere, particularly because his background was in marketing. He worked tirelessly for no financial reward, yet was a constant target for the professional GAA media who had latched on to him. He then became something of a hate figure in the corridors of power after he gate-crashed the GAA's Congress in Galway in April 2000 and had to be removed. Ironically, I was supposed to be with him and only pulled out at the last minute because my son Frankie took ill. His presence at the Congress was seen as a publicity stunt but, I wonder, had I been alongside him, would the perception have been the same? Even if I was without an invite, would they have ejected me? I really think the fact that Donal wasn't actually a current player was used as a stick with which to beat him.

We were accused at the time of being 'all style, no substance', but I always found it hard to fathom how we were expected to evolve overnight. Publicity, even it was a little shallow and opportunistic, was vital if we were going to raise the consciousness of the players. We also knew that we had to win over a section of the media, convince them that we were on the right track, a potential force for good.

Progress was painfully slow. The back room in my parents' house became the GPA's temporary office. My mother Anne volunteered to do the paperwork for us, while my father Seán also helped out. Then we started to bring a lot of professional experts on board to advise us about our development. Barrister Aaron Shearer, who was then a playing colleague of mine in Na Fianna, and solicitor David Burke, a former Waterford footballer and one of the key men in setting up the GPA in Munster, agreed to give us legal advice, as did our founding member, Fergal Logan. Civil Servant and union activist Cathal Ó Torna explained how to organise our meetings properly. GAA analyst Gerry McDermott, the man who had plotted many of Dublin's downfalls, also came on board as one of the few people in the country who was *au fait* with the GAA rulebook, while a number of journalists also explained the importance of PR and getting the media on side.

Former players like Longford's Frank McNamee (who still sits on our executive committee) and veterans, such as Stephen Melia and Cathal O'Rourke, were also of great assistance. Their considerable experience of the 'bad old days' meant their contributions were always succinct and forthright.

While we were still fairly disorganised, we were starting to get a handle on where we should be going. The anecdotal evidence starting to pour in about the treatment of players in the past and, disturbingly, in the present, was reason enough to pursue our goals.

I must stress that the countless people who helped us to get off the ground did so voluntarily and didn't even receive expenses. They believed in the GPA's potential for reform. In fact we probably survived because so many people, not just players, but grass-roots members, were fed up with how GAA officials carried out their work. If the GPA could help change the GAA itself, then they felt it was worth pursuing and supporting.

The assistance of the ad hoc committee of players, former players, professionals and experts helped give us confidence. Slowly but surely membership increased, and by the summer of our first year in existence, we had about 250 players signed up.

New GAA president, Seán McCague, was far more amenable to the GPA than his predecessor. He held an informal exploratory meeting with Donal and David Burke which quietly opened up the channels of communication between the two groups.

However, we turned up the heat in August when, with the help of PR consultant Declan Kelly who became a staunch ally, we launched a £50,000 promotion deal with recruitment agency, The Marlborough Group, involving ten top GAA players. The announcement invoked the wrath of the GAA. McCague had developed the Players' Advisory Group further by setting up an 'official' Players' Committee appointed by the GAA and chaired by former Armagh footballer Jarlath Burns. Burns launched a stinging attack on the GPA in the wake of the Marlborough deal, accusing us of elitism. 'It would appear that those who have claimed in the past that the GPA is elitist and only representative of a greedy minority may well have been proven right,' Burns blasted in the newspapers. While Burns' comments spawned a new title, the 'Greedy Players' Association' – one of the many definitions of our acronym – the publicity surrounding the deal increased our profile significantly. People started to take notice of the GPA.

Unfortunately, the deal subsequently collapsed when The Marlborough Group ran into difficulties. The players only received half their money but, significantly, they succeeded in bringing the GPA to the wider public. Ultimately, the whole pioneering event cleared a path for players to endorse products without any restrictions, a move that was hailed as a mighty concession by the GAA and nothing to do with the GPA. But the ill-fated Marlborough deal was the catalyst for change. It transcended the sports news and hit the front pages of the papers. Now, of course, the faces of GAA players can be seen on billboards across the country and rivalling the Premiership and international rugby stars on our television screens.

In September 2000, GAA president Seán McCague, announced a £250,000 players' endorsement package managed by Murray Consultants. Ten blue-chip companies were to commit £25,000 apiece but, apart from Toyota, this never really materialised. The GAA vehemently denied that this was in response to the GPA's activities.

Although we were getting noticed, we still had no firm foundation. Our first AGM in The Gleneagle Hotel, Killarney, in November that year was attended by forty-five players, many of them high-profile footballers and hurlers, which seemed to convince our critics further that Burns was right about elitism in the GPA. However, the status of these players was the very thing that gave them the clout to stand up and be counted. During our formative years, intimidation by county officials of new GPA members was rampant. Players were warned not to become members. Donal had been hounded out of Hyde Park by Roscommon officials and had to escape through the kitchens in the Canal Court Hotel in Newry when Down boss Pete McGrath arrived at a team meeting, because the players didn't want their manager knowing he was there. But county-board officials were unlikely to stand up to the likes of Jamesie O'Connor, DJ Carey, Brian Lohan or Kieran McGeeney.

I was still somewhat sceptical. Donal and I had put in a huge amount of work organising the AGM and the gala night in the hotel. Prior to travelling to Killarney, I had told my wife Noreen, already on my case about time commitments to my family, that this would be my last act as a GPA activist and that I would pull back from front-line involvement in the association. The following day, I was elected chairman.

Jamesie was voted in as our first president, Séamus Moynihan was elected secretary and a number of players were recruited onto our first official committee. Some commentators, not prepared to allow the GPA time to evolve, scoffed at our meagre attendance. They could scoff; the GPA was now officially up and running.

We addressed the basic questions surrounding the new players' body: Were we about pay-for-play? What were the welfare issues common to inter-county players? How would we deal with the GAA? How could we improve insurance schemes? The discussion was fruitful, but everyone was conscious that we were treading on new ground. Pretty quickly, pay-for-play was dismissed. I had thrown this out to the floor because I was already on record some years previously as stating I would be in favour of players receiving a small payment for appearing in games. I had never thought out the practicalities of such a proposal and was keen to hear what others felt. Most believed it was unpractical and could damage the fabric of the GAA. They also feared that to go down such a road would jeopardise the GPA's future from the off. However, they agreed that the issue of out-of-pocket expenses be examined, along with mileage rates, provision of proper facilities for county squads and adequate ticket allocations for big matches. It was also proposed that we open discussions with Croke Park and, if necessary, put forward a representative (me as it turned out, although this didn't happen) to join the GAA's Players' Committee to improve relations between the two organisations.

What was really encouraging was the press conference afterwards. Although there was poor media representation, I sat at a table flanked by McGeeney, Logan, O'Connor and Brian Lohan. These were intelligent, articulate men, experienced and respected. They reached out to all players. Our strength, they argued, would come with numbers. I felt that the ground beneath us was beginning to harden. A network of ambitious players was being woven together, people who could think their way forward. It also took some of the heat off Donal O'Neill, who could now concentrate behind the scenes on the many commercial initiatives he had in mind for the GPA.

A couple of hundred players from different counties showed up for the gala night after the AGM, the first time so many had gathered for a function outside of the All Stars. We employed the services of Mícheál Ó Muircheartaigh as guest speaker. Yet, as if to highlight just how difficult it is to gather large groups of footballers and hurlers together at any one time, myself and McGeeney had to head back to Dublin before the dinner as we were playing Abbeylara in the Leinster club championship in Longford the following day. RTÉ Radio's GAA correspondent, Brian Carthy, gave the pair of us a lift back to Dublin, not the first act of kindness carried out by the RTÉ man, who has been straight up and fair to the GPA since its inception.

Early in the New Year, the cold war between the GPA and the GAA thawed somewhat when Burns invited me to a formal meeting. We had already met informally with the Players' Committee and found the whole set-up to be very ad hoc, not unlike the GPA in the early days. What was funny about that initial meeting was that Kieran McKeever, Derry footballer and one of the Players' Committee appointees, was also a member of the GPA. He wasn't the only one testing the water at that point.

My meeting with Burns was cordial and we identified areas of common ground where our objectives were identical. If nothing else, the meeting helped to defuse some of the incendiary criticism that was being dished out by both sides. Burns also arranged another date for us to meet with McCague. There was a touch of 'talks about talks' at this point, but neither side had any choice. We had to move forward.

Although there had been a small turnout at our AGM, the impetus gained from the gathering strengthened our hand considerably. We went on a big recruitment drive and our membership almost doubled to about four hundred and fifty. During the subsequent months, however, much of the media focus centred on the size of our membership. We were under constant pressure to reveal the names of our members, something that we steadfastly refused to do as we knew only too well that it could lead to a witch hunt. A tabloid newspaper had offered a substantial sum (it was actually an unbelievable £10,000) to Donal for the list of players, a move that seemed to confirm our fears even if we couldn't be sure it was a genuine offer. It didn't make any sense for us to give out the names of our members. We were still evolving slowly as an organisation, trying to work out our best course of action and what issues were most critical to the players. We didn't want journalists selecting members randomly and phoning them to ask them about GPA policy. There was also a confidentiality agreement with each member, stating that his name would not be released to a third party without his consent.

Instead we published a list of our county-by-county breakdown and the numbers signed up from each squad. While it was clear the GPA was certainly growing, it also revealed that we were particularly weak in many counties. For example, no Meath players had come on board, while Cork hurling was also a black spot for us, with only two registered members: Dónal Óg Cusack and

Brian Corcoran. Before long though, the Cork hurlers would become our bulwark.

Under pressure to increase our mandate, we targeted one individual in every county squad to act as our representative whose job was to persuade his fellow panellists to join up. It proved a very effective strategy, although the success of the recruitment drive depended largely on identifying the right player in each county. We discovered that one person, if sufficiently respected within the dressing room, could harness entire panels.

Another significant development for the GPA in 2001 was the arrival of The Carphone Warehouse as a sponsor for our annual player awards which we proposed to establish. They also subsequently agreed to finance a scholarship programme for students. The agreement with The Carphone Warehouse came about because our solicitor, David Burke, was an acquaintance of the company's chief executive, Stephen Mackarel, a man whose vision and support were to prove fundamental to the development of the GPA.

Conscious that a lot of the publicity surrounding the Players' Association centred on endorsement deals, we were keen to highlight our burgeoning service to players in terms of welfare and advancement. The scholarship scheme was aimed at giving assistance to college students whose commitment to Gaelic games precluded their ability to work part time. A bursary of £3,000, funded by The Carphone Warehouse, was offered to successful applicants.

Perhaps the most important step for us in our first year as an elected executive was to have an actuary's report commissioned to highlight the potential loss of earnings incurred by an inter-county player throughout his career. The results were incredible. The report indicated that players whose careers averaged between ten and sixteen years, taking into account the different tax brackets, were likely to suffer a loss of income between £80,000–£140,000 (€100,000–€180,000). The losses would occur typically as a result of training, match commitments, shorter working hours, loss of overtime, loss of shift work, loss of bonus payments and diminished promotional prospects.

Armed with this factual vindication, I threw myself into the job as chairman. The learning curve was steep, but progress began to accelerate, as did our membership, particularly when news of the actuary's report started to filter through.

Unfortunately, there was one very rocky passage to negotiate before we took the next step up and it was one that I had steered us into due to my stubbornness. Prior to our AGM in November 2001, The Carphone Warehouse agreed to sponsor our Player of the Year Awards at the gala night, which was due to be held in The Montague Hotel in Portlaoise. The winners were to be chosen by our members in a postal vote. As the ceremony approached, I informed Galway's Pádraic Joyce, one of the stars of the county's successful All-Ireland campaign, that he was the winner of the football accolade. He told me he would be delighted to attend and booked a number of rooms for his travelling party. However, just before the event, we discovered from one of his colleagues that he wouldn't be coming as he was playing for Connacht in the Railway Cup down in Kerry. I rang him to confirm what I'd heard and offered to arrange transport for him from Kerry to Portlaoise, stressing the importance of his attendance. He declined. I was furious. How, I asked, could we be expected to get this organisation off the ground if players would not act for one another?

As it transpired, a lot of late votes arrived on the day for Joyce's team-mate, Declan Meehan. Although I was advised otherwise by some of our executive, because we had not stipulated a closing date for nominations, I decided that Meehan should be awarded footballer of the year. After all, the late votes had swung it in his favour. In hindsight, it was a rash move on my part, having already told Pádraic that he was the recipient. The decision had been born out of sheer frustration. As if to highlight my stubbornness, Meehan had already informed us that he couldn't attend the ceremony and Michael Donnellan accepted it on his behalf. A fortnight after the gala night, Meehan returned the trophy, dismantled, in a cardboard box.

It was a major embarrassment for the GPA and a big mistake on my behalf. With my naive disregard for the bigger picture, our critics in the media were only too delighted at our *faux pas*. Even RTÉ's Michael Lyster mentioned it at the All Stars when Meehan received his gong: 'You won't be giving this one back, will you?' Lyster joked. As an All-Star nominee, I was seething in the audience.

Our awards ceremony is an important statement of our solidarity. And while I was wrong to tamper with, or at least pre-empt, the result, I still feel

Joyce let us down terribly. I don't bear a grudge towards Pádraic Joyce and I am a huge admirer of him as a footballer, but no player would consider missing the All Stars – a set of awards selected by journalists. Now, with a chance to accept the recognition of fellow players, at an event organised solely by fellow players, some were prepared to take it or leave it. Needless to say, we haven't had any problems with indifference since the award-winners started to receive a car! I met Meehan at a subsequent All-Stars banquet and he apologised for returning the trophy, explaining that it had been an awkward situation for him.

After the debacle, the executive decided that the whole gala night needed to be transformed. In future, the voting process for the awards would be formally structured. We also decided to seek major sponsorship to increase the profile of the whole ceremony.

Because of the furore surrounding the awards gaffe, the outcome of our second AGM was largely ignored. Jamesie and I were returned to office, while Glenn Ryan replaced Séamus Moynihan as secretary. The most significant outcome of the meeting was the passing of a motion calling on the GPA executive to enter negotiations with the GAA to achieve a flat weekly rate of expenses. Following the publication of our actuary's report earlier in the year, the issue of a flat rate had become something of a political hot potato. The media had latched on to the idea of a £100-a-week (€127) reimbursement for every player from commencement of pre-season training to championship exit. The *Sunday Independent* ran a poll among GAA players that showed that up to 85 per cent of them were in favour of receiving the weekly expenses.

Another stand-off developed with the GAA who claimed they were being railroaded into a pay-for-play situation. If the parent body was annoyed, then it was nothing to what the players felt. For the first time, a real militant streak could be detected throughout the GPA. Our membership continued to increase, boosted massively by Dónal Óg Cusack's success in bringing the Cork hurling panel on board. This was a huge benefit, not only to our bottom line figures and our recruitment drive, but because the Rebels don't just carry their moniker for fun, it's in their nature – something they would prove in the future.

Having sensed that we had, at last, got our act together as an organisation, there was quite a lot of support from the media for the notion of the €127-a-week issue. It was neatly packaged for them and it gave the papers a reason to smoke out a few hot-headed GAA officials who spoke out with typical anachronistic rhetoric. But this time, fire was met with petrol. The players spoke about the possibility of a strike if Croke Park did not meet their demands for proper reimbursement. More significant still, the Cork hurlers informed us of the intolerable treatment that was being dished out to their panel. They were also compiling a dossier of their grievances in preparation for a campaign of action. Several officials were implicated, including county-board secretary Frank Murphy – one of the most powerful figures in the GAA.

With emotions running so high and players pressing for us to turn up the heat on Croke Park, an EGM was arranged for 27 April 2000 in the Killeshin Hotel in Portlaoise. Besides the issues at stake, the GPA executive knew this meeting was a kind of make-or-break affair. If, after months of teeth-gnashing and threats, we couldn't muster a big, passionate crowd to attend, then the GPA's very future was in doubt. This was the big one. The Minster for Finance, Charlie McCreevy, agreed to address the meeting, as did Brendan Batson from the English Professional Footballers' Association, who we had contacted for advice and whose organisation we would visit at a later date.

When I accepted the position of GPA Chairman in 2000, I had no idea what lay ahead. I was certainly no Lenin-type revolutionary coming out of exile with a satchel full of theories and grand plans. My designs were pretty simple and were based on a real feeling of players being exploited by an Association's ruling body that had shown little regard for them. Many county board officials were, by and large, political animals, concerned with their own survival and power. The gulf between their way of thinking and the changing reality of playing inter-county games was, in my experience, growing. Something had to be done.

Despite my naivety and occasional uncertainty during my two years at the helm, we had begun to travel with a wet sail.

Now, the EGM would tell us if we could clear the choppy waters for good.

Chapter 21

Rebel Yell

The turning point for the GPA happened on 27 April 2002. Our EGM was attended by over 200 players from all over the country who were no longer tiptoeing around the issues. Many more of our members were engaged with training commitments and sent their apologies along with strong messages of support.

Brendan Batson of the English Professional Footballers' Association got the blood flowing in the room when he emphasised the need for players to stand together. It was music to my ears. He also stressed the importance of image rights, how the future power for players lay in the substantial TV revenue which was changing hands between the broadcasters and the GAA. Batson attended our EGM after a simple request over the telephone and never even charged a penny for his journey. He recalled the experience of soccer players in England and, although the status of Gaelic games and professional soccer were very different, he saw striking similarities between our struggle and that which preceded the formation of the Footballers' Association in England.

The confidence of the assembled players seemed to grow when a very lively debate occurred between the floor and the then Minister for Finance, Charlie McCreevy. He was asked about possible tax breaks for players as well as the issue of the €127 a week. He was more than positive. In fact, he confirmed what most of us already knew, that €127 was a paltry figure and we should be setting much higher targets. However, McCreevy was at pains to point out that it was the parent organisation's responsibility, not the government's, to sort out these issues. Tax breaks, he argued, could only be considered if the GAA paid the players. We were already sowing the seeds of a plan in this regard, but McCreevy's witty performance helped the overall mood.

The debate among the members over our negotiations with Croke Park was passionate and extremely militant. For the first time, players spoke openly about the possibility of a strike. The Cork hurlers, furious over their treatment by their county board, outlined their plan for a visual protest at the forthcoming national league final against Kilkenny, where they agreed that they would parade with their socks rolled down and their jerseys out, actions which would incur a fine for the county board. It may have seemed tokenistic, but it was highly symbolic and, significantly, the first step in a campaign that ultimately led to a complete transformation of the set-up in the county and weakened Frank Murphy's vice-like grip on the panel structures. The bravery of the Cork players to speak up, to take action, was extraordinary. There was a palpable sense of solidarity about the assembly.

It was decided at the meeting that both Cork and Kilkenny would carry out the protest at the league final. However, only a handful of Cork players and one Kilkenny man, Andy Comerford, were courageous enough to see it through, highlighting the difficulties we faced in forging a sense of solidarity. Comerford, in particular, showed exceptional steel in the face of enormous criticism within his own camp and county.

I knew that there was a gulf between talk and action. The Portlaoise meeting was highly militant with even talk of an all-out strike by players in demand for improvements. The reality reflected in the subsequent league-final protest was at odds with the tone of the meeting. Nonetheless, the fact that certain men were brave enough to register their discontent was hugely heartening. Their courage, in time, would motivate others.

One way or another, after that gathering in Portlaoise, things would never be the same again.

By the following month, the GPA had over a thousand members. The Carphone Warehouse also agreed to become our title sponsor and fund the setting-up of a full-time post of chief executive. While we were terribly excited about the prospect, we knew we had a difficult task on our hands to find a suitable candidate. Executive experience was all very well, but we needed a figure who could command respect in the dressing room, someone who players could relate to.

I was part of an interview panel set up to find a chief executive and, as the process got underway, the extent of our task became apparent. Genuinely, I had no designs to take the job myself, although I've no doubt the chattering classes bitched about the idea of 'jobs for the boys'. However, I was overwhelmed with calls from players urging me to consider taking the job.

The more I thought about it, the more nervous I became at the prospect. Not only was I unsure whether I would have the necessary skills to administer the GPA, but I was doing well in my job with Jansen Cilag Pharmaceuticals. I had already spent a number of years as a medical rep for Park Davis, Pfizer and Knoll and, with each move, my reputation and career prospects were increasing. Was I now going to chuck all that aside and take over an association that was still finding its feet? I was also nervous about the impact such a role might have on my football. I informed Dublin manager, Tommy Lyons, who was supportive of the idea.

What convinced me ultimately to apply for the position was the attractive notion that I could consolidate everything we had done since the GPA's inception by dedicating myself full time to the players' body. The support of so many strengthened my resolve and confidence. I discussed the idea with my family and informed the executive committee that I was interested in the post. After a series of meetings, they agreed to match my current wages and I signed a contract to become the first chief executive of the GPA.

It was a step into the unknown. I wasn't fooled by the loftiness of the job title. After all, I was still licking envelopes and processing membership applications. I was sure, however, that I'd have a huge amount of free time to concentrate on the GPA. Little did I realise how the position would expand to fill every conceivable minute of the day. Subsequently, GAA director general, Liam Mulvihill, related his own experience of moving from a voluntary position to a professional one in the organisation and how attitudes towards him had changed. Things would never be the same again, he counselled. He was right.

News of my appointment was announced on Thursday, 23 May 2002. It never hit the radar. That afternoon, word filtered through from Saipan that Roy Keane had been sent home from the Irish World Cup camp. As civil war broke out in Ireland, I quietly assumed my new position.

Dessie Farrell

Before I could get a clear picture of my priorities, Croke Park agreed to meet us, following our demands for reimbursement over loss of earnings. Seán McCague, Liam Mulvihill and Jarlath Burns were all present, while the GPA representation consisted of Glenn Ryan, Donal and me. While the mood was convivial enough, we soon reached an impasse over the expenses issue. We highlighted the anomaly, as we saw it, whereby the GAA was happy to pay the international rules players a daily expense for their involvement in the annual series against Australia. It stumped them somewhat. Initially they claimed that it wasn't Gaelic games, although Gerry McDermott had already tipped us off that the games, once sanctioned by the GAA, fell under the Association's rules.

We didn't reach any kind of agreement, though further meetings were arranged. The next time we met, McCague had to be excused, so we insisted that Mulvihill play a more prominent role in the meeting (he had just taken minutes on the previous occasions). The director general ruled out any idea of a flat rate of €127, but said he would look at expenses in general. We stuck to our guns. Mulvihill said he felt a flat rate constituted pay-for-play. I brought up the fact that a flat rate had been paid to the touring Irish international rules players while they were in Australia. I suggested that this was something of a precedent. Mulvihill hit back, saying that the only reason this money was paid was because players were out of pocket.

Then one of our committee members, Aaron Shearer, a barrister by profession, pushed this issue further, suggesting that there was a strong analogy between the touring rules players and inter-county players in general. After all, both groups of footballers were out of pocket. Mulvihill got really annoyed with this full-court press about the flat rate. The more the GPA insisted on it, the more likely it would be, he countered, for expenses to be withdrawn for the touring squad. 'Then players won't play,' replied Shearer. 'Then I'll shed no tears if that happens,' Mulvihill stressed.

We then asked to adjourn for a few minutes to consider the response. However, things had calmed down when we returned and we revisited our merry-go-round discussions, seeking a meeting with the new president-elect, Seán Kelly, in the process.

It was an interesting experience. Mulvihill stands above GAA officialdom. His reputation is solid as a highly skilled and incredibly successful administrator who has overseen the enormous capital redevelopment of Croke Park and helped drag a deeply conservative organisation into the twenty-first century. So it was with some surprise that, during that fractious meeting, he became so animated. He had never really engaged with us in previous meetings, yet we knew he was the constant power figure in the organisation. We had been told repeatedly that he was the one who would make the big decisions, regardless of the bureaucratic labyrinth of Congress and Central Council. Whether that is the case or not, I don't really know. Nonetheless, on this occasion, he may have let his guard slip.

The meetings with the GAA were important even if we didn't actually achieve any major concessions. Although they refused to recognise us officially, and while many of the rank-and-file officials continued to despise us, we could point to the ongoing working relationship as a step towards official status.

After assuming my new professional position as head of the GPA, what became apparent pretty quickly was that the role consisted of two strands that were not mutually exclusive, but that required two very different approaches.

Firstly, I had to deal with direct player-welfare issues which were increasing by the month. Players, not prepared any longer to put up or shut up, were asserting themselves to a much greater extent and this was leading us into direct conflict with their respective county boards. Facilitating our members in this regard was a huge task. We often had to confront officials for the first time because the players were too reticent to do so. We had to educate our members on how to organise themselves properly, how to document their grievances and how to present them to the officials. Then there was the difficulty with mediation, particularly tricky when representing exasperated players in a conflict with obdurate officials whose antipathy for the men who wore their county jerseys was barely concealed. After intervening in a number of disputes, I started to detect a regular pattern: expenses not being paid, lack of basic training and medical facilities, medical bills left unpaid, intimidation of GPA members.

We also had to prepare Gaelic players for the introduction of rigorous drug-testing. Some of our members opposed the idea, not because they favoured the use of drugs, but simply because they found the imposition of such strictures as yet another professional demand for amateurs. The GPA executive actually took quite an amount of flak for its stance in upholding policy in accordance with the guidelines issued by the Sports Council of Ireland.

Knowing that drug-testing would make the paradox of increasing 'professionalism' among its amateur ranks all the more stark, the GAA dragged its heels somewhat over the issue until forced by the authorities – with the threat of a withdrawal of funding – to embrace the new structures for testing and assume responsibility for them.

Besides the countless welfare issues coming to the fore, the second major strand of my new brief concerned our financing and commercial activities. We had to fund the GPA properly to secure its future, to provide the services pledged to our members. Obtaining a permanent office and an administrative staff were crucial if we were to carry out our basic operations. To do this, we had to generate an ongoing income through some sponsorship initiative.

At the end of November 2002, our 'union' status was strengthened considerably when the Cork hurlers took matters into their own hands after a long-running dispute with their county board and called a strike. They outlined a substantial list of grievances, involving poor travel arrangements, problems over gear, gym accessibility, support structures and membership of the GPA. Accusations of intimidation and bullying were rife. Mark Landers, who had captained the team to their All-Ireland hurling victory in 1999, painted a vivid picture of the type of treatment that was being dished out when he was quoted during the strike. 'Just before the league final,' Landers explained, 'and just after the GPA EGM in Portlaoise, an unnamed individual said to me during a training session in Páirc Uí Chaoimh: "Take a good look around because you won't be seeing this place again".' A couple of days after the threat, Landers was dropped from the Cork panel but, after the side were subsequently beaten in the Munster championship by Waterford, the selectors reinstated him.

Their problems had reached an impasse, with the Cork county board showing little willingness to address the problems. Because the Cork players had included reimbursement for loss of earnings on their list of demands, they were being branded as greedy mavericks who were trying to tear the GAA's core values apart. A few days later, the Cork footballers joined their colleagues in solidarity and the officials were backed into a corner. Frank Murphy, for all his established power, couldn't browbeat the Cork hurlers any longer. Officials would have to concede to the players' demands. A fortnight later, the victorious players called off their strike after brokering a satisfactory deal with the county board. One of the stumbling blocks – the demand for reimbursement for loss of earnings – was overcome by the county board's pledge to pursue the issue on a national basis.

By standing together, the Cork men had proven their power. Images of Joe Deane, Seán Óg Ó hAilpín and Dónal Óg Cusack making their public stand sent out a potent message to the GAA. The massive support enjoyed by the players also indicated to officials everywhere how out of touch they were with their own grass roots.

Since our inception, the GPA has been accused of being elitist; only interested in the top counties, only interested in endorsement deals for the star players. However, we had already opened up a can of worms in the weaker hurling counties. We were swamped with complaints from hurlers from nearly every county outside of the top-flight counties. Before the stand taken by Cork's 'top players' no one was particularly interested in the plight of the minnows. Now their voice was strengthened and they too would become empowered to speak out against poor treatment.

The case of the Louth hurlers was particularly galling. We discovered that, on one occasion, they had to train close to midnight because the facilities were unavailable earlier in the evening. Cold showers, no meals, no gear – they were an irrelevance in the eyes of some county officials. Sadly, they weren't alone either.

Ironically, when we highlighted these problems, they were met with a lot of indifference by our critics in the media. Some of the columnists, who normally revelled in the romance of the GAA, were uninterested in the plight of the Louth hurlers. Worse still, the county board officials were equally unconcerned. With no ambition and little respect, they were happy to treat their players like dirt.

Having witnessed the state of play for many of the weaker hurling counties, we decided to lend our weight to the 'Hurling Re-development Group' a body comprising of representatives from the game's poor relations and spearheaded by Kerryman Roy Dineen. We organised a series of meetings for players operating at this level and presented Dineen's report on the state of hurling as they saw it to the players. Incorporating the response of the players and elements of the report, we compiled our own blueprint, which identified problems and offered solutions to hurling's problems, both as a game and with regard to its exponents. DJ Carey and Brian Whelahan attended a number of these discussions to offer their advice and their very presence was encouraging to these players.

Top of the list was the precarious state of the sport in many parts of Ireland, a situation that was all too real despite the endless lip service paid to it by the GAA's politicians. Regardless of the aspirations of Croke Park's top men, who were trying to improve the state of hurling with various initiatives, the reality was a lot different at county board level where some of the ruling bodies were proving to be at best uncaring and apathetic and, at worst, antagonistic and abusive.

After compiling our report, we presented it to the GAA's Hurling Development Committee, a body of high-profile hurling figures. We brought along Louth hurler Donnach Callan and Pat Coady of Carlow who explained clearly what was happening at the lower level. The Committee members, men like Ger Loughnane, Cyril Farrell and Nicky English, couldn't believe what they were hearing. After a litany of woe, Loughnane intervened: 'Lads will ye stop before I overdose on horror stories!'

While the HDC is continuing to address the structures of the game, in particular the championship, many of the more pressing concerns still need to be tackled.

Some officials will argue that my focus in regard to promoting games is too narrow, too concerned with the inter-county strata. However, I maintain that the inter-county teams remain the ideal and, if well attended to, will nurture all levels beneath it, inspiring young players to persevere with the game.

While some progress has been made since we issued our hurling report back in 2003, it has been all too sporadic. I need look no further than my own back yard, where inter-county hurling in Dublin has deteriorated alarmingly in recent years.

Behind the scenes and in between the countless bushfires igniting in dressing rooms around the country, me and Donal were busily trying to strengthen the business end of the GPA. Our profile reached a new level when we had our first major gala night in the Citywest Hotel in November 2002, where Seat sponsored two cars for our Player of the Year Awards. Nearly 1,000 players, friends, politicians, officials, sponsors and guests showed up and, for many, especially some sceptics in the media, it was tangible evidence that we weren't going to disappear.

However, we still had the not insignificant matter of generating funds to run the GPA and, at our first Seat gala night, we were presented with an idea that would ultimately secure the association's future. David Burke had introduced us to a Waterford businessman by the name of Peter Queally, who owned the Glenpatrick Drinks Group. He suggested that the GPA should develop its own sports drink and invited us down to Tipperary to discuss the idea at one of their plants. We invited fitness expert Dr Liam Hennessy to accompany us. While the idea was excellent, the deal on offer stretched us too much. We would have had to come up with a substantial sum of money that we simply didn't have to get the product off the ground and there were issues surrounding distribution and marketing which we couldn't manage. On the journey back from Clonmel, we discussed approaching C&C, the only big drinks company in Ireland that didn't have an isotonic sports drink on the market.

So, I rang C&C's top man, Maurice Pratt, who put me on to their Ireland executives, Colin Gordan and Michael McArdle, and Club Energise was born. With direct player involvement, the whole project has been a remarkable success. We thrashed out a ten-year multi-faceted deal with C&C estimated to be worth over €10million to the GPA, securing our future and giving us a vital independent platform on which to operate. Not only that, there were fantastic spin-offs. The deal gives huge scope for players to benefit from the various initiatives which the funding has enabled us to establish: increased scholarship schemes, benevolent fund, coaching seminars and the initiation of official player GPA funds (a pool of money for county squads controlled by players). The relationship with C&C has even led to several employment opportunities for players.

By securing the GPA, which now boasts over 1,400 members, this landmark deal has ensured that players will have a voice in the future. It has also increased the profile of the game. Because of Club Energise's energetic and highly visual advertisement campaign, drinks rivals have followed suit and put GAA players at the core of their marketing.

Ironically, we did actually approach Lucozade in the early stages of our search for a long-term sponsor and they offered us a donation of £500 to our gala night, stating that their budgets wouldn't allow them to get involved. This from a multi-million euro operation in Ireland, for which Gaelic games is becoming an increasingly important part.

Club Energise was launched in August 2003 and has thrived in a ferociously competitive market place. However, not every player has rowed in behind us and we have had our problems with a small number who have accepted deals with rival companies. It is vital for the GPA and all inter-county players that we stick together. Before any deals, before any major sponsorship, we were told by experienced players' associations in England and Australia that unity and solidarity was vital for GAA players to improve their lot.

So we were very disappointed, as were a lot of other players, when Oisín McConville, Dessie Dolan, Brendan Cummins and Eoin Kelly (who also received a £3,000 GPA scholarship from The Carphone Warehouse) chose to ignore our request for them not to promote a rival product. We offered to match the money they were being offered by the rival and we emphasised that they would not be out of pocket in any way. However, they went ahead with the campaign to promote the rival product while Waterford's Paul Flynn, who had also been lined up for the deal, agreed to the GPA's request at the last minute and pulled out.

By making that choice, which of course they are perfectly entitled to make, these players have benefited only themselves. They have not helped their playing colleagues in any way. By siding with the GPA product or allowing the GPA to negotiate on their behalf for general endorsement deals, each player is strengthening the hand of the other. There is no creaming off the top done by the GPA – our advice and representation is done for free. Peter Canavan and DJ Carey turned down far more lucrative offers to ensure that the Club Energise project would get off the ground before the deal had even been finalised. Had Canavan and Carey not been committed to the collective ideal behind the GPA, then the C&C arrangement would have been scuppered. Of course the only reason rival products are now competing for player endorsement is because of our deal and their fear of a decline in market share.

Other players have also broken ranks since and have endorsed other drinks products and I suppose it's something we're going to have to live with. All we can do in the GPA is implore our members and all players to try and stick together for the collective good.

It's hard to fathom the GAA's blatant hostility towards Club Energise which they have banned as an advertiser from their grounds. Despite slating us for elitism and greed in our early days, they are now denying players the chance not only to earn money, but also to benefit the players' organisation in general. This is a collective goal, one being hampered by that great bastion of collectivism, the GAA.

So, you see, both strands of the GPA, our union work and our commercial work, are equally emotive. Both strands involve a struggle for recognition, for power; a fight to raise the players' voice, to take some control of our futures. But if all the major battles which we have fought to date have brought the GPA to where it is today, then one remains which could catapult it into a different orbit.

Chapter 22

Strength in Unity

No one in the GPA is foolish enough to believe that our struggle is in any way over, or nearly at an end for that matter. It's not. Many more battles remain to be fought. Yet an increasing number of players who are prepared to defy convention and stand up for their rights are emerging. The young player stepping into the dressing room for the first time is now a lot more *au fait* with player power. He is much more likely to confront and agitate. He sees the models in other sports, he rubs shoulders with professional athletes of other codes in the gym and he is no longer walking back into his county dressing rooms cowering from some official with a sackful of jerseys. His status has changed in the GAA and there is no going back.

The assertion of rights has become a point of principle for the modern GAA player. In the past, players were terrified to make any public gesture. They were immediately branded a prima donna if they acted out of step in any way. In the summer of 2005, we witnessed how players stood in solidarity in the dispute with RTÉ over the display of Club Energise drinks in post-match interviews. The broadcaster refused to allow players to drink from the bottle while on camera, an action for which they received €500 from the GPA. Dublin player, Alan Brogan, declined to accept his RTÉ man-of-the-match award, which exemplified this attitude. This was a bold and courageous stance to take and resulted in numerous other high-profile players and squads doing likewise. Undoubtedly, the GAA have observed this player unrest with great interest.

In the early days, when we were struggling to make an impact, one supportive columnist described the group of militant players as no longer suffering from the 'mushroom' syndrome, whereby we were prepared to be kept in the dark and fed shite. Young county players reflect the massive changes which have occurred in Irish society in general. Increasingly, they are better educated and this is reflected in their ability to make decisions without fear of rebuke. They are all too aware that their commitment to the game means between twenty-five and forty hours a week. They are never off duty.

While the relationship between the GAA and the GPA continues to evolve, it cannot flourish in its current state of vacuum. There is no contract, no official bond between the players whose skill and commitment fills Croke Park and the people who run the sport. This cannot continue. History has a habit of repeating itself and, unless the GAA puts structures in place to properly reimburse players for their unprecedented commitment to the sport, they could well be facing the increased possibility of unlegislated player payments.

While pay-for-play remains something of an 'evil' concept in the GAA, having observed the changes within the games and the attitudes of players, it is my opinion that we will be looking down the road to semi-professionalism. A lot of young players are already searching for ways in which to dedicate themselves full time to their sport. It is not because they have any hare-brained ideal of making wads of cash from playing for their counties, but because their ambition is to improve as players or athletes and to maximise their own potential. This already has been the motivation for some players to take sabbaticals, or to seek part-time work only, in their endeavour to pursue success.

This trend is set to continue. During my own rehab from my knee injury, I took a week's holidays to train and I made huge progress because I was able to comfortably train twice a day while recovering properly, eating well and undergoing physio. It may seem improbable, but an ambitious county panellist operates on an almost full-time basis. I heard commentators refer to the Tyrone footballers under Mickey Harte's management as 'only training twice a week'. If they had checked a little more thoroughly, they would have discovered what each individual in Harte's squad is doing on a daily basis, away from group sessions. The drive for success is an irrepressible force. Better to embrace it and put in proper support structures than make ludicrous attempts to curtail training.

The fear that any form of professionalism will destroy the very fabric of the GAA is a real one. It is well-founded. But it is based on the idea that something beyond the control of the Association will draw the lifeblood from it and lead to a haemorrhage of voluntary help. However, our experience in the GPA has shown that, in theory, there could be sufficient funding available to county panels to create a semi-professional structure without a detrimental effect. It remains to be seen whether this will actually happen or not. The GPA have already put in place a network of 'player pools' where county squads can raise their own monies, outside of the control of the county board, which they can spend however they decide: on a team holiday, on a training week or simply to reimburse themselves for their expenses. This does not cut across county board financing, nor does it tap into the enormous revenue generated by the players who raise millions (for the GAA) during the championship season. Supporters' clubs are also having an increasing influence in the game, an influence that has not always been greeted with open arms by intransigent county board officials who fear an erosion of their power.

However, the most significant change of all could centre on image rights and their impact on television revenue. As things stand, the GAA refuse to acknowledge the GPA's ownership of the players' image rights. When a player becomes a member of the GPA, he assigns his image rights to the player body. During the dispute with RTÉ, we discovered that part of the contract between the national broadcaster and the GAA refers to the accessibility of players to do interviews for RTÉ. The GPA is quite prepared to challenge the GAA on this issue as we believe that they do not have the authority to assume ownership of these rights, particularly when negotiating a package with a broadcaster that essentially relies on the performances of players. For the privilege of negotiating on the backs of players, a percentage of the GAA's television revenue should be forthcoming to footballers and hurlers as is common practice in other codes across the world. We do not believe that the current 'arrangement', of which even the most informed Gaelic-games supporter knows little, can continue.

When the government was trying to protect a number of sporting events against their removal from terrestrial television – Irish soccer internationals, the All-Ireland semi-finals and finals – it was very interesting to see how trenchant the GAA was in asserting their right to determine how their games are broadcast. Though it might be a while before we see pay-for-play in the GAA, how long will it be, I wonder, before we see pay-per-view in the championship? And of course it's already happening in other jurisdictions through satellite TV.

The GPA aims to highlight a player's right to assert ownership of his own image. Internationally, sporting bodies have all had to concede in this matter. Players elsewhere have successfully claimed ownership of this fundamental right and we are confident that the Irish experience will not be treated differently.

While the image-rights issue is sure to reach a critical point in the near future, the high-profile transfer of GAA stars to Aussie Rules has already turned the spotlight on our own games. Players are now aware of the structures in place Down Under and are wondering why it is such heresy to aspire to something similar in Ireland. The Australian Football League has a three-tier structure: a professional level, a semi-professional level and an amateur level. This came about when the AFL came under huge pressure from the AFL Players' Association to change and they made a bold move: they stood back and allowed experienced business consultants to set up their three-tier structure. These consultants restructured the whole league and put in place a collective bargaining agreement with the players' body, which now essentially defines how the AFL operates. The success of the Australian model is based on the simple logic that everyone knows where they stand within the organisation.

Young GAA players breaking onto today's inter-county stage are children of the information age. They are already competent young athletes, aware of modern-training methods and very aware of the lifestyles on offer in professional sport, particularly in rugby. Can we always take our success in the GAA for granted – that our young talent will always remain loyal to our games and not jump ship to seek out a better existence? I'm not so sure. The very fact that kids are now debating the issue seems to suggest that they are already ahead of the game.

County board debt is usually one of the arguments used against any form of professionalism for GAA players. However, bringing this issue into the equation only strengthens the position of those who look to the Australian model as a good way to proceed, rather than allowing mismanagement to continue. The cost of running county teams is not just something that can be fumed over at county board meetings. It is a necessary requirement. Without properly prepared teams, the magnificent structure in Jones' Road wouldn't be long turning white and growing a trunk.

Of course any radical transformation of the GAA's structures has to be done while safeguarding the club structures and grass roots. No one wants to see a transfer system in place because they know it would jeopardise the county dynamic which drives the game. A semi-professional structure, where every player received the same amount of money, entitlements and welfare, might resolve this issue. However a semi-professional tier could only be introduced if the ongoing problems which beset club structures are tackled properly. For example, the absence of a defined club season with a sacrosanct fixture list is ridiculous. Numerous attempts to address this problem have all failed and I know from my own experience with Na Fianna just how frustrating it is for committed club players to be left in suspense by the uncertainties of the inter-county championship season.

Other issues of huge concern, not just to county players but also to club players, are the insurance and injury schemes which are in place at the moment. The cover for loss of earnings and for medical bills due to injury is grossly inadequate and must be improved. Something else that must be improved is the availability of information so that proper coaching and physical conditioning structures can be implemented from underage to adult level for all clubs. This will ensure that players can train in an environment that reduces the risk of injury and ensures that skills and talent can be properly nurtured. The new training regimes, which have come about due to the advances in sports science, need to be applied to the club game as well.

I believe that the change towards a tiered structure of semi-professionalism will come about regardless of all the emotive arguments. It is inevitable. In fact, it is already upon us if one takes into account the large sums of money being paid to certain managers and, indeed, a number of club players. But of course there is no transparency in the current arrangements, which leaves officials at a loss to explain it properly. The immortal line of a previous GAA president comes to mind in this regard when, after trying to investigate payments to managers, he remarked, 'Never mind finding evidence of under-the-table payments, we couldn't even find the table!'

However, I hope that these issues are addressed properly very soon.

Ignoring them will not protect the GAA's future. The parent body must be proactive in this regard; it must promote and control the development of any new structures rather than turning a blind eye. But to do that, they must negotiate with players and they must harness the support of our association in the process.

The decision by RTÉ to ban players from displaying their Club Energise bottles at the beginning of the 2005 championship was most disheartening and there is a question over who was influencing the move. It's very difficult from our perspective to accept the decision, even if it is backed up by legislation concerning 'surreptitious advertising'. However, our interpretation of this legislation differed from that of the broadcaster. Therefore, it was decided to refer the matter to an independent body in the EU that deals with disputes arising from broadcasting legislation. In the interim, in return for co-operation from the GPA and players, RTÉ has agreed to grant extensive benefits to the GPA, including exposure of various GPA events. Confidentiality prohibits me from elaborating on the deal between the two bodies, but suffice to say we were satisfied with the outcome. Thankfully, we had a strong hand in the negotiations because of the solidarity shown by the various squads during the dispute. Once again, the Cork hurlers were in the vanguard. This powerful display of unity will be needed again in the future when the substantive issue of image rights is thrashed out. And it is certainly worth repeating, for the benefit of players and the public, that the whole episode highlighted how the GAA assume 'control' of players to benefit their own interest in contractual negotiations.

Though the GPA's struggle to be officially recognised by the GAA has been an emotive one, my appointment to their central council as the players' representative is a significant step. Seán Kelly's presidency has been an inclusive one and his pragmatic reference to the GPA in his 2005 Congress address was recognition that we are, de facto, now the official players' body.

However, the GPA will remain autonomous, independent of the GAA and my contact with Croke Park's ruling body will not, in any way, jeopardise our separate standing. We believe we are best placed to be heard as an outside voice. On central council, I will be representing all players, even those who are not signed up to the GPA. It is a positive step for both bodies and I am certainly honoured by the appointment. It is highly symbolic for the GPA and I sincerely hope it will be productive as there are issues of huge importance for players which remain unaddressed by the GAA's hierarchy, despite the best efforts of Kelly. His presidency will be hailed as an era of huge progression for the GAA. The abolition of Rule 42 warrants no further mention. His relationship with the GPA and with individual players has been equally significant, though it has not had as much publicity. On a personal level, I have always found him to be forthright and extremely amenable to the players' plight and my only hope is that his successors will operate in a similar vein.

I'm looking forward to representing players on the council, particularly as I believe there are a number of 'progressive' officials coming to prominence at executive level in the GAA. It heartens me to see it. There are wonderfully skilled administrators and officials in clubs the length and breadth of the country, but way too few of them step into the county board arena. Clubs should encourage their top administrators to becoming more involved in county-board matters and, although I'm sure it's not going to happen in the short term, I would love to see more former players become involved in GAA politics. The experience they bring to the table is invaluable.

For me, the defining moment of the GPA will always remain the Cork hurling strike. It provided a template for every county squad, not just because of the remarkable display of courage and solidarity, but because the whole protest was conducted with great dignity.

Casual observers of the ongoing dynamic between the Players' Association and the GAA often forget the status of our members. Dónal Óg Cusack, our current GPA chairman, was a pivotal figure in mobilising the Cork squad to take on the might of the strongest county board in Ireland. But Dónal Óg is not just a brave, progressive character; he is an exemplary GAA man. His undying love of and commitment to both club and county is unquestioned. He lives for Cloyne and Cork, so when he made his pioneering stand, he was treated with respect. Players who still fear the wrath of officialdom must take stock of their standing within the broader GAA community. When the Cork hurlers took their historic step, they could not have been sure what way their actions would be perceived. It was a leap into the dark. But their success has shown the way forward for all players, from the Cavan hurler to the Galway footballer.

Grass-roots GAA people will, by and large, support players who strive for better conditions, better treatment, a fair deal in a rapidly changing environment. They can ignore the doomsayers; the officials who claim the GPA will drive a wedge between an elite and the ordinary GAA folk. This claim is spurious. Players remain the product of their clubs; they are intrinsically linked to a club and a community. Now, however, they have a real opportunity to help transform the GAA for the better; to shift the balance of power away from the committee rooms and onto the playing fields, particularly in areas pertaining to player issues. But this shift is not a destructive move. Inter-county footballers and hurlers are wonderful GAA men, an accolade usually preserved for long-serving officials.

I will always be indebted to the players who stood in the front line during our formative years when there was an enormous price to pay for failure. It's worth reiterating that Peter Canavan and DJ Carey were pioneers, standing with their fellow players so that the collective could benefit in the long run without fear of recrimination. Kieran McGeeney has been a forthright, articulate voice within the GPA and in the wider sports community. Many GPA county representatives have always been defiant and their enduring commitment has had a knock-on effect, providing a model for player representation in every county squad. Particular mention should be made of Brian Lohan, Tommy Dunne, Paddy Bradley, Jason Sherlock, Gregory McCartan, Glenn Ryan, Brendán Ó hAnnaidh, Brian McFall, Muiris Gavin, Brian Whelahan, David O'Connor, Ronan Sweeney, Dara McGarty, Damien Diver, Ross Munnelly, Liam Hassett and Fergal Hartley.

In time, the work of these men, and many others, off the field may be forgotten by a generation of players who won't have any experience of what it is like to be disrespected, to be bullied and ill-treated. Yet it is vital to record what these footballers and hurlers did. They were told that GPA activity could destroy their careers. They were asked how they could prepare properly for championship if their heads were full of this 'nonsense'. But they stuck to their guns. They paved the way for others because they were strong enough and intelligent enough not to allow themselves to be browbeaten by the myopic traditionalist.

There was a time when the GPA could close down for the championship season as players didn't want to be distracted or at least didn't want the finger pointed at them if results didn't go according to plan, but that is no longer the case nowadays as players realise how important it is to fly the flag, even during those busy summer months. The Cork hurlers stand as a testament to this by being both pro-active off the pitch and successful on it.

The pioneers have not always had a high profile. The GPA has been incredibly well served by men like Donnach Callan of the Louth hurlers, Leitrim hurler Kevin Glancy, Tyrone hurler Thomas Colton, Armagh hurler Paul McCormack, Pat Coady from Carlow and Mark McEntee from the Cavan hurling squad, who have utilised the association to highlight their own struggle to promote hurling in the most adverse conditions. A true passion for hurling is what drives these men to strive for recognition and equality on the playing field.

Players can be proud of what the GPA has achieved since Donal O'Neill first put the wheels in motion. Nearly six years later, we find ourselves at the heart of the matter, central to the development of the game at the top level. Players are now represented and they have a strong voice. My only regret is that some people still take this groundbreaking achievement for granted. I do know that, in time, future generations will be unaware of our great struggle in these formative years, but the GPA has already left a lasting legacy. On occasions, players of my era may lament the fact that previous generations didn't take this stand for us, as apparently the idea had been mooted several times. However, it is reasonable to assume that it would have been virtually impossible to set up a players' body in the circumstances which pertained in the past. Times and attitudes have changed and players now place a value on their worth, individually and collectively.

The importance of solidarity to the GPA cannot be overstated. Every player who breaks ranks with the GPA because of a perceived threat, because of fear of an official, a manager, the press or the public, or even just for a quick buck, is letting down his comrades, the ones who really matter. The Cork hurlers' united stand has become the GPA's model. They continue to lead the way for hurlers and footballers throughout the land. More must now follow their example.

Faoi scáth a chéile a mhaireann na daoine. Our strength is in our unity.

SECTION 6

Chapter 23

Chamber of Horrors – 2004–2005

Summer 2004

Year three of Tommy Lyons' reign looked as if it would be a Dessie Farrell-free zone. The fallout from the previous summer had, in most people's minds, ended any chance of me playing for Dublin while he was at the helm. Pundits sensed that with a poor relationship between me and the manager, allied to the miles I had already clocked up, my retirement was imminent.

I kept training with a comeback in mind, however. I stuck to my individual programme in the gym and trained hard with Na Fianna in the off chance that the call-up might come again. My belief was bolstered by the fact that Lyons' selector, Dave Billings, stayed in contact with me and kept a check on my progress.

Some may find this attitude hard to tally with my contention that Tommy Lyons should have gone after the 2003 championship. Was I being hypocritical? Well, to be honest, I just wanted to play football, to play for Dublin, contribute in any way my ageing body would allow. But it didn't look good.

Adversity opened the door for me, just as it had the previous year. Dublin crashed out of the Leinster championship in the quarter-final to a Westmeath team invigorated by the arrival of Páidí Ó Sé. The reaction of Dublin supporters was one of anger, though Lyons' small coterie of sycophants in the media tried to heap the blame on a fickle, uneducated Dublin public. Nothing could be further from the truth. Solid football folk in the capital were furious with Lyons' approach, believing that he had disregarded some of the traditions associated with the Dublin game. No one suggested, however, that he should be ditched mid-championship. The consensus was that we'd have to plough on. But among Lyons' critics, there was also considerable support for my re-introduction, based on my club form and availability.

After Dublin played London in the All-Ireland qualifier series, Dave Billings suggested that I ring Lyons with a view to discussing a possible return. Billings was adamant that if it was put to the management team, the selectors would support my inclusion in the panel. So I broke the ice and phoned Tommy. I told him that I was still interested in playing and felt I'd something to offer. He was gracious to me, saying he would discuss the matter with his selectors. He also added that he always maintained that no one could question my commitment to the cause. He subsequently called me and said he had addressed my possible return with the management team and that they would have a look at me in an upcoming Dublin championship match against Naomh Barróg.

As it transpired, I played against Barróg with a bad Achilles tendon problem, though I managed to do enough, grabbing an important late score to help seal a victory.

Following that game, Tommy rang and we arranged to meet in Jurys Hotel. At the meeting, Tommy was straight about how he saw the situation. He spelled it out that, if I was to come back, there could be no repeat of the post-season team revolt. I would have to accept my lot. I saw no problem with this; I assured him that, after giving the players the option to act in the wake of the Armagh game, an option which they ultimately failed to exercise, I wouldn't be going out on a limb again.

So I returned to training afterwards with the squad. It was my first night back with the squad since the attempted coup and there was a palpable tension at the session. The panel had been together throughout the league and early rounds of the championship. Now I was back in from the cold. Some players came over and shook my hand in front of Lyons. Others were more circumspect, waiting until we were out of sight, fearing a bit of 'guilt by association'.

It was tough, physically, at first, because I didn't want to re-emerge carrying yet another injury. So I spent my days rushing from work to intensive physio with Alan Kelly, back to work, up to collect the kids, down to training.

I don't know what I'd do without Kelly. He has got me back in contention more times than I care to remember. Ian Robertson first introduced me to him when both of us had good cause to find an expert in deep friction massage and the likes. But Kelly is more than a great pair of healing hands. The torture aside, he is a pure tonic to spend an hour with. As a therapist who treats a lot of the GAA's top players and the rugby stars, he is a mine of information and gossip. There is also something of the psychologist about him because he is generally dealing with athletes in a race against time for a big game and, although he has repeatedly told me to give it up, he always comes back with a positive spin. He worked wonders on Peter Canavan's ankle prior to the 2003 All-Ireland final. AK is also a great supporter of players and the GPA because he has seen, first hand, how poor training and ill-treatment has caused serious physical problems for players. When we played Donegal in the All-Ireland quarter-final in 2002, I managed to get him some passes for the players' lounge afterwards and he brought Pádraig Harrington, Denis Hickie and Brian O'Driscoll with him. After arriving, he made a bee-line for GAA president Seán McCague to introduce the lads and, with the formalities out of the way, AK proceeded to inform McCague why they were present. 'Oh, we're here as guests of Dessie Farrell and the GPA.'

With regular visits to AK's chamber of horrors, my niggling injuries began to clear up and my fitness started to improve greatly. Dublin, meanwhile, were being nursed along through the qualifiers. I made my return as a late substitute against Leitrim in Carrick-on-Shannon where the travelling Dublin supporters (who made up most of the attendance) gave me a rapturous welcome. During fifteen years in a blue jersey, I can't recall my name being chanted too often on the terraces, but in the unlikely surrounds of Páirc Seán Mhic Diarmada, the fans made their point.

Things had changed under Lyons from what I could see. Gym programmes had been re-introduced, there was no more tramping around Leopardstown racecourse, and he was inviting much more opinion from the players. He was also less animated. He seemed to have accepted his lot, and the media frenzy had dissipated.

Another appearance as a sub against Longford in Portlaoise saw me through to our final game in the series, a clash with Roscommon in Croke Park. Victory would secure a quarter-final berth, a tantalising prospect given that I wasn't even on the panel when we crashed out of the Leinster championship. I was moving really well at training, so much so that Billings asked me before the Roscommon game if I thought I had seventy minutes in me. The management decided that the prudent option was to hold me on the bench and hope that we could negotiate the final qualifier.

Everything was going pretty much to plan. We had got on top of Roscommon in the second half when Tommy called me down to the sideline to introduce me for the final fifteen minutes. Two minutes after coming on, a ball arrived into my corner, between the Hogan and the Canal End. I got out in front of my man but, instead of winning it cleanly, I shielded him to ensure that he didn't get it and that I would at least draw the foul if I didn't get my hands on the ball. Just as I turned, I felt a searing pain shoot through my right knee. My leg collapsed under me. I knew it was bad; I'd been down this road too often to even hope for the best. I was carried off to the line. My championship was over. Everyone who looked on must have felt that the injury would end more than my championship. Farrell's finished.

Tommy Lyons commiserated with me in the immediate aftermath and paid tribute to my contribution. The Dublin players also rallied around and, despite having to face into a tortuous rehabilitation process to deal with yet another cruciate ligament injury, I was lifted a little by the invitation by the management to help out with Dublin's training matches in preparation for the All-Ireland quarter-final against Kerry.

It all mattered little, however, when Kerry demolished Dublin in the second half of our quarter-final, marking the end of Lyons' three-year tenure.

In the end, Tommy went graciously with the usual confusion in the county board as to whether or not he'd been offered an extension to his contract. Yet, if there was confusion surrounding Tommy's decision to go, it was nothing to the ensuing mayhem that accompanied the protracted process of appointing his successor. Brian Mullins was seemingly set to take over, but he fell foul of the county board who rejected the demands he placed on the table.

Whether Mullins was everybody's favourite choice to replace Lyons is a moot point, but the way the appointment was dealt with was a bloody joke. I don't believe county-board officials or the delegates alone should appoint the manager. A select committee comprising former players, managers and a number of officials should be formed to nominate a shortlist and interview the candidates. There is a wealth of expertise available in most counties, but it often remains untapped because, I suspect, officialdom fears that there would be an erosion of control and power if it were harnessed.

John Bailey was at the centre of the controversy surrounding the on-off appointment of Mullins and, because of the status of the candidate in Dublin, the county board took a lot of flak at the time.

The drama finally ended on 28 November 2004 when Pillar Caffrey was handed the job, with Dave Billings, Paul Clarke and Brian Talty named as selectors. My first reaction to the news of Pillar's appointment was a sceptical one. A lot of the players believed that there needed to be a clear-out, so when two of Tommy Lyons' selectors were renamed, there was a lot of deflation at the county board's perceived failure to clean the slate.

I had issues with Pillar. Knowing him so well, both as a playing colleague and subsequently as Na Fianna manager, I didn't feel he had stood his ground with Lyons, particularly in regard to the treatment of the Na Fianna players under him. I also felt that Pillar had sort of sold out on his very successful coaching and man-management philosophy which had been adopted in the club.

However, the first indication I received that things were about to change dramatically came almost directly after Pillar's appointment when he called and asked to meet me. Bearing in mind I was facing crucial surgery on my knee, I was taken aback when he told me he wanted me to be involved in the panel and to undergo my rehab while staying in touch with the squad. I laid my cards on the table, expressed my concerns about his role under Lyons, told him how I'd felt let down by his stance. Pillar defended his position saying that loyalty to the manger in his circumstances was vital; he would not break ranks. He also said that he was hurt by our attempted coup in 2003, although I did point out that Lyons was the central figure in that aborted move. But our meeting wasn't acrimonious. I could sense Pillar's determination to move on, to get going with his own ideas and his own team.

I was glad of the conversation. I had soldiered long and hard on the field with Pillar during the unglamourous days with Na Fianna. He was one of the best club footballers in the county, played national league with Dublin, and was really a mainstay of our club for years. During that period, I was very friendly with him though, naturally enough, that changed somewhat when he became Na Fianna's trainer. As our club coach, he was smart and hard-working. He always paid great attention to detail and our relationship was a dynamic one, so I was glad when he stipulated that things would be changing dramatically in the Dublin camp. We agreed to move forward, hopefully together.

My scepticism about the new Dublin management proved misplaced. Throughout Lyons' reign, Billings had remained a close ally of mine, and he remains so. Paul Clarke is a huge addition, having performed at the highest level himself, while Brian Talty's experience in Dublin is almost unrivalled. Not only has Pillar a very solid management team around him, he has cast the net further and utilised the expertise of some great former players like Kieran Duff, Barney Rock and, in particular, Stephen Wade, whose influence cannot be underestimated.

Whether success comes our way or not, two significant things have happened under Caffrey. Firstly, there has been a return to tried-and-tested approaches to Dublin management. The tradition established in the 1970s has been brought back to the table: defiance on the field and deference off it. The Lyons publicity rollercoaster has been shunted off track. Instead, Pillar has adopted a reserved, functional approach to what is a seriously pressurised position. It is a measured approach, one that helps in no small way to defuse the hype that accompanies any summer victory in Dublin. Secondly, modern training and coaching techniques have been embraced wholeheartedly from the outset, and this training is nicely embellished by the rich experience of the former footballers who are now present at squad sessions. As he was with Na Fianna, Pillar is an excellent man to delegate and to listen.

Steel – mental and physical – has proven to be the determining factor in the destination of the Sam Maguire in recent years. Hopefully, the new Dublin sideline team can forge that precious ingredient with their squad and land an All-Ireland back in the capital.

St Mary's Ward, Cappagh Orthopedic Hospital, January 2005

Why is it that boxing writing seems to capture the essence of sport better than any other kind of sportswriting? My mate was at me to read more sports books, so I've just finished *The Fight* by Norman Mailer. What is it about boxers? Is it the bleak exposure, the endurance, the fearlessness? I love boxing, no hiding place. Can't stop thinking about Ali, how he didn't want to ruin the aesthetic of the punch that floored Foreman in Kinshasa by battering him to the canvas. I love boxers. Loved Ali, loved Sugar Ray Leonard, Marvin Hagler, McGuigan, Carruth, Collins. Jayzus, I even love Johnny Magee. The night he fought snooker player Quentin Hann in the National Stadium, I got to go into the dressing room beforehand: the tension, the smell of winter green, grease. Brilliant. I'm thinking, 'I'd have loved a go at this.'

Mailer's name keeps popping up in all the boxing books. Some man; married six times. Here's a quote from Mailer: 'Writing books is the closest men ever come to childbearing.' He must never have severed his cruciate. Then again, I know what he means.

'He fought in World War II, ya know,' me mate informs me.

'Did he do in his knee there?'

Now, the nurse is back to check the wound. 'That's coming on fine, Dessie, but the doctor'll be around in an hour to talk to you. You know you won't be going home for a few days. Can't risk infection.' Bollix! Back to the pile of sports books. I never liked January: no football, though the pain of the heavy training would dull the pain of, well, January. Famous American sports hacks, pound for pound: who was the best? Sugar Ray Robinson. I love boxing.

Dr Ray Moran has just performed surgery on a severed anterior cruciate ligament in my right knee. What a gobshite I am. Tore the ligament against Roscommon in Croke Park in August. I didn't have to turn the way I did, I was just making sure I'd at least draw the foul. That pitch is so hard, there's no give. Two months later and the doctors are telling me the knee is coming on fine. You don't always need surgery for it to heal, just follow the rehab.

On the mend, I decide to come on as a sub and play for Na Fianna in a league play-off against St Vincent's. I do another proper job on the knee. Going for a ball, I plant the leg in the ground and turn. Trouble is, my leg doesn't turn with me. Now I tear the fucking thing apart completely. What a gobshite.

'Well Dessie, you've done about as much damage as you could have,' they tell me. 'You'll need the knife now.'

Almost fifteen years have passed since I tore the ligaments in my left knee. They told me then that I wouldn't play again and sure they may as well have been pissing in the wind.

'How do ya do it Farrell? How can you go back carrying your leg like that, put yourself through the mill? Have you a real high threshold for pain?' my mate asks.

'It's nothing to do with threshold, we all have the same threshold. It's to do with tolerance.'

'Ah, you're full of that science shite Farrell,' he blasts. 'You're a mad fucker who won't give up. You're finished, get over it.'

Now, I'm thirty-three years old. The operation has gone very well. Before the procedure, I asked Ray Moran without asking him (if you know what I mean) to do the job as if I was going back playing. He's some man, Ray. He understands footballers, specially injured ones – he *really* understands them, knows what the deal is.

Rehab is going to be a nightmare, but that's the kind of ball-breaking stuff that I'm good at. Training twice a day, up on the bike, exercises every night, health supplements, physio sessions, treatment table with AK. Obsession. It worked for Keano.

Rehab, a nightmare. Not as bad as the other nightmare though.

'What's the other nightmare?' my mate asks.

'The end.'

'So you're going back?'

'Ya. A "mad fucker" who won't give it up.'

'It'll give you up Farrell.'

10.15 a.m., 15 May 2005

It's funny, but while I wasn't a big fan of Lyons during my truncated playing days under him, I had made up my mind to close off on his era by stating that I respected him for having the balls to take me back into the fold, even though it was perceived by some as a weakness on his part. He accepted the high-pressure job, which is a lot harder than criticising someone in that position, and he was pretty successful in the short term. A Leinster senior championship and an All-Ireland under-21 victory are noteworthy achievements and I reiterate that Dublin players didn't want for anything off the field during his tenure.

I was going to close that way. That was until I got a text message from a friend early this morning. Now my mood has changed. Today, Dublin take on

Longford in the first round of the Leinster championship, Pillar's first big game in Croker. The text message reads: 'Pick up the *Sunday Tribune*, you won't believe it.' Oh no, I'm thinking, who's the latest mouthpiece being wheeled out to have a go at the GPA?

I drive up to the shops and pick up a copy of the *Sunday Tribune*. Before pulling out of the carpark, I thumb through the sports section before reaching the headline 'Where it all went wrong. Tommy Lyons explains the reasons behind his departure and why this Dublin side won't go the distance.'

So he's decided that he wants to have the final word on his troubled reign as Dublin manager. I need a cup of coffee for this.

For the past two years, Lyons has vociferously defended himself against criticism from past players in the newspapers. Now, having only recently stepped aside, he is doing exactly that. His former charges are just getting their heads sorted for their first championship game under Pillar and he decides to highlight the team's shortcomings in a national newspaper. This from a man who had the audacity to question Tommy Carr's loyalty to his former players when he accepted an advisory role with the Wexford footballers.

So what's wrong with Dublin footballers, Tommy?

'Too many players from the country playing for Dublin clubs.' Great answer. Rather pointedly, he selects Na Fianna for his example, which is rich coming from the manager who won an All-Ireland with a Crokes' team that had five country players in the starting fifteen. I don't buy this at all. If a young player isn't good enough to make his club senior team because of the presence of a few country players, how will he ever be good enough to play for Dublin?

He suggests putting a 'cap' on the amount of country players. Essentially this would mean that players from all over Ireland who happen to earn their living in the capital would be unable to play for a nearby club if the quota has been reached. Hmmm, now that he's chairman of Kilmacud, will he be implementing this policy in his own club?

I read on. 'I should have had a complete clear-out when I came in.' Ah, now that's it. I'm wondering how to be magnanimous to a manager I didn't get on with while he's suggesting he should have ditched me from the start, and maybe Jason too. Sure Senan Connell could have joined us and anyone else who stood by Tommy Carr. Well, if the complete clear-out was something in his mind, something he now feels at liberty to discuss in a national newspaper, he made seriously heavy weather of doing it, considering he brought me back twice.

What's next? Who else is to blame?

I see he's trying to get back at Charlie Redmond, delivering a serious dig in the process. Good man Tommy, that'll endear you further in the hearts of Dublin folk.

'He never blamed Stephen Cluxton for losing to Armagh,' says the journalist. Yes you did, Tommy, no revisionism you attempt will change that.

The former players. Ah yeah, the former players with 'nothing positive to contribute' says Tommy; unlike this ungracious summation before my eyes. I must text Curran and Barr.

'He [Lyons] is from the west of Ireland and a member of Kilmacud Crokes.' Ah Jayzus, Tommy, where are you off to now? Tommy Carr was from Tipp and was loved in Dublin and none of us ever had issues with the Crokes' lads in our squad.

'He [Lyons] lost the media.' That's strange, I thought that some of the top GAA writers were more than sympathetic to Lyons. It was usually the Dublin players or their fans who got the blame. In fact, is this piece before me not a sympathetic treatment? The *Evening Herald*. Ah yes, the failed *Dublin Daily* experiment that pissed off all the hacks. That's why the papers were having a go, they didn't forgive him for being involved in a new paper, one outside of the Independent Group, and here's me thinking that it was because we were dumped out of the bloody championship.

I need more coffee.

'"No regrets" is his [Tommy Lyons'] mantra.' Ah, they're taking the piss. No regrets? No Gooches, no Colm Coopers 'until we look at the flaws in the system.'

I'm now thinking one of us inhabits a parallel universe. Flaws in the system? Of course we all know the one flaw in the system that he doesn't mention.

When Lyons first took over, he suggested to me that I may have done one press conference too many by publicly standing by Carr after his sacking. Well, now methinks Tommy Lyons has done one interview too many.

Enough.

'What are you doing Dad?' asks Frankie as I stuff the paper into the bin. 'Ah nothing Frankie, just throwing out the old paper.'

'Is that not today's paper, Daddy?'

'Ah, it is, but I'm finished with it.'

'Is Jason in the paper, Daddy?'

'No Frankie, no he's not. But we'll see him today in Croker. Come on *a stór*, put your jersey on and get Emma, we've to go down and get Granny and Granddad for the match.'

EPILOGUE

13 July 2005

12.30 a.m. Back in my living room after testing out my leg on the green in front of the house – still in my gear, ice pack on leg, a handful of anti-inflammatories washed down with a pint of protein drink. Got up to 80 per cent tonight; need to make 100 per cent at some point before Sunday. Now for the hard bit.

So this is it. The last shout. I've hauled myself back from the precipice for one final rattle. On Sunday, I will sit on the Dublin substitutes' bench for the Leinster final against Laois, six months after the knife. I may have won an All-Ireland, I may have won Leinster and county championships, but this is perhaps my greatest victory – to get from Cappagh Hospital back to Croke Park at the age of thirty-four. Some of the lads I will sit alongside were six years old when I played in my first provincial decider against Kildare in 1992.

All week I've quietly nursed a thigh-muscle tear, just reward for trying to beat a player fourteen years my junior in a sprint. That is my nature; I have always ignored advice to hold back, to preserve. I'll stand and fall by my desire to perform as well as I can. I always pushed myself to endure, to deliver, to improve – ignoring the risks, physical and mental.

One way or another, I will wear the blue jersey for the last time this summer. Romantic from a distance, the reality of my last stand is perpetual motion:

family, training, work, physio, one long and hellish car journey through Dublin's gridlock. The end should bring freedom, a release from the one responsibility that shapes every moment of my waking life: getting myself right for the big game. In time, it might be more difficult; the stark realisation that Croke Park is no longer a stage on which to perform.

I have many regrets in my career, which time will hopefully diminish. They were never exclusive anyhow. I've cherished everything football has thrown at me, my magnificent memories will not fade: The adrenaline rush before big games; the amazing experience of running towards Hill 16 with a blue shirt on my back; looking a team-mate in the eye after acquitting ourselves properly; walking back into the Na Fianna clubhouse with some of my closest friends as county champions; embracing my father, my mother and my sister as an All-Ireland champion; sitting in Hanlon's Pub with Mick Galvin and Pat Coffey the day after a championship match; training with an August sun on my back; slugging it out with Eamon Heery; getting clocked by Paddy Moran; watching Keith Barr lash away at Tom Harris; joking with Paul Curran, Jim Gavin, Paul Bealin, Dermot Deasy, Vinny Murphy and Darren Homan; watching Charlie Redmond's frees go over, Jason Sherlock's goals go in; standing by Tommy Carr and his selectors; playing alongside Kieran McGeeney; watching Senan Connell in action, on and off the field; being around long enough to play with some of the new Dublin greats, Alan Brogan, Bryan Cullen and Barry Cahill.

This year, like a man on borowed time, I appreciate my involvement with Dublin all the more: collecting young Aiden Downes and Niall Cooper for training, the banter in the car, the *craic* with the lads in the dressing room and, above all else, the bond and sense of belonging that comes with donning the sky blue jersey.

Most of all, I've cherished the competition, the challenge, the test, especially when the odds were against me – pitting myself, my skill, my fortitude and my attitude against others, at training or in a match, always searching for the answers to the ultimate questions in sport: Who is the best? And why do the skills that elevate a player to greatness often desert him and reduce him to a bystander at the crucial juncture?

Whether I follow in the footsteps of McCaul, Cullen, O'Neill, Whelan, Carr, Lyons and Caffrey, I cannot say. Only by stepping away will I know what the future holds. One thing I do know for certain is that what I look forward to most of all is watching over my two best pals, Frankie and Emma, and doing my best to make life as good for them as it was for me.

For now, I await destiny's hand. My last summer tangled up in blue.

Dessie Farrell – Record Card

Honours

All-Ireland Senior Championship title – 1995

Six Leinster Senior Championship titles – 1992, 1993, 1994, 1995, 2002, 2005

National Football League title –1993

All Star Award – 1995

Leinster Minor Championship title– 1988

O'Byrne Cup title – 1999

Three Dublin Senior Championship titles – 1999, 2000, 2001

Leinster Club Senior Championship title – 1999

Dublin Captain – 1998–2001

CHAMPIONSHIP APPEARANCES 1992–2004

Tullamore, 31 May 1992   *Dublin 2-17; Offaly 1-9*
Dublin: J O'Leary, M Deegan, G Hargan, T Carr, P Curran, K Barr, E Heery,
P Clarke (0-4), P Gilroy (0-2), C Redmond (1-2), J Sheedy (0-2), N Guiden,
D Farrell (0-2), V Murphy (0-3), P Doherty (1-0). *Subs*: C Walsh for Barr,
M Galvin for Doherty.
Offaly: A Daly, V Byrne, G O'Brien, T Coffey, F Cullen, K Kelleghan,
J Stewart (0-1), P Dunne (0-1), M Plunkett, S Grennan, M Devine, V Claffey
(1-0), D Reynolds (0-3), P Brady, B Lowry (0-3). *Subs*: P Moran for Coffey,
S Dunne (0-1) for O'Brien, J Hughes for Plunkett.

Portlaoise, 28 June 1992   *Dublin 1-18; Wexford 0-11*

Dublin: J O'Leary, M Deegan, G Hargan, T Carr, P Curran, K Barr (0-1),
E Heery, P Clarke (0-3), P Gilroy, C Redmond (0-7), J Sheedy (0-2),
N Guiden (0-2), D Farrell (0-2), V Murphy (1-0), P Doherty. *Subs*: M Galvin
(0-1) for Guiden.

Wexford: G O'Connor, G Halligan, J O'Gorman, D Stafford, B Kirwan,
P Fitzhenry, B O'Gorman, L Rafter, G Waters, J Harrington (0-1), E Cleary
(0-1), J Roche, M Hanrick (0-1), S Fitzhenry, B Dodd (0-7). *Subs*: P O'Gorman
for Stafford, C Jevans for Kirwan, N Fitzhenry (0-1) for Hanrick.

Croke Park, 12 July 1992   *Dublin 0-15; Louth 1-9*

Dublin: J O'Leary, M Deegan, G Hargan, T Carr, P Curran, K Barr, E Heery
(0-1), P Clarke, P Gilroy, C Redmond (0-6), J Sheedy (0-2), N Guiden, D Farrell
(0-2), V Murphy (0-2), M Galvin (0-2). *Subs*: D Foran for Gilroy.

Louth: N O'Donnell, P O'Neill, D Mulligan, S Melia, P Fitzpatrick, D Reilly,
K Rooney, S O'Hanlon (0-2), J Osborne (0-1), P Butterly, R O'Neill, M Malone,
C O'Hanlon, C Kelly (0-5), S White (1-1). *Subs*: P Kirk for P O'Neill,
K O'Hanlon for R O'Neill, D Brady for Butterly.

Croke Park, 26 July 1992   *Dublin 1-13; Kildare 0-10*

Dublin: J O'Leary, M Deegan, G Hargan, T Carr, P Curran (0-1), K Barr (1-0),
E Heery (0-1), P Clarke (0-1), D Foran, C Redmond (0-5), J Sheedy, N Guiden,
D Farrell (0-1), V Murphy (0-3), M Galvin (0-1). *Subs*: P Gilroy for Sheedy,
P Bealin for Foran.

Kildare: C Gannon, D Dalton, J Crofton, S Dowling, P McConnon, G Ryan,
A Rainbow, S McGovern, N Buckley (0-4), D Kerrigan, T Harris, B Fahy (0-1),
M Lynch (0-2), J Gilroy, J McDonald (0-1). *Subs*: P McLoughlin (0-2) for Fahy,
B Nolan for Dowling, N Donlon for Gilroy.

Croke Park, 23 August 1992   *Dublin 3-14; Clare 2-12*

Dublin: J O'Leary, M Deegan, G Hargan, T Carr, P Curran (0-1), K Barr, E Heery, P Clarke (0-2), D Foran, C Redmond (0-5), J Sheedy (0-2), N Guiden (0-1), D Farrell (0-1), V Murphy (2-1), M Galvin (1-1). *Subs*: P Bealin for Foran.
Clare: JJ Hanrahan, S Clancy, G Kelly, C O'Mahoney, F Griffin, JJ Rouine (0-1), C O'Neill, T Morrissey (0-1), A Moloney, N Roche, F McInerney (0-2), G Killeen (1-3), P Conway (1-2), C Clancy, M Flynn (0-1). *Subs*: M Daly (0-1) for O'Neill, M Roughan (0-1) for Kelly, D Coughlan for Killeen.

Croke Park, 20 September 1992   *Donegal 0-18; Dublin 0-14*

Dublin: J O'Leary, M Deegan, G Hargan, T Carr, P Curran, K Barr, E Heery (0-1), P Clarke (0-2), D Foran, C Redmond (0-3), J Sheedy (0-2), N Guiden (0-1), D Farrell (0-1), V Murphy (0-2), M Galvin (0-2). *Subs*: P Bealin for Foran.
Donegal: G Walsh, B McGowan, M Gallagher, N Hegarty, D Reid, M Gavigan, JJ Doherty, A Molloy, B Murray, J McHugh (0-1), M McHugh (0-3), J McMullan, D Bonner (0-4), T Boyle (0-1), M Boyle (0-9). *Subs*: B Cunningham for Murray.

Wexford Park, 23 May 1993   *Dublin 0-11; Wexford 0-7*

Dublin: J O'Leary, C Walsh, D Deasy, P Moran, E Heery, P Curran, M Deegan, P Bealin, J Sheedy (0-1), J Gavin, V Murphy (0-2), N Guiden (0-2), D Farrell (0-2), M Doran, P Clarke (0-4). *Subs*: P Gilroy for Bealin, P O'Donoghue for Gavin.
Wexford: J Cooper, P O'Gorman, J O'Gorman, G Halligan, B Kirwan, J Dunne, B O'Gorman, L Rafter, G Waters, S Doran (0-3), J Harrington, N Darcy, S Byrne, S Roche, B Dodd (0-3). *Subs*: N Fitzhenry for Byrne, N Guinan (0-1) for Rafter, P Fitzhenry for Waters.

Tullamore, 7 June 1993   *Dublin 2-11; Westmeath 0-8*

Dublin: J O'Leary, C Walsh, D Deasy, P Moran, E Heery, P Curran (0-1),
M Deegan (0-1), P Gilroy, J Sheedy (0-1), P Clarke (0-3), K Barr (1-2),
N Guiden, D Farrell (0-1), V Murphy (1-1), M Doran. *Subs*: J Gavin (0-1) for
Clarke, C Redmond for Deegan.

Westmeath: D Ryan, P Smith, T Darcy, J Conlon, M Fagan, A Collins,
J Murray, T Ormsby (0-1), J Cooney, J Fleming, N Lynch, M Broder, G Heavin
(0-7), D Prendergast, L Giles. *Subs*: P Corcoran for Broder, J Healy for Lynch.

Croke Park, 4 July 1993   *Dublin 1-10; Meath 0-12*

Dublin: J O'Leary, C Walsh, D Deasy, P Moran, E Heery, P Curran,
D Harrington, P Gilroy, J Sheedy (0-1), J Gavin, K Barr, N Guiden (0-1),
D Farrell, V Murphy (0-1), C Redmond (1-7). *Subs*: P Bealin for Harrington,
M Galvin for Gavin.

Meath: M McQuillan, R O'Malley, E McManus, K Foley, G Geraghty,
M O'Connell, C Murphy, C Brady, J McDermott (0-1), D Beggy, PJ Gillic (0-2),
J Devine, C O'Rourke (0-5), B Stafford (0-3), T Dowd (0-1). *Subs*: L Harnan for
Foley.

Croke Park, 25 July 1993   *Dublin 0-11; Kildare 0-7*

Dublin: J O'Leary, C Walsh, D Deasy, P Moran, P Curran, K Barr, P O'Neill,
J Sheedy, P Bealin (0-1), E Heery, D Farrell (0-1), P Gilroy (0-1), J Gavin,
V Murphy (0-1), C Redmond (0-5). *Subs*: M Galvin (0-1) for Gavin, J Barr (0-1)
for Galvin.

Kildare: C Byrne, S Dowling, D Dalton, N Donlon, D O'Connell, G Ryan,
B Fahy, M Lynch, S McGovern (0-1), K Doyle, N Buckley (0-4), A Rainbow,
P McLoughlin, J McDonald (0-1), L Miley. *Subs*: D Kerrigan (0-1) for Miley,
T Harris for Doyle.

Croke Park, 22 August 1993   *Derry 0-15; Dublin 0-14*

Dublin: J O'Leary, C Walsh, D Deasy, P Moran, P Curran (0-1), K Barr,
P O'Neill, J Sheedy, P Bealin (0-1), E Heery (0-1), P Gilroy (0-2) , P Clarke
(0-1), D Farrell, V Murphy, C Redmond (0-8). *Subs*: M Deegan for Deasy,
M Galvin for O'Neill, J Barr for Clarke.

Derry: D McCusker, K McKeever, D Quinn, T Scullion, J McGurk (0-1),
H Downey (0-2), G Coleman (0-1), A Tohill (0-2), B McGilligan (0-1),
D Heaney, D Barton, D Cassidy, J Brolly (0-1), S Downey, E Gormley (0-7).
Subs: K Diamond for Quinn, D McNicholl for Cassidy, F McCusker
for Barton.

Croke Park, 18 June 1994   *Dublin 0-11; Kildare 0-11*

Dublin: J O'Leary, C Walsh, D Deasy, P Moran, P Curran, K Barr, M Deegan,
J Sheedy (0-1), P Bealin, P Gilroy, T Carr, V Murphy (0-1), N Guiden, D Farrell
(0-1), C Redmond (0-8). *Subs*: B Stynes for Bealin, J Barr for Carr, P O'Neill
for Walsh.

Kildare: C Byrne, S Dowling, D Dalton, A Rainbow, B Fahy, G Ryan,
N Donlon (0-1), S McGovern, M Lynch (0-1), G Dunne (0-4), D O'Connell
(0-2), N Buckley (0-2), D Kerrigan, D McKevitt, J McDonald. *Subs*: K Doyle
(0-1)
for McDonald.

Croke Park, 3 July 1994   *Dublin 1-14; Kildare 1-9*

Dublin: J O'Leary, C Walsh, D Deasy, P Moran, P Curran, K Barr, M Deegan
(0-2), B Stynes (0-1), P Bealin (0-1), P Gilroy, J Sheedy (0-2), N Guiden (0-1),
D Farrell (0-1), M Galvin (0-1), C Redmond (1-4). *Subs*: P Clarke (0-1) for
Galvin, V Murphy for Gilroy.

Kildare: C Byrne, S Dowling, D Dalton, A Rainbow, B Fahy, G Ryan,
N Donlon, S McGovern, M Lynch (0-1), G Dunne, D O'Connell, N Buckley
(1-6), D Kerrigan (0-1), D McKevitt, K Doyle (0-1). *Subs*: D Doyle for K Doyle,
J Gilroy for Dunne.

Croke Park, 10 July 1994   *Dublin 1-15; Louth 1-8*

Dublin: J O'Leary, C Walsh, D Deasy, P Moran, P Curran, K Barr, M Deegan, B Stynes (0-1), S Cahill, P Gilroy (0-1), J Sheedy, N Guiden (0-2), D Farrell (0-2), M Galvin (0-5), C Redmond (1-4). *Subs*: J Barr for Sheedy, P O'Neill for Curran, G Regan for Walsh.

Louth: N O'Donnell, P Fitzpatrick, B O'Connor, D Reilly, D McDonnell, S Melia, K Rooney, G Curran, K Reilly, A Doherty, C Kelly (0-2), P Butterly (0-2), S White (0-1), F Murphy (0-2), E Judge (1-1). *Subs*: D Staunton for Rooney, O McDonnell for Curran, C Nash for Murphy.

Croke Park, 31 July 1994   *Dublin 1-9; Meath 1-8*

Dublin: J O'Leary, C Walsh, D Deasy, P Moran, P Curran, K Barr, M Deegan, B Stynes (0-2), P Bealin, P Gilroy, J Sheedy, N Guiden (0-1), D Farrell (0-1), M Galvin, C Redmond (1-4). *Subs*: P Clarke (0-1) for Bealin, V Murphy for Gilroy, G Regan for Deasy.

Meath: M McQuillan, R O'Malley, M O'Connell, C Coyle, G Geraghty (1-2), C Murphy, B Reilly (0-1), C Brady, J McDermott, J McGuinness (0-1), C O'Rourke (0-1), T Giles, B Flynn (0-1), T Dowd (0-1), B Stafford. *Subs*: PJ Gillic (0-1) for Stafford, J Devine for McGuinness.

Croke Park, 21 August 1994   *Dublin 3-15; Leitrim 1-9*

Dublin: J O'Leary, C Walsh, D Deasy, P Moran, P Clarke, K Barr, M Deegan, B Stynes (0-1), P Gilroy, V Murphy (0-2), J Sheedy, N Guiden (0-2), C Redmond (1-6), M Galvin (1-1), D Farrell (1-2). *Subs*: P Bealin (0-1) for Galvin, L Walsh for C Walsh, T Carr for Sheedy.

Leitrim: M McHugh, F Reynolds, S Quinn, J Honeyman, N Moran (0-1), D Darcy (0-1), G Flanagan, P Kieran (0-1), P Donohue, P Kenny, G Dugdale, M Quinn, A Rooney (0-4), C McGlynn (1-1), L Conlon. *Subs*: B Breen (0-1) for Dugdale, J Ward for Kieran, B Duignan for Reynolds.

Croke Park, 18 September 1994   *Down 1-12; Dublin 0-13*
Dublin: J O'Leary, P Moran, D Deasy, P Curran (0-1), P Clarke (0-1), K Barr,
M Deegan, B Stynes (0-1), P Gilroy, J Sheedy (0-2), V Murphy (0-1), N Guiden
(0-1), D Farrell (0-1), M Galvin, C Redmond (0-4). *Subs*: P Bealin for Gilroy,
S Cahill (0-1) for Galvin, J Barr for Guiden.
Down: N Collins, M Magill, B Burns, P Higgins, E Burns, B Breen, DJ Kane,
G McCartan (0-1), C Deegan, R Carr (0-3), G Blaney, J McCartan (0-1),
M Linden (0-4), A Farrell (0-1), G Mason (0-3). *Subs*: G Colgan for Deegan.

Navan, 18 June 1995   *Dublin 0-19; Louth 2-5*
Dublin: J O'Leary, K Galvin (0-1), D Deasy, P Moran, P Curran, K Barr,
M Deegan, P Bealin, B Stynes (0-1), S Cahill, V Murphy (0-1), P Clarke (0-2),
C Redmond (0-9), M Galvin (0-2), D Farrell (0-2). *Subs*: J Sherlock (0-1) for
Cahill, J Gavin for Murphy, E Sheedy for Redmond.
Louth: N McDonnell, P Fitzpatrick, G O'Neill, B O'Connor, D McDonnell,
S Melia, G Curran, S O'Hanlon, K Reilly, C O'Hanlon (0-1), C Kelly (0-4),
A Doherty, B Kearns, S White (1-1), O McDonnell. *Subs*: P Butterly for Kearns,
A Rooney for McDonnell, K O'Hanlon for C O'Hanlon.

Navan, 9 July 1995   *Dublin 1-13; Laois 0-9*
Dublin: J O'Leary, K Galvin, C Walsh, P Moran, P Curran, K Barr, M Deegan
(0-1), P Bealin, B Stynes, D Farrell (0-1), S Cahill, P Clarke (0-3), C Redmond
(0-7), M Galvin, J Sherlock (1-0). *Subs*: J Gavin for Galvin, V Murphy (0-1)
for Cahill, P Gilroy for Bealin.
Laois: E Burke, A Phelan, M Dempsey, T Conroy, E Delaney, D Lalor,
G Doyle, T Maher, D Sweeney, T Bowe, H Emerson, M Lawlor (0-3), N Roe,
D Delaney (0-6), L Turley. *Subs*: T Smith for E Delaney, D O'Connell for Roe.

Croke Park, 30 July 1995   *Dublin 1-18; Meath 1-8*
Dublin: J O'Leary, P Moran, D Deasy, K Galvin, P Curran (0-2), K Barr,
M Deegan, P Bealin, B Stynes, J Gavin (0-1), D Farrell (0-3), P Clarke (1-2),
C Redmond (0-7), J Sherlock (0-2), M Galvin (0-1). *Subs*: V Murphy
for Galvin.
Meath: C Martin, R O'Malley, M O'Connell, C Coyle, G Geraghty (0-1),
C Murphy, B Reilly, J McDermott, PJ Gillic, J Devine (0-1), T Giles (0-3),
E Kelly (1-0), C O'Rourke (0-2), B Stafford (0-1), T Dowd. *Subs*: C Brady for
Stafford, E McManus for O'Malley, O Murphy for Kelly.

Croke Park, 20 August 1995   *Dublin 1-12; Cork 0-12*
Dublin: J O'Leary, K Galvin, D Deasy, P Moran, P Curran, K Barr, M Deegan,
P Bealin, B Stynes, J Gavin, P Clarke (0-1), D Farrell, C Redmond (0-7),
J Sherlock (1-0), M Galvin (0-4). *Subs*: P Gilroy for Bealin, C Walsh for Galvin,
V Murphy for Clarke.
Cork: K O'Dwyer, M Farr, M O'Connor, N Cahalane, C O'Sullivan, S O'Brien,
B Corcoran, L Honohan, D Cullotty, D Davis, L Tompkins (0-2), P O'Mahony,
M O'Sullivan (0-2), J Kavanagh (0-1), C Corkery (0-7). *Subs*: S Calnan for
O'Mahony, S Fahy for Davis, P O'Regan for Calnan.

Croke Park, 17 September 1995   *Dublin 1-10; Tyrone 0-12*
Dublin: J O'Leary, K Galvin, C Walsh, P Moran, P Curran (0-1), K Barr (0-1),
M Deegan, P Bealin, B Stynes, P Clarke (0-2), D Farrell (0-4), J Gavin (0-1),
M Galvin, J Sherlock, C Redmond (1-1). *Subs*: P Gilroy for K Galvin, R Boyle
for M Galvin, V Murphy for Farrell.
Tyrone: F McConnell, P Devlin, C Lawn, F Devlin, R McGarrity, S McCallan,
S McLaughlin, F Logan, J Gormley (0-1), C Corr, Pascal Canavan,
C Loughran, C McBride, Peter Canavan (0-11), S Lawn. *Subs*: M McGleenan
for Loughran, B Gormley for S Lawn, P Donnelly for McCallan.

Navan, 9 June 1996   *Dublin 1-18; Westmeath 0-11*

Dublin: J O'Leary, M Deegan, D Martin, P Moran, P Curran (0-1), K Barr (1-0), E Heery (0-1), B Stynes (0-1), P Bealin (0-1), J Gavin (0-1), D Farrell (0-3), N Guiden (0-1), C Redmond (0-5), J McNally (0-3), D O'Brien (0-1). *Subs*: J Sherlock for Guiden, R Boyle for O'Brien.

Westmeath: D Mitchell, D Brady, J O'Brien, D McKinley, O Keating, M Fagan, A Coyne, R O'Connell, T Ormsby (0-1), C Ryan, J Cooney (0-1), G Heavin, M Flanagan (0-1), K Lyons (0-1), N Dolan (0-6). *Subs*: P Conway (0-1) for O'Connell, L Giles for Ryan, E Casey for Cooney.

Navan, 30 June 1996   *Dublin 1-9; Louth 0-8*

Dublin: J O'Leary, P Moran, D Martin, M Deegan, P Curran, K Barr, E Heery, B Stynes, P Bealin (0-1), J Gavin (0-1), D Farrell, N Guiden (0-1), C Redmond (0-5), J McNally (1-1), D O'Brien. *Subs*: P Clarke for O'Brien, P Gilroy for Bealin, J Sherlock for Gavin.

Louth: N O'Donnell, N Malone, G O'Neill, B Kerin, G Curran, J Donaldson, S Melia, S O'Hanlon, K Reilly, O McDonnell, D Reilly, A Rooney (0-1), C Kelly (0-3), C O'Hanlon (0-2), A Doherty (0-2). *Subs*: J Osborne for McDonnell.

Croke Park, 28 July 1996   *Meath 0-10; Dublin 0-8*

Dublin: J O'Leary, P Moran, D Deasy, M Deegan, P Curran, K Barr, E Heery (0-1), B Stynes (0-1), P Bealin, C Whelan (0-2), P Gilroy, J Gavin, C Redmond (0-4), J Sherlock, D Farrell. *Subs*: D O'Brien for Gilroy, D Harrington for Bealin, S Keogh for O'Brien.

Meath: C Martin, M O'Reilly, D Fay, M O'Connell, C Coyle, E McManus, P Reynolds, J McGuinness, J McDermott, T Giles (0-4), T Dowd (0-2), G Geraghty, E Kelly (0-1), B Reilly (0-2), B Callaghan (0-1).

Croke Park, 15 June 1997   *Meath 1-13; Dublin 1-10*

Dublin: J O'Leary, P Christie, I Robertson, C Walsh, P Curran (0-1), K Barr (1-0), E Heery (0-1), B Stynes (0-2), P Bealin, J Gavin (0-1), D Farrell, P Clarke, C Redmond (0-4), M Galvin, J Sherlock. *Subs*: M Deegan for Clarke, P Ward (0-1) for Gavin, P Moran for Walsh.

Meath: C Martin, M O'Reilly, D Fay, C Coyle, N Nestor, E McManus, D Curtis, J McDermott (0-2), J McGuinness (0-1), E Kelly (0-1), T Giles (0-3), G Geraghty (0-1), T Dowd (0-2), B Reilly (0-2), O Murphy (1-1). *Subs*: J Devine for Kelly.

Croke Park, 7 June 1998   *Dublin 0-10; Kildare 0-10*

Dublin: D Byrne, P Moran, P Christie, B Barnes, P Curran, K Barr, D Harrington (0-1), B Stynes (0-1), P Bealin, C Whelan, D Farrell (capt) (0-1), I Robertson, J Gavin (0-2), D Darcy (0-4), J Sherlock (0-1). *Subs*: M Deegan for Barnes, R Boyle for Whelan, E Heery for Bealin.

Kildare: C Byrne, B Lacey, D Dalton, K Doyle, A Rainbow, G Ryan, J Finn, N Buckley (0-2), W McCreery, E McCormack (0-2), D Kerrigan, D Earley, M Lynch, K O'Dwyer (0-2), P Gravin (0-4). *Subs*: R Quinn for Dalton, B Murphy for K O'Dwyer.

Croke Park, 21 June 1998   *Kildare 0-12; Dublin 1-8*

Dublin: D Byrne, E Heery, P Christie, P Moran, P Curran (0-1), K Barr, D Harrington, B Stynes (0-1), C Whelan, D Darcy (1-5), J Gavin (0-1), I Robertson, D Farrell (capt), M Deegan, J Sherlock. *Subs*: P Bealin for Robertson, P Croft for Harrington, R Boyle for Sherlock.

Kildare: C Byrne, B Lacey, R Quinn, K Doyle, J Finn, G Ryan (0-1), A Rainbow (0-1), N Buckley (0-3), W McCreery, E McCormack (0-2), D Kerrigan, D Earley, M Lynch, K O'Dwyer (0-1), P Gravin (0-4). *Subs*: S Dowling for Doyle.

Croke Park, 6 June 1999   *Dublin 2-15; Louth 0-14*

Dublin: D Byrne, P Christie (0-1), P Moran, T Lynch, P Curran, S Ryan, K Galvin, C Whelan (0-4), B Stynes (0-2), E Sheehy, J Gavin, D Darcy (0-5), D Farrell (capt), I Robertson (1-0), B O'Brien (0-3). *Subs*: M O'Keeffe (1-0) for J Gavin, D Homan for Sheehy, L Walsh for Ryan.

Louth: N O'Donnell, B Philips, G O'Neill, S Gerrard, A Hoey (0-1), N Malone, S Melia, S O'Hanlon (0-2), K Reilly, O McDonnell, S O'Neill, M Farrelly (0-1), D Reilly, C O'Hanlon (0-1), A Doherty (0-5). *Subs*: C Kelly (0-3) for O'Neill, S White for McDonnell, P McGinnity (0-1) for Hoey.

Croke Park, 27 June 1999   *Dublin 1-11; Laois 0-14*

Dublin: D Byrne, P Moran, P Christie (0-1), T Lynch, P Croft, P Curran, K Galvin (0-1), C Whelan, B Stynes (0-1), E Sheehy, J Gavin (0-3), D Darcy (0-2), D Farrell (capt) (0-1), I Robertson (1-2), B O'Brien. *Subs*: J Sherlock for O'Brien, D Homan for Stynes, S Ryan for Curran.

Laois: F Byron, E Delaney, D Rooney, P Conway, D Conroy, K Fitzpatrick, J Higgins, T Maher (0-1), G Doyle, I Fitzgerald (0-1), H Emerson (0-2), T Kelly, S Kelly (0-2), D Delaney (0-5), C Conway. *Subs*: M Lawlor (0-1) for C Conway, D Sweeney (0-2) for T Kelly, G Ramsbottom for Fitzgerald.

Croke Park, 18 July 1999   *Dublin 0-16; Laois 1-11*

Dublin: D Byrne, P Moran, P Christie, T Lynch, P Croft, J Magee, K Galvin, C Whelan (0-1), B Stynes (0-3), E Sheehy (0-1), D Farrell (capt) (0-1), D Darcy (0-5), J Gavin (0-1), I Robertson (0-4), J Sherlock. *Subs*: P Andrews for Lynch, D Homan for Sheehy, N O'Donoghue for Robertson.

Laois: F Byron, E Delaney, D Rooney, P Conway, D Conroy, K Fitzpatrick, J Higgins, T Maher, G Doyle, I Fitzgerald (0-4), H Emerson (0-2), D Sweeney, S Kelly (0-2), M Lawlor, D Delaney (0-2). *Subs*: N Garvan for Rooney, C Conway (1-1) for Sweeney, B McDonald for Lawlor.

Croke Park, 1 August 1999   *Meath 1-14; Dublin 0-12*

Dublin: D Byrne, K Galvin, P Christie, P Andrews, P Croft, J Magee,
P Moran, C Whelan (0-1), B Stynes, E Sheehy, D Farrell (capt), D Darcy (0-6),
J Gavin (0-5), I Robertson, J Sherlock. *Subs*: R Cosgrove for Farrell, D Homan
for Cosgrove, P Ward for Sheehy.

Meath: C Sullivan, M O'Reilly, D Fay, C Murphy, H Traynor (0-1),
E McManus, P Reynolds, N Crawford, J McDermott, E Kelly, T Giles (0-5),
N Nestor (0-1), O Murphy (1-5), G Geraghty (0-2), D Curtis. *Subs*: R Kealy for
McManus.

Croke Park, 2 July 2000   *Dublin 1-14; Westmeath 0-11*

Dublin: D Byrne, S Ryan, P Christie, C Goggins, P Curran (0-1), J Magee,
P Andrews, B Stynes (0-2), E Sheehy, J Gavin (0-3), C Moran, S Connell (0-3),
J Sherlock (1-2), I Robertson (0-1), D Farrell (capt) (0-1). *Subs*: V Murphy for
Moran, D Homan (0-1) for Stynes.

Westmeath: A Lennon, D Brady, D Mitchell, F Murray, D Healy, J Cooney,
M Murtagh, R O'Connell, D Gavin, G Heavin (0-1), P Conway, D Heavin,
J Fallon (0-5), M Flanagan (0-1), D Dolan (0-2). *Subs*: P Rouse for Brady,
J Brennan for Gavin, S Colleary for Cooney, K Lyons (0-1) for Dolan,
S Deering for G Heavin.

Croke Park, 30 July 2000   *Dublin 0-14; Kildare 0-14*

Dublin: D Byrne, S Ryan, P Christie, C Goggins, P Curran, J Magee (0-1),
P Andrews, B Stynes (0-3), C Whelan (0-1), S Connell, D Farrell (capt) (0-1),
J Gavin (0-1), C Moran (0-3), I Robertson, J Sherlock (0-3). *Subs*: V Murphy
(0-1) for Robertson, E Sheehy for Connell, D Homan for Stynes.

Kildare: C Byrne, K Doyle, R Quinn, B Lacey, J Finn, G Ryan, A Rainbow
(0-1), M Lynch (0-1), D Earley, E McCormack, J Doyle (0-3), W McCreery,
P Brennan (0-5), R Sweeney (0-1), T Fennin (0-3). *Subs*: B Murphy for
McCormack, D Hughes for Lacey, A McHugh for Sweeney.

Croke Park, 12 August 2000   *Kildare 2-11, Dublin 0-12*

Dublin: D Byrne, S Ryan, P Christie, C Goggins, P Curran, J Magee,
P Andrews, B Stynes (0-1), C Whelan (0-2), S Connell, C Moran (0-3), J Gavin
(0-1), D Farrell (capt) (0-2), V Murphy (0-2), J Sherlock (0-1). *Subs*: E Sheehy
for Connell, D Homan for Gavin, T Lynch for Ryan, W McCarthy for Murphy.
Kildare: C Byrne, R Quinn, K Doyle, B Lacey, J Finn, G Ryan, A Rainbow,
M Lynch (0-1), W McCreery (0-2), E McCormack, J Doyle (0-2), D Earley (1-0),
P Brennan (0-5), R Sweeney, T Fennin (1-0). *Subs*: K O'Dwyer for McCormack,
B Murphy (0-1) for Sweeney, D Hughes for Finn.

Croke Park, 27 May 2001   *Dublin 2-19, Longford 1-13*

Dublin: S Cluxton, M Cahill, P Christie, C Goggins, T Lynch, P Curran (0-1),
P Andrews, C Whelan (0-5), D Homan (0-1), S Connell (0-5), J Sherlock (0-2),
E Sheehy (0-2), N O'Donoghue, D Farrell (capt), W McCarthy (1-1).
Subs: J Magee for Andrews, C Moran (1-0) for O'Donoghue, V Murphy (0-1)
for Sheehy, J Gavin for Farrell, S Ryan (0-1) for Curran.
Longford: G Tonra, C Drake, D Ledwith, M Mulleady, P Jones, D Blessington
(0-1), E Ledwith (0-1), D Hannify, I Browne, P Barden (0-2), E Barden,
T Smullen (0-1), J Martin (0-2), N Sheridan, P Davis (1-5). *Subs*: C Hannify for
Jones, A O'Connor for Browne, D Barden (0-1) for E Barden.

Croke Park, 17 June 2001   *Dublin 1-12; Offaly 0-13*

Dublin: S Cluxton, M Cahill, P Christie, C Goggins, P Curran, J Magee,
P Andrews, C Whelan, D Homan, C Moran, D Farrell (capt) (0-2), S Connell
(0-2), J Sherlock (0-1), I Robertson (1-1), W McCarthy (0-4). *Subs*: K Darcy for
Whelan, V Murphy (0-2) for Connell, N O'Donoghue for McCarthy,
T Lynch for Cahill.
Offaly: P Kelly, C Daly, B Malone, G Rafferty, B Mooney, F Cullen, K Slattery,
C McManus (0-1), S Grennan, C Quinn (0-2), M Keenaghan (0-1),
G Comerford (0-1), N Coughlan, A McNamee (0-2), V Claffey (0-3).
Subs: R Malone (0-2) for Coughlan, P Keelaghan for Quinn, D Ryan for
Keenaghan, B O'Brien for Comerford.

Croke Park, 15 July 2001   *Meath 2-11; Dublin 0-14*
Dublin: D Byrne, M Cahill, P Christie, C Goggins, P Curran, P Andrews,
J Magee, C Whelan (0-3), D Homan, S Connell, D Farrell (capt) (0-3), C Moran
(0-4), W McCarthy (0-3), I Robertson, J Sherlock (0-1). *Subs:* S Ryan for Cahill,
E Sheehy for Robertson, V Murphy for Connell.
Meath: C Sullivan, M O'Reilly, D Fay, C Murphy, H Traynor, N Nestor,
P Shankey, N Crawford, J McDermott, E Kelly (0-3), T Giles (0-3), R Kealy
(1-1), O Murphy (0-1), G Geraghty (1-0), D Curtis (0-2). *Subs:* R Magee (0-1)
for Curtis.

Croke Park, 22 July 2001   *Dublin 3-17, Sligo 0-12*
Dublin: D Byrne, S Ryan, P Christie, C Goggins (0-1), P Curran (0-1),
J Magee, P Andrews, C Whelan (1-2), D Homan, E Sheehy (1-0), D Farrell
(capt) (1-4), C Moran, D Darcy (0-5), I Robertson, J Sherlock. *Subs:* S Connell
(0-2) for Homan, V Murphy for Robertson, T Lynch for Goggins, W McCarthy
(0-1) for Moran, K Darcy (0-1) for D Darcy.
Sligo: J Curran, P Gallagher, M Cosgrove, B Philips, P Naughton, M Langan,
D Durkin, P Durcan (0-2), K Quinn, S Davey, E O'Hara (0-1), D McGarty,
D Sloyan (0-5), J McPartland, G McGowan (0-2). *Subs:* K O'Neill (0-1) for
McGarty, N Clancy for Gallagher, P Taylor (0-1) for Davey, K Killeen for
O'Neill, P Doohan for Cosgrove.

Thurles, 4 August 2001   *Dublin 2-11; Kerry 1-14*
Dublin: D Byrne, P Christie, S Ryan, C Goggins, P Curran, J Magee,
P Andrews, C Whelan (0-1), D Homan (1-1), C Moran, J Sherlock (0-1),
E Sheehy, D Darcy (0-6), I Robertson, D Farrell (capt) (0-1). *Subs:* K Darcy for
Robertson, S Connell for Sheehy, V Murphy (1-0) for Moran, W McCarthy
(0-1) for D Darcy.
Kerry: D O'Keeffe, M Lyons, S Moynihan, M McCarthy, T Ó Sé,
E Fitzmaurice, T O'Sullivan, D Ó Sé, D Daly, A Mac Gearailt (1-1), E Brosnan
(0-1), N Kennelly, MF Russell (0-2), D Ó Cinnéide (0-6), J Crowley (0-3).
Subs: D Dwyer for Kennelly, M Hassett for McCarthy, M Fitzgerald (0-1) for
Mac Gearailt, W Kirby for Daly, D Quill for Ó Cinnéide.

Thurles, 11 August 2001   *Kerry 2-12; Dublin 1-12*

Dublin: D Byrne, P Christie, S Ryan, C Goggins, P Curran (0-1), J Magee,
P Andrews, C Whelan (0-1), D Homan (1-0), E Sheehy, J Sherlock (0-1),
K Darcy, D Farrell (capt) (0-1), C Moran (0-1), D Darcy (0-4). *Subs:* S Connell
(0-1) for K Darcy, V Murphy for Sheehy, W McCarthy (0-2) for D Darcy,
N O'Donoghue for Moran.

Kerry: D O'Keeffe, M Lyons, S Moynihan, M McCarthy, T Ó Sé,
E Fitzmaurice, T O'Sullivan, D Ó Sé, D Daly, A Mac Gearailt, D Ó Cinnéide
(0-4), N Kennelly (0-2), MF Russell (0-3), E Brosnan, J Crowley (2-2).
Subs: M Fitzgerald (0-1) for Brosnan, W Kirby for Daly, D Quill
for Ó Cinnéide.

Carlow, 1 June 2002   *Dublin 0-15; Wexford 1-10*

Dublin: S Cluxton, B Cahill, P Christie, C Goggins, P Casey, J Magee,
P Andrews, D Homan, C Whelan (0-2), S Connell (0-1), S Ryan, C Moran
(0-2), A Brogan (0-1), D Farrell (0-1), R Cosgrove (0-5). *Subs:* P Curran (0-1) for
Goggins, D Magee for Curran, T Mulligan for Moran, J Sherlock (0-1) for
Brogan, J Gavin for Connell.

Wexford: O Murphy, N Murphy, P Wallace, C Morris, D Murphy, D Breen,
L O'Brien (0-3), D Kinsella, W Carley, P Forde, R Barry (1-2), M Forde (0-4),
J Hegarty, J Berry, J Lawlor. *Subs:* S Doran (0-1) for Lawlor, R Mageean for
Murphy.

Croke Park, 23 June 2002   *Dublin 2-11; Meath 0-10*

Dublin: S Cluxton, B Cahill, P Christie, C Goggins, P Casey, J Magee,
P Andrews, Ciaran Whelan, D Homan (0-1), C Moran (0-4), S Ryan,
S Connell, A Brogan (0-3), R Cosgrove (2-3), J McNally. *Subs:* D Magee for
Homan, D Farrell for McNally, D Henry for Andrews, J Sherlock for Moran.

Meath: C Sullivan, D Fay, C Murphy, M O'Reilly, P Shankey, H Traynor,
P Reynolds, N Crawford (0-1), J Cullinane, E Kelly (0-2), T Giles (0-1),
N Nestor (0-1), R Magee (0-2), G Geraghty (0-2), D Curtis. *Subs:* A Moyles for
Cullinane, R Kealy for Curtis, O Murphy (0-1) for Moyles, A Kenny for Kealy.

Croke Park, 14 July 2002   *Dublin 2-13; Kildare 2-11*

Dublin: S Cluxton, B Cahill, P Christie (0-1), C Goggins, P Casey, P Andrews, P Curran, C Whelan (0-1), D Homan, C Moran, S Ryan, S Connell (0-2), A Brogan (1-2), R Cosgrove (1-4), J McNally (0-3). *Subs*: D Magee for Curran, J Sherlock for Connell, D Farrell for McNally, D Henry for Homan.

Kildare: E Murphy, B Lacey, P Mullarkey, K Doyle, K Duane, D Hendy, A Rainbow, K Brennan, D Earley, E McCormack, K O'Dwyer (0-1), R Sweeney, T Fennin (2-2), M Lynch, J Doyle (0-7). *Subs*: G Ryan for Hendy, P Murray (0-1) for O'Dwyer, S McKenzie-Smith for Lynch, T Harris for Duane.

Croke Park, 5 August 2002   *Dublin 2-8; Donegal 0-14*

Dublin: S Cluxton, J Magee, P Christie, C Goggins, P Andrews, P Casey, B Cahill, C Whelan (0-1), D Homan, C Moran, S Ryan (0-1), S Connell (0-1), A Brogan (0-1), R Cosgrove (2-2), J McNally (0-1). *Subs*: D Magee for Casey, D Farrell for Connell, J Sherlock for Moran, S Connell for Ryan, K Darcy for Homan.

Donegal: T Blake, S Carr, E Doherty, N McGinley, R Sweeney, B Monaghan, K Cassidy, J Gildea (0-1), J McGuinness (0-1), C Toye, M Hegarty, B Roper, A Sweeney (0-5), B Devenney (0-4), P McGonigle (0-1). *Subs*: D Diver (0-2) for Monaghan, B McLaughlin for Roper, K Rafferty for Toye, B Boyle for McGuinness.

Croke Park, 17 August 2002   *Dublin 1-14; Donegal 0-7*

Dublin: S Cluxton, B Cahill, P Christie (0-1), P Andrews, P Casey, J Magee (0-1), C Goggins, C Whelan (0-4), D Magee, S Connell (0-2), J McNally (0-1), C Moran, A Brogan (0-2), R Cosgrove (1-3), D Farrell. *Subs*: J Sherlock for Farrell, S Ryan for Moran, P Curran for McNally, D Homan for D Magee.

Donegal: T Blake, S Carr, E Doherty, N McGinley, R Sweeney, D Diver, K Cassidy, J Gildea, J McGuinness, C Toye, M Hegarty (0-1), B Roper (0-1), A Sweeney (0-2), B Devenney (0-2), P McGonigle. *Subs*: K Rafferty (0-1) for McGuinness, B Boyle for Gildea, C McFadden for Toye, R Kavanagh for Roper, C Dunne for McFadden.

Croke Park, 1 September 2002   *Armagh 1-14; Dublin 1-13*

Dublin: S Cluxton, B Cahill, P Christie, C Goggins, P Casey, J Magee, P Andrews, C Whelan (1-1), D Magee (0-1), S Connell (0-2), D Farrell, S Ryan, A Brogan (0-2), J McNally, R Cosgrove (0-6). *Subs*: C Moran (0-1) for Ryan, D Homan for D Magee, J Sherlock for McNally, D Darcy for Moran.

Armagh: B Tierney, F Bellew, J McNulty, E McNulty, A O'Rourke, K McGeeney, A McCann, J Toal, P McGrane, P McKeever (1-2), J McEntee (0-3), O McConville (0-5), S McDonnell (0-1), D Marsden, R Clarke (0-1). *Subs*: K Hughes for McCann, P Loughran for Toal, B O'Hagan for Marsden, C O'Rourke for McKeever.

Clones, 28 June 2003   *Dublin 3-9; Derry 1-9*

Dublin: S Cluxton, D Henry, P Christie, P Griffin, S Ryan, J Magee, C Moran, C Whelan (0-1), D Homan (0-1), S Connell (1-1), D Farrell (1-1), J McNally, A Brogan, T Mulligan, R Cosgrove (0-2). *Subs*: D Magee for Mulligan, J Sherlock (1-3) for McNally, C Goggins for Henry, T Quinn for Cosgrove, B Cullen for Farrell.

Derry: M Conlon, K McGuckin, N McCusker, SM Lockhart, G Doherty, P McFlynn, D Crozier (0-1), A Tohill (0-1), F Doherty, M Harney, E Muldoon (0-1), J McBride, P Bradley (1-2), G McGonigle (0-3), D Dougan. *Subs*: P O'Kane (0-1) for G Doherty, K McCloy for McCusker, C Gilligan for Gilligan, F Glackin for McBride, J Gray for Harney.

Croke Park, 5 July 2003   *Armagh 0-15; Dublin 0-11*

Dublin: S Cluxton, C Moran, P Christie, P Griffin, D Henry, J Magee, S Ryan, C Whelan, D Homan (0-1), S Connell (0-1), B Cullen, A Brogan, D Farrell (0-2), R Cosgrove (0-5), J Sherlock (0-2). *Subs*: D Magee for Homan, B Murphy for J Magee, D O'Callaghan for Brogan, T Mulligan for Connell.

Armagh: P Hearty, E McNulty, F Bellew, A Mallon, A O'Rourke, K McGeeney, A McCann, P McGrane (0-1), P Loughran, P McKeever (0-1), J McEntee (0-4), O McConville (0-1), S McDonnell (0-5), D Marsden (0-2), T McEntee. *Subs*: R Clarke (0-1) for McConville.

Carrick-on-Shannon, 3 July 2004   *Dublin 1-13; Leitrim 0-4*

Dublin: S Cluxton, B Cahill, P Christie, C Goggins, P Casey (0-1), B Cullen (0-1), P Griffin, J Magee, D Magee, S Connell (1-2), C Whelan, D Lally, A Brogan (0-3), J Sherlock (0-2), T Quinn (0-3). *Subs:* I Robertson for Lally, D Farrell (0-1) for Quinn, R Cosgrove for Sherlock, D O'Mahony for D Magee, S Ryan for J Magee.

Leitrim: G Phelan, S Quinn, M McGuinness, D Reynolds, N Gilbane, P Flynn, C Regan, N Doonan, C Carroll, B Prior (0-1), J Guckian, J Glancy, M Foley (0-2), P Farrell, J McGuinness. *Subs:* F McBrien (0-1) for J McGuinness, S Canning for Farrell, P McGuinness for Glancy, D Gilhooley for Foley.

Portlaoise, 10 July 2004   *Dublin 1-17; Longford 0-11*

Dublin: S Cluxton, B Cahill, P Christie, C Goggins, P Casey, B Cullen, P Griffin, D Homan, D Magee, J Sherlock (0-2), C Whelan (0-3), S Connell, T Quinn (0-5), I Robertson (1-1), A Brogan (0-4). *Subs:* S Ryan (0-1) for Casey, D Farrell (0-1) for Brogan, J Magee for Homan, R Boyle for Robertson, R Cosgrove for Connell.

Longford: D Sheridan, D Brady, C Conefrey, B Burke, D Reilly, E Ledwith, M Mulleady, L Keenan, D Hanniffy, A O'Connor, P Barden, T Smullen (0-2), D Barden (0-2), N Sheridan, P Davis (0-7). *Subs:* S Carroll for Mulleady, S Mulligan for Carroll, J Kenny for O'Connor, P O'Hara for Smullen.

Croke Park, 1 August 2004   *Dublin 1-14; Roscommon 0-13*

Dublin: S Cluxton, B Cahill, P Christie, C Goggins, P Casey, B Cullen (0-2), P Griffin, D Homan (0-1), D Magee, C Keaney (0-1), C Whelan (0-2), S Connell (0-1), A Brogan (0-3), I Robertson, J Sherlock (1-4). *Subs:* J Magee for Homan, S Ryan for Goggins, D Farrell for Keaney, T Quinn for Farrell.

Roscommon: S Curran, R Cox, M Ryan, J Whyte, A McPadden, D Casey, E Towey, S O'Neill (0-1), S Lohan (0-3), J Hanly, F Grehan, G Cox (0-1), G Heneghan (0-5), N Dineen (0-2), J Dunning. *Subs:* J Tiernan (0-1) for G Cox, K Mannion for Lohan, F Dolan for Dunning, J Rogers for Towey, B Higgins for Hanly.